# MS-DOS
# *REVEALED*

## – Tips, Tricks and Expert Advice

GW00482465

# Rex Last

*SIGMA PRESS – Wilmslow, United Kingdom*

**First published in 1991 by**

Sigma Press, 1 South Oak Lane, Wilmslow, Cheshire SK9 6AR, England.

**British Library Cataloguing in Publication Data**

A CIP catalogue record for this book is available from the British Library.

**ISBN:** 1-85058-223-8


**Typesetting and design by**

Sigma Hi-Tech Services Ltd, Wilmslow, UK


**Distributed by**

John Wiley & Sons Ltd., Baffins Lane, Chichester, West Sussex, England.


**Acknowledgement of copyright names**

Within this book, various proprietary trade names and names protected by copyright are mentioned for descriptive purposes. Full acknowledgment is hereby made of all such protection.


**Cover Design**

Anchor Design, Macclesfield, UK

**Printed by**

Manchester Free Press, Paragon Mill, Jersey St., Manchester M4 6FP.

# *Preface*

This is a book for all those of you keen to dig beneath the surface of MS-DOS and derive even greater benefit and pleasure from your computing. My basic intention is to help you to make the transition as painlessly as possible from being a mere ''user'' of the computer to someone who has a pretty reasonable insight into what is actually going on under the bonnet of your PC. Not only that, I'll be showing you how to exploit that knowledge to your full advantage.

As an added bonus, the techniques and programs described and listed in the book build up into a valuable library of utilities to add punch and power to your programming. In the unlikely event of your being too lazy to key in all the programs yourself, there is a disk of the book, so to speak, containing all the programs and batch files presented in these pages.

You will be able to get to grips not just with advanced batch file techniques, screen handling, and keyboard management, but also with the crucial MS-DOS program DEBUG, which in turn will enable me to give you a gentle and fairly painless introduction to assembly language programming.

My aim has been to bridge the gap between the flood of introductory guides to MS-DOS which weigh down the bookshop shelves on the one hand, and the horrendously advanced–and horrendously priced–technical manuals on the other. So, while I shall be exploring the more challenging aspects of MS-DOS, I won't leave those of you behind who aren't too sure of the technical aspects of computer number systems or disk layouts.

At the end of the book, there are five appendices which cover in detail hexadecimal, DEBUG, assembler instructions, and the different versions of MS-DOS. The final appendix is a tutorial guide to using EDLIN without pain in order to help you key in the assembler listings and edit them.

It is all rounded off with a list of books which you will find useful in your further explorations of the MS-DOS operating system. The purpose of the appendices is to serve both as a primer for aspects of computing like number systems, and as a point of reference for your own future explorations of the PC computing system, as well as to keep a clutter of detail out of the body of the text. In addition, the chapters on DEBUG each conclude with a summary, in which points raised in the chapter are discussed and, where appropriate, ideas are explored more fully.

I start with a few preliminaries to enable you to tune your PC up to full power. Then we explore the amazing tricks you can play with MS-DOS batch files, and after that there is a long lingering look at DEBUG and the many ways in which it can add beef to your programming. Add to that an investigation of the keyboard, the line editor EDLIN, and the MS-DOS environment, and I hope you will find here an exhilarating cocktail of insights and explorations which will help you enjoy and profit from your PC more than you ever thought possible.

## The disk of the book

To order a copy of the disk which accompanies this book, please send a cheque for £6.50 made out to Lochee Publications Ltd to:

LocheeSoft
Oak Villa
New Alyth
Perthshire
PH11 8NN

Please state whether you require a 5.25 inch or 3.5 inch disk, and please do not forget your name and address for return. The price includes VAT, post and packing.

# *Contents*

# 1

# *Getting Under Way*

---

The world of microcomputing has come a long way since the first "games computers" landed on the electrical retailers' shelves and captured the imaginations of a generation of young people of all ages. For a time, the home computer market may have been regarded as no more than a collection of electronic toys, but consumers soon became aware of the fact that computers were capable of achieving even more productive heights than zapping aliens or guiding Horace goes Skiing into the nearest tree.

Spreadsheets and wordprocessors led the way into a computing boom which even now appears to have no limits to its horizons. Now DTP, graphics, hypertext, CD-ROM, and music MIDI interfaces are constantly expanding the power and range of microcomputing applications; and there is even talk of supercomputer power sitting on your desktop for an affordable price.

Many people are content just to sit at their keyboards and make use of these electronic marvels without worrying excessively as to who or what waves the magic wand to make it all happen, just like the many drivers who press the buttons and push the pedals without being excessively aware of the mechanical consequences of their actions. But there are, thank goodness, many of us not happy to be mere passive users of computers, but who are keen to take the lid off and see what makes their micro tick, and maybe learn a new trick or two in the process. It is for computer enthusiasts just like you that this book has been written.

## What is MS-DOS?

One of the things I don't intend to do is to make assumptions about what you may or may not know about the PC computer. Everyone is assumed to know what MS-DOS is, and the general feeling is that it has been vaguely around somewhere since the beginning of time and that it is the only operating system in existence. Both those assumptions are very wide of the mark indeed.

First, the name: it stands for Microsoft Disk Operating System. And while we are at it, PC simply stands for Personal Computer. Next question: what is an operating system and why do we need one? There are really two answers to that question in relation to the PC: the first and most important is that an operating system takes over all the highly technical, error-prone, complicated and messy business of dealing with the practicalities of how information gets on the screen, what happens when you press a key on the keyboard, how you get yellow on a blue background if you have a colour monitor, how files are stored on disk, how memory is allocated – I could go on for several pages, but I suspect you have already got the general drift.

In other words, the operating system deals with all those fiddly bits and more, and via the commands it provides us with it allows us access to and control over the various parts of your computing system. If you want to put it another way, an operating system is a set of computer programs which perform tasks like listing, copying and deleting files, formatting disks, and so forth, together with a number of routines to handle all the various parts of the machine to allow them to function in something resembling a state of harmony.

In the early days of computing, when only white-coated boffins were allowed near the expensive, space-consuming, slow, unreliable and noisy monsters that passed for computers, not only were there no operating systems – you had to deal with each and every finicky detail yourself – there weren't even programming languages. Everything had to be typed in in machine code, and you can imagine the potential for the huge expenditure of time and effort chasing housekeeping bugs in the program even before you got on to the business of debugging the real meat of the program itself.

Nowadays, we are spoiled. If you key in a command like:

```
DIR C:\MYFILES\*.*
```

– we don't have to worry about the precise way in which the system finds out which disk drive to access, where the file names are on the disk, how it decodes the date and time of creation or update of the file, how it determines the length and so on and so forth. If we had to worry about all those aspects of file access down to every last detail every time we needed to list a directory, the grey hair count on computer programmers would be even higher than it currently is.

The second very important reason for the existence of an operating system, and what has so significantly contributed towards MS-DOS becoming so universally accepted, is that it is designed in such a way that it will work with a whole range and variety of different machines with different chips, screen types, disk drives and so forth. If you like, it is not too dissimilar to what happens when you sit at the wheel of an unfamiliar car. As long as it has a gear lever, three pedals and a steering wheel, together with a few more levers and buttons, it doesn't matter to you whether it's a four cylinder one litre engine under the bonnet, or a sixteen cylinder five litre monster.

The controls all work more or less the same. It is just the power you get that varies. The same applies to computing systems running under MS-DOS. The operating system doesn't deal directly with the nuts and bolts of the computer, but via a special set of programs, which the individual manufacturer supplies, called the ROM BIOS (standing for Read-Only Memory Basic Input Output System), and which acts as a go-between halfway between MS-DOS and the actual hardware itself.

This means that it doesn't matter to MS-DOS itself what make of machine, or what kind of screen system or disk drives are hung on to it, and much more importantly, it doesn't matter to you. Give or take a few technicalities, using one MS-DOS machine is very much like using another, and that's one key reason why the PC and its younger and more powerful relatives have risen to such a totally dominant position in the small to medium home and business computing market place.

As with our car analogy, the only real difference is in the power of the engine, the computer itself, and also in the way in which the controls operate. Some controls are more sophisticated than others, and MS-DOS has been through a number of different versions since it orginally came into the world at the beginning of the 1980s with Version 1.0. In those days, life was very different indeed. It was a world of crash gear boxes and double declutching, rather than the synchromesh five-speed box and cruise control we now take more or less for granted.

## The role of CP/M

At the beginning of the 80s, the most common operating system on microcomputers was called CP/M, the Control Program for Microcomputers, and it was found running on computing systems using the Intel 8080 chip – or Zilog's Z80 chip. These were 8-bit systems, which limited their speed and the amount of memory they could address directly (a mere 64K) although in those days that seemed like a vast amount of memory that even the greediest programmers couldn't fill up, however hard they tried.

We shall be looking in more detail at bits and bytes later on in this book, so I won't pause now to explain them in detail. Nowadays you really need ten times as much, if not more, memory to run much of the memory-hungry software in the market place. That makes 8-bit machines more or less obsolete, with the notable exception of Amstrad's PCW range of home computers, which did more than any other computer to bring wordprocessing power within the reach of the man and woman in the street.

The IBM PC was designed as a faster and more powerful 16-bit machine. The very first version of MS-DOS was bought in by Microsoft and was a variation on CP/M. As we shall see when we come to look at programming with DEBUG, there are ways in which MS-DOS deals with commands and files which are deliberately put together in such a way that they are compatible with CP/M.

## MS-DOS grows up

MS-DOS really got under way with Version 2.0, and then it evolved into MS-DOS Version 3.0, with new commands and concepts being added all the time. Many of the changes are of the "behind the scenes" variety, in which the ability to handle ever larger amounts of computer memory and ever bigger disk formats is added on to the existing system, but other modifications, like installable device drivers have, as we shall soon see, a direct impact on the power the user can extract from his PC. For an explanation of what happened when in more detail, see Appendix D.

All the time, the emphasis has been on as high a degree of compatibility between the various versions of MS-DOS as possible, which enables you to continue using your own version on your own machine without having to upgrade every time an improved version comes out, although if you are a power user, it is in your interest to acquire the most recent version possible.

One thing you will have noticed about MS-DOS is that it is a traditional command line operating system; in other words, you type in an instruction at the keyboard and it tries to carry out that instruction. Version 4 of MS-DOS offers a better presentational interface or "visual shell" as it's called, and the OS/2 operating system developed by Microsoft allows for powerful graphics use as well as offering compatibility with Microsoft's windows.

So that very brief Cook's Tour of MS-DOS demonstrates that as an operating system it isn't set in concrete; it is an ever-developing and evolving programming environment with enough punch and flexibility to stay the course for many decades to come. Some people greatly involved in the hi-tech end of the business may well pour scorn on the notion that MS-DOS is a stayer, but they fail to recognise that there is a very great deal of inertia in the computing world.

If you have invested a great deal of time – and money – into learning a particular system, you are not over-keen to move from that system to a new one, especially if the existing framework has overwhelming support from the software companies. The same applies to programming languages: FORTRAN, the first real high-level(ish) programming language, is still with us, albeit in a much improved guise, and the antique business language COBOL has survived over the decades despite all the software innovations that have taken place since then, for the very simple reason that people have invested so heavily in writing programs in that language for their business environment that they can see no compelling reason to start all over again from scratch. It would be simply too costly and too disruptive.

So, whilst Unix and other operating systems may make minor dents in the market share, MS-DOS will still remain the dominant operating system for a very long time to come. In fact, as I write these lines, I see in the computing press that Microsoft is due to launch a new version – MS-DOS 5.0 – before the end of 1990. From the reports it seems that this will again be an evolutionary, rather than revolutionary, upgrade, working faster than existing versions and gobbling up less memory.

There are also indications that a form of multitasking will be introduced, and this is one area in which MS-DOS suffers a distinct disadvantage in relation to a machine like the Amiga, on which you can use the graphics interface and windows to run a whole number of different tasks at the same time.

While we are on the subject of introductory explanations, I said a little earlier that the CP/M operating system was designed for the 8080 and Z80 chips. The PC machines run on the 8086 family of chips, which are 16-bit microprocessors. You will read of variations from 8088 at the bottom end of the market, via 80286 and 80386 and beyond, but they are all essentially the same kind of processing system. When I refer to the chip at the heart of the PC, I shall call it the 8086 for the sake of consistency.

There is an equal rash of different names and titles in relation to the exact description of your microcomputer itself, whether it be a plain vanilla PC, or an AT or XT. The faster machines, with their more powerful chips can jump through fancier hoops than the humble PC, but they are all part and parcel of the same ever-growing band of computing systems.

So much, then, for our quick overview of MS-DOS and the PC series of machines it runs on. Let's now look at some of the specific aspects of the system we shall be exploiting in the rest of this book and how best to adapt them to our requirements.

# 2

# *The Tools for the Job*

What you need to derive the best possible advantage from this book is a PC, or PC compatible computer, ideally running MS-DOS Version 3.0 or above, although Version 2 will do at a pinch. You will also need to perform some minimal tinkering with a couple of files on your MS-DOS working disk, or on the root directory of your hard disk if you have one, but this is perfectly straightforward and should hold no terrors for you. A technical word for hard disk owners: for the sake of simplicity, I assume throughout the book that your MS-DOS commands are in the root directory. Some owners, I know, prefer to put the external commands in a subdirectory which, with a flash of inspiration, they usually call /DOS – but I will assume that you have a PATH set up to read that subdirectory. In other words, when I refer to the root directory, I assume a directory which can be accessed by the operating system from the root directory.

To help make the text as clear as possible, I have printed all the MS-DOS commands, file names and DEBUG commands in capital letters, but you can use either upper or lower case as you please, except on the odd special occasions where I advise otherwise. This also enables you to distinguish between, for example, the MS-DOS PROMPT command, and references to the MS-DOS prompt, usually A> or C>, depending on whether or not you have a hard disk.

On several occasions in this book, reference is made to different versions of MS-DOS, which we looked at in the previous section. If you aren't sure which version you have, there is an internal command designed to put you out of your misery. Just type from the MS-DOS prompt:

VER

– and your machine will oblige you with the relevant information. There have been some significant upgrades at Version 3.2 and 3.3, to which I shall be referring in the text, but even if you have Version 2 you will still be able to make use of most of the ideas I have on offer. Details of these changes will be found in Appendix D. It may even encourage you to upgrade, and indeed it is always best to have the latest version possible of MS-DOS, so long as it has been designed to run on your particular machine.

Most of the commands, program instructions and suchlike which you will find listed in the book are pretty well self-explanatory, but for those of you not too familiar with the conventions, here are a couple of important guidelines. First, if you are asked to press F3 or F6, this means not upper case F followed by 6, but the function key F3 or F6, which you will find nestled together on one part or other of your keyboard, depending on what kind of machine you have.

Point number two: if you see the sequence Ctrl+Z, the Ctrl refers to that key on the keyboard, and the plus sign means hold down the Ctrl key and while you are holding it down, press Z.

For the extended character set, you will have to press Alt+1+3+0, for example, to obtain an e acute in French. That means hold down the Alt key, then press, one after the other, the keys 1, 3 and 0 on the numeric keypad – not the ordinary numbers on the main keyboard, since, for reasons best known to themselves, they refuse to perform this menial task – and then let go of the Alt key. The chosen value will then appear on the screen. Note that the numbers you type in are decimal values, and that you can use the Alt plus number combination, if the fancy takes you, to generate any value you wish. So Alt+6+5 is a longwinded and pedantic way of creating an upper case A.

The same applies to another key combination, which goes by the delightful name of a warm boot, a term which refers to restarting the operating system, either in order to run it with new parameters or to extricate yourself from a system crash. The key combination is Ctrl+Alt+Del, which means hold down the Ctrl and Alt keys, and while they are depressed, press Del. Then release all three, and the computer will restart itself. If you are a floppy disk only owner, you will need your MS-DOS working copy in drive A to effect a restart.

Just in case you were wondering, the boot does not imply that you are kick-starting your computer, although there are times when I feel like doing that to mine. It is short for bootstrap, which came into being because starting up a computing system is rather like the improbable act of hauling yourself up by your own bootstraps.

One final introductory point: although it is not exactly forbidden to read this book on planes and boats and trains, you will derive the greatest pleasure and benefit from it if you are sitting at your PC, with a couple of blank formatted disks to hand, and your working copies of the MS-DOS disk or disks, if you don't have a hard disk, which I assume will have all the appropriate programs sitting on it. There is only one real way of becoming expert on your computer, and that is to work your way through the tips and example programs on offer in these pages, so that you can share the experience of getting to know more and more about the intricate world of MS-DOS.

Now it is time to explain about a couple of aspects of MS-DOS which you may already be familiar with – even so, it will be worth your while to refresh your memory by having a quick read through the next few paragraphs – and which are very important to the rest of the book. They are: how to create a file directly from the keyboard, how to set up the AUTOEXEC.BAT file, and how to install what is known as a device driver using the CONFIG.SYS file. Let's start with the easiest one.

## It is all a CON

One of the things which we shall be doing quite often in the course of the following pages is to create a short file for one purpose or another. Not only is it a pain having to load a fully featured wordprocessor just to type in a couple of lines, it also means in most cases that when you've typed in your mini-file, you have to convert it to a plain text file to get rid of all those control codes and other fiddly bits that word-processors insist on putting into their files.

So here is a very straightforward way of creating a one or two line file, which is simplicity itself as long as you follow the rules. From your MS-DOS prompt, type:

`COPY CON FRED`

(As elsewhere, unless I say so, I assume that you press the Enter key at the end of every line of input to the computer.) On some systems, it may be necessary to type:

`COPY CON: FRED`

– but most of the varieties of MS-DOS I've come across don't mind if the colon is left out. We shall see in much more detail later what the word CON, with or without colon, means and what the other similar words signify, but suffice it to say for now that what you have done is to ask for a new file to be created called FRED, for which you are going to key in text directly from the keyboard.

At the winking cursor now sitting under the COPY command, type in a line of text, plus Enter. Then find the F6 function key on the keyboard and press it. Up pops on the screen a mysterious-looking symbol: ^Z. That marks the end of the file, and carat plus Z stands for Ctrl+Z. You could, if the fancy took you, press Crtl+Z instead, but F6 is set up by MS-DOS to issue the code, so we might as well save our tired fingers and use it. Now press Enter again to tell MS-DOS that you want to close the file, and then:

`TYPE FRED`

The contents of the file FRED should now be listed on the screen; in other words, the line of text you typed. Also check with DIR to convince yourself that it duly exists and was created just a couple of moments ago. To abandon work on a file, press Ctrl+C.

This is a most effective way of creating short files, but as you might gather it is pretty limited. One shortcoming is that once you have pressed Enter at the end of a line there is no way of editing that line, short of pressing Ctrl+C, abandoning the COPY altogether and starting again. That isn't too much of a pain with just a couple of lines. When we get on to batch files later in this book, we shall be writing our own tiny wordprocessor which will makes things a great deal easier for you, and have the added benefit of enabling you to re-edit individual lines. Alternatively, you can use EDLIN as described in Appendix E.

The second point to remember is this: if you type F6 at the end of a line and then press Enter, the file you have created will contain that line, but it won't have a carriage return line feed sequence in it, and that will not create the desired effect in some of the examples we shall be working on.

If you do that in error, recreate the file by starting from scratch again. Remember that you will overwrite an existing FRED file if you use COPY CON FRED a second or subsequent time.

If the reference to carriage return and line feed puzzles you, it is really a throwback to the days of manual typewriters, when at the end of a line you reached out and gave the chrome-plated arm a hefty whack across from left to right. That did two things, apart from nearly dislocating your wrist: it returned the carriage to the lefthand side of the paper, and advanced the platen roller by a line space.

That is the equivalent to what happens at the end of a plain text file: two special control codes are inserted, one equalling carriage return, moving the cursor back to the start position, and the other representing the line feed, in other words moving the cursor down one row on the screen. The ASCII values of those two actions are 13 and 10 respectively, 0D and 0A in hex.

So, the COPY CON command is quite straightforward, but as with everything else in computing, do check that you have achieved the desired effect by using TYPE to list it on screen, and just do it all over again if you are not happy with the result.

## AUTOEXEC.BAT for starters

When your PC first arrives in its shiny new box and you've finally connected all the cables up so that the back of the machine bears a passing resemblance to a map of spaghetti junction, you will find that the first message you have to deal with, when the computer is powered up and you insert the MS-DOS master disk, is to provide the date and time.

This is an important set-up procedure, since all your files will be marked with the system date and time whenever they are created or updated, and if they are scattered around various floppy disks or in different directories – we all get untidy with our computers sometimes – one sure way of finding either the latest version or the one you used last Thursday is to check the time and date on the directory listing.

Most modern PCs have battery back-ups nowadays, whether a lithium battery, four AA-types or, on a portable, the battery that comes fitted with the machine, so that once the date and time are given there's no need to key them in every time you power up – unless the batteries fail and you are required to reset them.

But you will find in the case of many PC machines that, whether they have a built-in battery or not, every time you power up the machine they will ask you for the date and time, even though they know it already. This isn't some kind of mental challenge that the PC is issuing you – it is simply that it is set up to ask for date and time unless you make the necessary arrangements for it not to do so.

How is this achieved? The answer is by creating a special file called AUTOEXEC.BAT. As you probably know, the name of each file you use or create is divided into two parts: the first is the file name proper, and the second is called the filetype, or extension. While there are no limitations on what filetype you give your files, apart from that of a three-letter maximum, MS-DOS does make certain assumptions about some of them.

If you list the contents of your MS-DOS disk or directory, for example, you will see that most of the files have a file type COM or EXE. Both are variations on a theme – they are files which contain executable code, and which MS-DOS tries to run as a program when you type the name of the file, without the file type, from the keyboard.

The BAT file type is not quite the same. It is short for batch, and refers to an important class of files to which we shall be devoting a great deal of attention in the course of this book. The idea roughly goes like this. If MS-DOS is asked to execute a batch file, it doesn't treat it as a program, but as a series of instructions or commands which it considers as if they had been typed in from the keyboard.

It is a shorthand way of lumping together a group of instructions and letting MS-DOS do the work rather than you, and it is particularly valuable if those are instructions you'd otherwise be typing in time and again, like setup commands or a menu from which you can select a particular option or applications program.

The AUTOEXEC.BAT is a special case of this kind of file. When MS-DOS is booted, it looks for this file and if it finds it, carries out the instructions in it. The side effect of having an AUTOEXEC.BAT file on your operating system disk or root directory is that you are no longer asked for the date and time when you power up. The very existence of the AUTOEXEC.BAT file makes MS-DOS assume that you have sorted out the date and time.

So, if you don't already have an AUTOEXEC.BAT file, now is the time to create one – to begin with, a very simpleminded one with just one instruction in it. To find out if you have such a file and, if so, what is in it, just type from the A> prompt with your MS-DOS working disk in it, or from your hard disk root directory:

`TYPE AUTOEXEC.BAT`

If you are not the proud possessor of such a file, type:

`COPY CON AUTOEXEC.BAT`

– and type in the one line:

`CLS`

Then finish off in the usual way, with F6 and Enter. Now press Ctrl+Alt+Del to reboot, and you will find not only that you are not asked for the time and date, the screen is now neatly cleared for you and the prompt is sitting at the top lefthand corner waiting for your orders. As you will have guessed, CLS is the internal command meaning "clear the screen".

Just one additional point for the few readers who might not have a battery backup in their machines. You will need to have AUTOEXEC.BAT in existence, as we shall be using it to perform some useful tricks later on, but you unfortunate few will have to create a file which contains these lines:

`CLS`
`DATE`
`TIME`

– so that you can enter the information at power-up time. Who said computers were easy?

You can type TIME and DATE whenever you like from the keyboard, and when you are asked for the new date or time, just press Enter, and the existing values are retained. We shall be playing around with the date and time a great deal more at a later stage. But now we must look at our final setup instruction.

# Configuring the system

One other change will be necessary, and that is to the CONFIG.SYS file, if you have one. If you find the next bit baffling, you'll be pleased to know that there's a little utility on the disk which you can purchase for this book which looks for a CONFIG.SYS file and adds the necessary line if it isn't already there – it will even create a file for you with the line in it if you aren't the proud possessor of one already.

The purpose of this file, which MS-DOS looks for at boot up time, and executes as if it was a batch file if it finds it, enables the system to install what is known in the trade as one or more device drivers. This may sound frightfully technical and abstruse, but it is quite a simple way of dealing with a complicated problem.

Imagine what difficulties MS-DOS, or any other operating system for that matter, would find itself in if you had to completely rewrite the system and distribute it to vast numbers of users every time someone invented a new bolt-on goody for the computer, such as a mouse, a games joystick, a CD-ROM player, interactive video, and so on and so forth. Life would become impossibly complicated, and doubly so if a new set of similar changes had to be made every time MS-DOS itself was upgraded.

So the idea of a "device driver" was conceived, which means in non-technical terms that by using one particular set of instructions within MS-DOS, you can "train" the system into accepting a different kind of device and into using it as if it was one of the standard devices which MS-DOS already has built-in commands to deal with.

The standard devices include one familiar to us already, the console (CON), which stands for the keyboard and screen, and which works a character at a time, and the disk drives, starting with A and going on through the alphabet, which are block oriented devices, since they handle large chunks of data at a time. In the next chapter, we'll be examining how to kid the computer into coping with a high-speed non-existent disk drive, but for the moment we have to persuade MS-DOS to accept another kind of device, the "extended screen and keyboard control device", which will be of great value in our tinkerings throughout the rest of this book.

If you look on your main MS-DOS disk or root directory in your hard drive by typing:

```
TYPE CONFIG.SYS
```

– you may find a file of that name there already. If it does not contain the line:

```
DEVICE=ANSI.SYS
```

– which may have been inserted there by an applications program at some time in the past, it will need to be added. You should first of all ensure that there is space on your disk for this purpose, and if you only have a 5.25 inch drive and it appears to be completely full, the best approach is to remove a couple of external commands that you are never likely to use (they will still exist on your master copy which you should have secretly locked away somewhere), and then create a file using COPY CON, as I described a little while back.

A couple of candidates for files which are used once in a blue moon, or even less frequently, are:

```
GRAFTABL.COM
RECOVER.COM
```

Here is a recap on creating a little file to append to your CONFIG.SYS file. Type:

```
COPY CON FRED
DEVICE=ANSI.SYS
```

Then press F6, followed by Enter. Check that the file is correct by asking for it to be typed on screen. It should just contain that one line. Then add it to CONFIG.SYS like this:

```
COPY CONFIG.SYS + FRED CONFIG.SYS
```

Check that it has duly been added to CONFIG.SYS, and then you can erase FRED from your disk. The plus sign means take the first file, add – or append, to use the technical term – the second one to it, and put the result in the third file. If you don't have a CONFIG.SYS file at all, use:

```
COPY CON CONFIG.SYS
```

– and work from there. Now from the next time you boot up the system, you will have the ANSI.SYS driver installed. It uses up a small amount of memory, about 1500 bytes in all, but in today's PCs this won't be noticed, and the benefits are enormous. ANSI, by the way, stands for the American National Standards Institute, and the driver you have installed allows you considerable control over three key aspects of your PC.

First, you can manage the cursor position, locating it at will on the screen, moving it in any one of the four possible directions, saving the cursor position and restoring it. Next, you will be able to erase part or all of the screen, and change the screen colours and mode. Finally, you will be able to change the effect of pressing nearly every one of the keys on the keyboard, generating a series of keystrokes from just one keypress. All these fascinating aspects of ANSI.SYS we shall be exploring in the coming chapters.

When all those fiddly bits have been done, you need to reboot your computer to implement the changes. Do that with Ctrl+Alt+Del.

One final preparatory word: it is just about impossible to present all the material in a book like this in a smooth upwards learning curve, so you will find me more than once asking you to take something on trust for the moment, and I shall explain it fully later. The trouble with computing is that in order to learn any one aspect of it, you ought to already know every other aspect of it, including the one you are about to learn. If you think I'm joking, read on!

Seriously, though, although I have tried to arrange the material in some kind of order, I have now and then stepped out of sequence so as to be able to make the examples I give as useful to you as possible, rather than keep them artificially primitive. I have indicated where you should turn a temporary blind eye to something or other, and hope that, unlike some politicians I could mention, all my promises to do things later are actually carried out at a subsequent stage in the book.

# 3

# *Driving the RAM*

---

One of the features built into MS-DOS which tends to be sadly neglected by users is the RAM drive. This feature is available from Version 3.0 onwards. If you own an Amstrad PC, you will find that a small RAM drive is loaded by default; otherwise it will tend to be relegated to a remote corner of your reference manual and completely forgotten. Ironically, those of you brought up on the Amstrad PCW should be familiar with the concept, since much of the power of LocoScript is built around it. That's what makes the spelling checker in LocoScript 2 so fast, for example.

Let me first of all explain what a RAM drive is, and the ways in which it can increase the power and speed of your PC. There are basically two kinds of immediate access memory in your computer, ROM and RAM. ROM stands for Read-Only Memory, and refers to one or more memory chips into which instructions are permanently set and which cannot be changed. RAM stands for Random-Access Memory, which is strictly speaking not quite an accurate description of the way in which it works, but it is a punchy enough acronym for memory which you can read information from, and write information to.

## What is RAM?

The available RAM is the amount of memory referred to when you hear of a 512K or 640K machine, and that's the memory into which the kernel of the MS-DOS operating system is loaded at boot up time, and where applications programs, word-processors, spreadsheets and the rest sit when they are running on your PC. So that's why Amstrad called their first series of PCs the 1512 and the 1640.

The idea of a RAM drive is that part of this main memory is set aside and told to behave just as if it was another disk drive, but with two important differences. The first is that it is very fast indeed, since it is just like moving data around in the computer's memory.

That's the good news. The bad news is that when you switch off your PC, everything in the RAM drive is lost. This means either that the RAM drive should be used for programs or data which it is not necessary to save, or that you should ensure that you do save to floppy or hard disk before you switch off.

Let us first of all consider how to set up a RAM drive if you don't have one established for you, or how to vary the size of the drive if it is installed already. At this point you are going to have to dig out your manual, since this is a case where different systems tend to go their own way.

If you have an Amstrad, load disk 3 into your A: drive and type NVR. Then move the highlight bar down to 'Size of RAM Disk' and change it to 64K, which is the standard amount and more than you are likely to need for current purposes. That alters the settings in the non-volatile RAM, which means the battery-backed RAM which doesn't lose its contents when you switch off.

If you have a battery failure you will have to reset the RAM disk value – as well as the date and time – when you get back into business.

For the rest of us ordinary mortals, it is a matter of adding a line to the CONFIG.SYS file, which contains either:

`DEVICE=RAMDRIVE.SYS`

or possibly:

`DEVICE=VDISK.SYS`

– depending on which machine you have. Check with your manual for the exact format of the file name. In any event, you should not have to resort to using any of the list of parameters available for this command, since the normal, non-Amstrad default value is 64K bytes, unless you are one of those plutocrats with extended memory, that is, more than a megabyte of memory in your machine, in which event you use the /E parameter in order to locate the virtual disk there, and in that case you can make it as big as the Albert Hall if the fancy takes you.

To add the line to your CONFIG.SYS file, use the same technique as for the ANSI.SYS driver, which I described in the previous section.

## Accessing the RAM drive

You obviously have to reboot in order to install the RAM drive, and you should see a message of some kind on screen telling you about the drive. Now comes the question of accessing it.

What follows is a simple explanation of something which can get quite complicated. The main default drive letter is drive A: and that's where everything starts from. If you have a hard disk, it is usually given the drive name C:. If you only have one floppy drive, whether you have a hard drive or not, there is a "phantom" drive B: which can be extremely useful. The RAM drive is given the next available letter.

If you have picked your way through the logic of that, it means that if you don't have a hard disk, the next available letter is C:, but if you do, the next free letter is D:. So your RAM drive will either be C: or D: according to circumstances, unless you have been frightfully clever under Version 3.3 and partitioned your hard disk into a number of different logical drives. In that case the RAM drive will be whatever the next available letter of the alphabet is. I'll refer to it throughout as drive D: for the sake of consistency and to avoid embarrassing problems for hard disk owners, but do remember to convert it to C: or whatever if your system is different.

If you type:

```
D:
DIR
```

– you'll get a "File not found" message. Just to remind you this once only – if you have no hard drive, it should be C: that you type on the first line.

The message tells you two things. First, the RAM drive comes empty, which is fairly obvious, and secondly it comes already formatted by the system. It behaves just like a normal drive, which means you can write files to it, read files from it, delete them, and put subdirectories into it. Do watch out for the limitation on the number of files you can put into the root directory, which does seem to vary from one system to another but is generally around the one hundred mark.

Now that we have created our RAM drive, let us put it to work for a living. What follows is of most value of all for floppy-only owners, but it does greatly speed things up for hard disk persons too, especially where batch files are concerned.

## External commands and the RAM drive

One of the irritants of MS-DOS is that it consists of two classes of commands, "internal" and "external" commands. When you power up your PC, a program called COMMAND.COM – which we shall be tinkering with later in the DEBUG section – is loaded into memory, and sits there all the time the machine is running.

Among other things, COMMAND.COM checks all commands typed in at the keyboard, and looks to see if the current command is part of the COMMAND.COM program, like DIR, COPY, and so forth. These "internal" commands run without the system having to look for them on a disk drive.

The "external" commands, on the other hand, need to be loaded from disk, and that can cause problems, particularly if you are a floppy disk only user, not least because you have to fiddle about with disk swapping and, in some cases, with the phantom B: drive. With a hard disk, the system will pick the external commands off the root directory of the hard drive, but even so you can gain time if such commands are sitting in the virtual drive.

There are a number of external MS-DOS commands which we shall be using a great deal in this book, and it will make life a great deal easier for you if you copy these files automatically to your RAM drive when you power up your machine.

This means creating a little file like this (remembering to substitute C: for D: if you don't have a hard drive):

```
COPY CON FRED
COPY EDLIN.EXE D:
COPY DEBUG.COM D:
COPY FIND.EXE D:
COPY MORE.COM D:
COPY SORT.COM D:
```

– and if you have Version 3.2 or above, add also:

```
COPY XCOPY.EXE D:
```

This is a fast version of copy which is extremely useful if you are copying groups of files at a time, and you might as well have it sitting there within easy reach. There is a remote chance that you may not have this program, since it is an IBM product and not a Microsoft utility.

Then save FRED with F6 and Enter and add the contents to the AUTOEXEC.BAT file:

```
COPY AUTOEXEC.BAT + FRED AUTOEXEC.BAT
```

The first five commands will be of use to you throughout the rest of the book, and it will be worth your while to type:

```
D:
```

– or C: as the case may be, to change to the RAM drive when you are running through the programs we shall be devising.

If you only have 5.25 inch floppy disk drives, you may find that some of the above commands are on the supplementary disk for MS-DOS, so that it may well be worth the effort of setting up a special MS-DOS disk for use with the programs in this book. To do this, format a blank disk, and then use DISKCOPY to make a copy of your MS-DOS disk. Then erase a number of files you are unlikely to need, such as:

```
RESTORE.COM
SHARE.EXE
RECOVER.COM
GRAFTABL.COM
XTREE.EXE
```

– and copy across the files on the supplementary disk. There will also be plenty of room on the disk for the programs and batch files we shall be devising later.

## Batch files and the RAM drive

Batch files are executed a line at a time, and if they are loaded from a floppy disk it can take a while for them to carry out commands, particularly when you are trying to put an attractively laid out listing on screen, so loading your batch files into the RAM drive is an extremely effective way of adding punch and speed to your presentation. It may well be worth your while considering adding frequently used batch files to the list of files to copy to the RAM drive in the AUTOEXEC.BAT file.

One final point about RAM drives: clearly they take up chunks of memory, and that can be bad news if you switch from running MS-DOS to a power-hungry applications program like Ventura or a big spreadsheet.

### Paths and drives

Once you have set up drive D: – or whichever your RAM drive is – there is one more administrative matter to deal with. If you are currently using drive A, for example, and you summon up a batch file sitting on drive D, you will get an error message if you simply type its name from the keyboard, unless you happen to have a copy of it sitting on the disk which is currently in drive A.

Hard disk users will be familiar with what I am driving at (pun intended). MS-DOS, being stupid, has to be told where to look for commands you type in at the keyboard. If it isn't told any better, it looks in the current drive only, unless of course you override that situation by prefacing the command with the drive letter, like this:

```
D:MENU
```

That's a bit of a pain, especially if you don't want to be bothered remembering where exactly EDLIN, DEBUG and all the other useful programs are sitting. To overcome this, you need to make a further modification to your AUTOEXEC.BAT file. You will find that it may contain a line with the word PATH in it, either:

```
PATH=\
PATH=C:;\DOS
```

– or something similar. The idea is quite simple. A path is the full name, rank and number of a file, for example:

```
C:\MYFILE\LETTERS\BEGGING.WP
```

The PATH command tells MS-DOS which path or paths to look down for commands typed in at the keyboard. Each path is separated by a semicolon, and MS-DOS searches in the order you specify. So if your path is blank or unspecified, it means search only in the current directory. In the case of hard disk users, the system will be asked to look at the root directory of drive C, followed possibly by the subdirectory \DOS, on which you might keep all your MS-DOS external commands.

We need to extend this PATH search to the RAM drive. So, add to your AUTOEXEC.BAT file a line containing whatever is already in the PATH command, plus a reference to the RAM drive:

```
PATH=C:;\DOS;D:
```

Or, for floppy disk only users:

```
PATH=C:;A:
```

Check that it is working by creating a one-line batch file in your RAM drive called CHECK.BAT, using COPY CON CHECK.BAT, containing, for example:

```
ECHO Here I am
```

– or something equally imaginative, and then move to drive A, by typing:

```
A:
```

Then type the name of your batch file and, if all is well, you will see that MS-DOS finds it after looking first in drive A, then anywhere else you have currently asked for in your path specification, and finally in drive D.

Now you are in business to speed up your accessing of external commands enormously, especially those like EDLIN.EXE, DEBUG.EXE and the batch files and programs that we shall be designing in the coming pages.

# 4

# *Batch Files for All*

---

The world is full of chapters in guides to MS-DOS on Batch Files and How Terribly Useful They Are. In this part of the book, we are indeed going to explore batch files along with other aspects of MS-DOS, but this isn't going to be just another low-level introduction to the subject. Instead, we are going to have a stab at a number of quite tricky projects which exploit advanced features of batch files –together with PROMPT and SET – which will greatly enhance your understanding of MS-DOS and expand the power of your PC. In addition, we are going to write a couple of small designer-programs which will vastly increase the power of batch file writing and execution.

The projects we are going to have a crack at include persuading batch files to react to different keyboard inputs in a menu system, to put up a message box in the top righthand corner of the screen, giving details of date, time, active disk and directory and so forth, to design your own personal notepad, and to design much-improved variations on DIR and DEL. Later, in conjunction with DEBUG, we'll add to that list with a flexible loop counter which works inside batch files.

First, a general comment about batch files. As they can be slow in execution if you run them from a disk drive, especially if it is a floppy drive, it is well worth a few minutes' effort to set up a RAM drive as I explained earlier, and to develop and run batch files from there. This makes them a much more powerful and speedy tool and has the additional benefit of releasing a floppy drive for other purposes than sitting there holding the disk with the batch file on it. Even hard disk owners will notice a speed benefit from working in RAM.

## Creating a batch file

At this point many books will tell you to type in this or that batch file. Unfortunately, they don't tell you how to do so. It is all very well for the expert who knows his way round the editors and wordprocessors on MS-DOS, but for those of you just venturing out into the world of batch files, a little explanation is called for. A batch file is a text file which you can create in a variety of different ways.

First, there is COPY CON which, as you know, is quick and dirty in that, once you have typed it in and pressed Enter, there is no way of editing the output using the same command, unless you wipe the slate clean and start all over again. Then there is whatever wordprocessing package you use, but this will have the great disadvantage of having to be loaded every time you want to make a tiny correction. In many cases, too, you will have to go through the conversion routine of turning a document with control codes back into an ASCII file.

For Amstrad users, there is the RPED program which comes on the GEM disk (disk 3), but which runs quite happily under MS-DOS. This is a useful straightforward screen editor, but lacks word wrap, which limits the number of characters per line which you can type in. If you have the program, it is simple to use despite the drawbacks. Alternatively, you can try the notepad program which comes on the disk with this book and which is described later on in our discussions of batch files and DEBUG.

Finally, there is good old EDLIN, a line editor which comes with MS-DOS and which can be described as a blunt instrument for editing files which performs just about every trick in the book but certainly makes you work hard for it in its basic form. The appendix on EDLIN gives you a brief tutorial guide, and the chapter on EDLIN tells you all about it, and offers some simple hints and a batch file or two which make it far easier for you to use. If you don't have RPED, EDLIN plus the enhancements I give it is probably your best bet.

As well as being a text file – which should always have the extension .BAT, although you don't have to type the extension when you run it from the keyboard – a batch file is a list of commands to MS-DOS which are carried out as if you had typed them in from the keyboard. In other words, it is a program written in MS-DOS, and that's why I shall be referring to batch files either as files or as programs in what follows. There are a couple of additional points: the first is that there is the added bonus of a GOTO command, which allows you to jump from one part of the file to another, and also batch file specific commands like IF... and ECHO... which beef up its capabilities.

In addition, there is no limit to the number of programs which you write yourself in BASIC or assembler, or other people's programs which you can call from inside batch files. So, all in all, this is a pretty powerful tool, but as we shall see, it is not without its quirks and oddities.

## A better way to DELete

Let me get the ball rolling with a batch file which offers you a delete command that prompts for attention, rather than wiping files out without having the decency to check with you first. As you know, DEL or ERASE will simply delete the file or files you specify without further ado, unless you type:

```
DEL *.*
```

– or indeed:

```
DEL .
```

That second command is DEL followed by a full stop. This alternative version of DEL does not appear to work with Version 2, which simply generates the error message "File not found". In Version 1.0 of MS-DOS, you weren't even prompted if you asked to erase all files in a directory. In subsequent versions, you are at least asked if you are sure. Incidentally, the two DEL commands I've just listed don't strictly mean the same thing. The first states: Erase all files with whatever the file name and whatever the extension or filetype in the default directory. The second tells MS-DOS to erase "dot", and in MS-DOS the full stop or period means "the current directory".

# Getting dotty

The dot explains why every time you create a subdirectory, there are two "non-files" at the head of the list, one being "dot", which means this directory, and "dot dot", which means the directory immediately above this one. This is the way in which MS-DOS knows where it is in the tree of subdirectories which you establish for yourself.

If you are working on a hard disk, subdirectories are an essential organisational tool, but even on a floppy disk it is well worth dividing up into subdirectories, not least because, if you have a limited imagination and call files by the same kinds of names, you can inadvertently erase or overwrite a file you need if you've got everything jumbled up in the root directory.

In addition, it makes life easier if you are looking for a particular file to know that you keep personal correspondence in one subdirectory, accounts in another, your latest novel in another, and so on.

So if you create a subdirectory (using MD plus its name) and change to it using CD, again plus the directory name, you should be able to list the contents of the directory and then those of the one above by typing:

```
DIR .
```

– and then:

```
DIR ..
```

# Making DEL kinder

But, I digress. Back to DEL: I find it a vicious little command, not least because a slight slip on your part can have disastrous results, so any way of making DEL safer is fine by me. Here is an example of what can go wrong. If you intended to type:

```
DEL *.BAK
```

– and your finger slipped and you typed:

```
DEL *BAK
```

– by mistake, you will find something most unpleasant has happened. MS-DOS has deleted all the files in the current directory without a filetype. Anything after the wildcard asterisk is simply ignored. It's just as if you had typed:

```
DEL *.
```

– and there is no prompt query to you to ask if that is what you intended. So it would be of great benefit to mankind in general and you and me in particular if we were able to create a batch file which would prompt you every time that you wanted to delete a file or files, told you their names, and checked to see if you really did mean to wipe them from the face of the earth. Here is a primitive Mark One batch file to do this, which we shall call WIPE.BAT:

```
ECHO OFF
IF "%1" == "" GOTO ERROR
DIR %1/P
ECHO Do you want to delete %1? If not, press Ctrl+C
PAUSE
DEL %1
GOTO FINISH
:ERROR
ECHO You forgot to name a file. Please try again...
:FINISH
```

In order to run the batch file, you will need to type in something like:

```
WIPE *.BAK
```

– at which point it will list the files you intend to delete. Note the much-neglected /P parameter of DIR, which means that if the list runs on longer than a screenful, DIR will politely wait and tell you to press a key for the next part of the listing. The other parameter of DIR, which is /W, a wide screen listing, does not give any details of file size and access time and date. Moreover, if you have a particularly large directory, the /W command doesn't stop information scrolling off the top of the screen. You can, though, put both parameters after a DIR command, if you wish.

The PAUSE command simply prints on screen the message:

```
Strike a key when ready...
```

The operating system then waits for you to do just that. If you hit any keys, except the key combinations Ctrl+C or Ctrl+Break, the batch file resumes working from where it left off.

This means that PAUSE can be useful if, as in this case, you want to allow the user to look before he or she leaps, to consider whether or not he really wants to delete files or whatever; and alternatively, PAUSE gives the opportunity for the user to perform an operation which can't safely be undertaken without halting proceedings, as in this case:

```
ECHO Remove the disk in drive A and insert your data disk
PAUSE
```

The two panic button key combinations I referred to – either of which you can use whilst the batch file is pausing, or indeed while it is running – allow you to jump out of the batch file by typing Ctrl+C and back into the operating system. You first get a message "Terminate batch file (Y/N)?" which gives you the option of continuing if you wish. The option to press Ctrl+C or Ctrl+Break is always present when a batch file is running, and it is particularly useful to remember this when you are developing a batch file and get into an infinite loop.

The "%1" refers to the parameter used with the batch file name when it is called. In the sample call above, the parameter is *.BAK. We'll have an in-depth look at parameters later. The full meaning of the command line beginning IF goes like this: If the string "%1" is equal to "" then go to the label ERROR and print out the ECHO message. Note that, perversely, labels in batch files have a colon in front of them, rather than afterwards. I suspect strongly that this is a device purely for the convenience of whoever programmed the batch file commands section of COMMAND.COM, as it is easier to pick up a colon at the beginning of a line rather than try to make sense of a string of characters followed by a colon.

What happens when a batch file line is interpreted is that the contents of the first parameter are substituted for %1. In our example, then, the call:

```
WIPE *.BAK
```

turns the second line into:

```
IF "*.BAK" == "" GOTO ERROR
```

## Getting an ECHO

The command ECHO can be a little confusing at first blush, to put it mildly. It can be used in three ways. Its first and most important function is to switch between ECHO ON and ECHO OFF. What does this mean? If you are sitting at the keyboard with the MS-DOS prompt in front of you, you can type in any command you like and MS-DOS will try and make sense of it. Say you typed:

```
DIR *.BAT
```

MS-DOS obligingly toddles off and lists all the files with the BAT extension in the current directory. What you have done is to type the command on to the keyboard and it has been ECHOed on the screen for you as you typed each character in. That's fair enough, but when you are working within batch files ECHO ON will provide you with a pile of untidy screen clutter which is only of use if you are developing a batch file and want to find out what's going on.

If ECHO is left ON – and try it with the batch file we are currently looking at – the second line of the file containing the IF command will be repeated in full, preceded by the prompt, and with the %1 substituted for by whatever is in the first parameter, and so it goes on all the way down the file, making the screen look rather like a bowlful of alphabet soup.

That is why it makes sense during production runs of batch files to switch ECHO OFF, and to have ECHO ON when you are working from the keyboard.

There are two other uses of ECHO: the first is simply to type ECHO by itself, which doesn't, as you might at first think, generate a blank line – instead it tells you whether it is ON or OFF. This means that we shall have to find other ways of generating a blank line to improve screen layout, but we shall come to that one later. In addition, the state of ECHO is not necessarily passed on by one batch file when it calls another, unless you are working under Version 3.3, when it obligingly does remember.

The final use of ECHO is as a means of putting a message up on screen, which I found pretty confusing when I first got to know MS-DOS and was puzzling out why something was ECHOed when ECHO was OFF. The one point to remember about this is a matter we shall be examining at a more advanced stage of our exploration of batch files, and that is that ECHO is not like a REM line in BASIC, or indeed in batch files themselves, in which the interpreter ignores the whole of the rest of the line.

In batch files, unless certain conditions are met, it seems to be the case that all lines are scanned and any special characters or character combinations are interpreted. If you invoke our WIPE batch file like this:

```
WIPE *.BAK
```

– the line containing:

```
ECHO Do you want to delete %1?
```

– appears on screen as:

```
Do you want to delete *.BAT?
```

– or whatever you have put as the first parameter. That is a great advantage in a case like this but, as we shall see later, in a different context this feature can also be the cause of a pretty baffling error message.

## Dealing with parameters

To return to our consideration of parameter substitution: if there is no parameter present, a null string is returned. That's why you need to surround the %1 with double quotes, because otherwise if there wasn't a parameter the line would read:

```
IF == GOTO FINISH
```

– and MS-DOS would, not surprisingly, grumble that syntactically the line doesn't make sense because it hasn't been given anything to compare anything else with. Incidentally, it doesn't have to be a double quotes sign round the two strings being compared. This means that you can put what you like, so long as it comes out in the wash that, if there isn't a parameter, the two sides of the equation match as in:

```
IF "%1" == "" GOTO FINISH
IF !%1 == ! GOTO FINISH
```

The double equals is the batch file convention, which goes back to programming languages of the distant past where a double equals sign was one of the string comparison operators as opposed to numerical comparison operators.

## Substituting parameters

Anyway, let's return to the %1 parameter. This is a powerful tool in a number of different ways. One of them is to allow you to make the new WIPE.BAT facility far more flexible by permitting you to have more or less as many parameters as you like. Here's a complete listing of how it might work first. Explanations come afterwards:

```
ECHO OFF
IF "%1" == "" GOTO ERROR
:AGAIN
DIR %1/P
ECHO Are you sure you want to erase %1? To exit, type Ctrl+C
PAUSE
DEL %1
SHIFT
IF "%1" == "" GOTO FINISH
GOTO AGAIN
:ERROR
ECHO You haven't specified a file name. Please try again.
:FINISH
```

First of all, we check to see if there are no parameters at all. In that case, an error message is issued and you are invited to try again. Then comes the DIR listing of the file or files specified in parameter %1, and you are asked if it is all right to erase the file(s) concerned.

If so, the erasure takes place, and now the interesting bit occurs. You are allowed to have up to nine parameters after the batch file name when you call it, and they are represented as:

```
NAME %1 %2 %3 %4 %5 %6 %7 %8 %9
```

These parameters are usually separated by spaces, but you can use a comma or semicolon – in fact, if you have nothing else to do on a rainy evening, you can play around with the parameter separators in MS-DOS and find out some surprising things like, for example, the fact that it quite happily swallows a command such as:

```
COPY FILE1;;;;;;FILE2
```

In cases where nine is felt to be a limitation, or you have written your file in such a way – as we have – that we are dealing with %1 all the time, SHIFT comes to the rescue. SHIFT moves all the parameters one to the left, so if your WIPE command is:

```
WIPE *.BAT X?.WP
```

– the first time round %1 contains *.BAT, and the second time round, after the SHIFT, it conveniently contains X?.WP. Third time round, it is empty. The great advantage of SHIFT is that you can have a variable number of parameters to a batch file without having to specify in advance how many you are going to use. You simply keep testing %1 until you have shifted past the last existing parameter.

If you are not too clear how that all works, run the batch file with ECHO ON and half a dozen parameters and just watch what happens. The simplest way of doing that is to add REM to the first line:

```
REM ECHO OFF
```

– so that all you have to do later is to remove the REM, which stands for REMark, just as in BASIC. And to avoid wiping out everything for miles around, you could do the same with the DEL line while you are experimenting:

```
REM DEL %1
```

## SHIFTing along

This means that you can have – almost – as many parameters as you like. To experiment with SHIFT, try this short batch file which we will call MOVEIT.BAT, for the simple reason, as you will remember, that if we called it SHIFT.BAT MS-DOS would ignore it because SHIFT is an internal command and internal commands always take precedence over everything else:

```
:AGAIN
ECHO %0 %1 %2 %3 %4 %5 %6 %7 %8 %9
SHIFT
IF NOT "%1" == "" GOTO AGAIN
```

Then call the file like this:

```
MOVEIT A B C D E F G H I J K L M N
```

– and you can watch the effect of SHIFT on the parameters from the comfort of your own computer screen.

You will have noticed that I said that you can have "almost" as many parameters as the fancy takes you. There is a limitation, which is common to all lines of text input to a batch file or generated by the batch file interpreter, and that number is 127, which is the maximum length of buffer which can be referenced by a single byte, as you can work out if you read through the appendix on hex and binary.

If a line is longer than that, the rest of the line is simply ignored. Note that, as MS-DOS converts %1 and so forth into their full-blooded equivalents, it can be easier to run up against the 127 limit than you think. To demonstrate to yourself how this might occur, here is a batch file which we will call TOOLONG.BAT:

```
ECHO %1%1%1%1%1%1%1%1%1%1%1%1%1%1%1%1%1%1%1%1%1
```

Call it with parameters of varying length:

```
TOOLONG HI
TOOLONG HELLO
TOOLONG GREETINGS
TOOLONG SALUTATIONS
TOOLONG FELICITATIONS
```

– and you will see the result for yourself.

In case you have been wondering, there is a tenth parameter called %0, and in order to find out what it contains, create a one-line batch file containing the command:

```
ECHO I want to know what the zero parameter is. It's %0
```

And you will find when you run it that %0 contains the name of the batch file itself.

If you insist on having a percent sign printed out in a batch file line, you have to double up:

```
ECHO This result is expressed as a %%tage.
```

One per cent sign is duly echoed on screen.

In case you have been wondering, what happens to the value in %0 when you SHIFT is that it is lost, unless you make use of the SET command which we look at later in these pages.

# Vagaries of MS-DOS

You may have noticed a number of drawbacks to our user-friendly delete batch file, despite the fact that it is a clear improvement on plain vanilla DEL.

The first points to one of a number of irritating little discrepancies in MS-DOS. You will find that the commands:

```
DEL FRED*
DIR FRED*
```

– do not produce the same results on screen, and in fact DIR and COPY are another similarly mismatched pair. With copy, you have to tell MS-DOS if there is an extension. These two commands have different results:

```
DIR *
COPY * B:
```

– as you will find if you try them out. The outcome as far as DIR and DEL are concerned is that DIR might put up on screen more files than you intend to delete, maybe causing you to press the panic button and exit from the batch file prematurely.

Here is an illustration. If you have the following files in your directory:

```
FRED.1
FRED
FREDA
FRED.BAK
```

– the DIR command above will list them all, but the DEL command will delete only those with no extension or filetype; in other words FRED.1 will be left unscathed, and COPY will also behave like DEL.

The next drawback relates to the PAUSE command. It doesn't allow you to accept or reject the current %1 parameter contents and then go on to continue the batch file. It would be nice to be able to interact with the batch file, typing Y or N, and continuing even if you don't want to delete one particular set of files. We shall be seeing soon just how to do that.

The third, and biggest drawback of all is that the batch file is called WIPE. It would be very nice indeed if it was called DEL.BAT, but if you called the file by that name it would never be executed. The reason for this is central to the way in which MS-DOS operates, as you may recall from our earlier discussion of COM-MAND.COM. If you type in a command at the keyboard, MS-DOS first looks for an internal command which matches – like DIR, COPY, DATE, DEL, VER and so on – then it looks for an .EXE. or .COM file, and only then for a .BAT file to carry out.

The search for the .EXE, .COM and .BAT files takes place in the directories specified by whatever PATH command you have currently in effect.

This means that if there is an internal command called DEL, MS-DOS won't even bother to look for a batch file by that name. So our attempt to overcome accidental erasing appears to be stopped in its tracks by the fact that we have to give it the rather offbeat name of WIPE, which we shall probably forget to use just at the moment when we carelessly seek to erase a file or files which we desperately need to keep.

However, there is a way round the problem which we shall be exploring later in our discussion of DEBUG, and we shall return then to a full-blooded version of our WIPE.BAT batch file which, by sleight of hand, we shall actually be able to call DEL.BAT and persuade MS-DOS to accept it as the real thing. We shall come to the matter of bending DIR again when we have considered the PROMPT command in batch files, and something by the catchy name of redirection operators.

# 5

# *Playing with PROMPT*

---

Now that we have cut our teeth on batch files, let us be a little more daring and boldly go where few programmers have gone before.

What we are going to have a stab at in this section is to put up on the top righthand side of the screen in a neat little box a message containing the date, time, path specification and any other information you require.

This is quite a challenge, the most interesting aspect of which will be the problem of how to put a message in the top righthand corner of the screen and yet return the cursor to sit winking where it belongs just alongside the prompt "A>" or whatever you care to use.

It is quite easy to customise your prompt. The command PROMPT serves this purpose – as well as being able to achieve a great deal more, as we shall soon see. Before we try and put up our customised prompt on screen by means of a batch file, we need first to know what PROMPT can do, so here is a rundown of the variations on PROMPT which MS-DOS has given you to manipulate. First, let us look at the basic set of PROMPT commands, which work whether or not you have ANSI.SYS in your CONFIG.SYS file, and which are limited to dealing with the actual prompt itself.

## PROMPT lines

If your prompt is currently "A>" or "C>", this is what is known as the default prompt, and it is the equivalent of issuing the following command:

`PROMPT $N$G`

– or, as it is the default:

`PROMPT`

Each of the "meta-strings", as they are known in techno-gabble, begins with a dollar sign, followed by a single character which can be either upper or lower case. The $N string means the default drive letter (in other words, the drive you are currently working from, and $G stands for the ">" character. You can also incorporate into the command other keyboard characters which are printed out as they stand, so:

`PROMPT You are working from $N$G`

– will create the prompt:

`You are working from A>`

– or C>, as the case may be. Incidentally, if at any time in your tinkerings with PROMPT you get yourself into a mess, simply type:

`PROMPT`

– and the default prompt will be restored.
  So this means you could establish a prompt to impress your friends, like:

`PROMPT MS-DOS Version 99.5 $N$G`

– or to remind yourself to do something or other:

`PROMPT Backup before switch off $N$G`

Among its other abilities, PROMPT can give you access to the time and date:

`PROMPT $T $D $N$G`

will print out the time, plus a space, the date, plus a space, and then the default drive and ">". The sequence $V will give the version of MS-DOS under which you are running, and $P tells you the current directory on the default drive.
  The $P meta-string is, in my view, an essential tool for any serious MS-DOS user, since it tells you the drive and directory or subdirectory you are working from, and particularly for hard disk users, it is an indispensable guide to reminding you which branch of the directory tree you are currently swinging from.
  Of course, it would be a bind to have to set up PROMPT manually at power-up time, so here is one more occasion where AUTOEXEC.BAT comes to the rescue. Simply add to your AUTOEXEC.BAT file the line:

`PROMPT $P$G`

using the same technique as I showed you for adding to the CONFIG.SYS file, and you will find that your prompt will change to one of the following:

`A\>`

`C\>`

In other words, you are in the root directory of your default drive. Change to a subdirectory further "up" the tree, and the prompt obligingly changes with you. If you are confused about the concept of a tree directory which starts with the root and grows downwards through the branches, I too believe I detect a mixed metaphor here, particularly if you start talking about paths through trees!

# If you want to know the time...

If you ask for the time, using the $T meta-string, you will be swamped with information. The time I am currently writing this chapter at – and I'll leave you to guess whether it is am or pm – is, according to the information generated by the PROMPT command:

```
12:20:10.44
```

I don't really want to know the time down to the last hundredth of a second, so here is a case where one of the "drawing characters" which are available with PROMPT comes into its own. The character in question is $H, which backspaces one space and erases the character over which it has moved. So, to get rid of all but the hour and minute, we need half a dozen of them:

```
PROMPT $T$H$H$H$H$H$H $P$G
```

That PROMPT, as you have probably worked out, generates the time in hours and minutes, plus a space, and then the current path and the ">" sign.

On the slowest PC systems, you will note a fractional delay as the characters are wiped out. We have met one of the other drawing characters before – $G for > – and the whole of the list of drawing and special characters goes like this:

| | |
|---|---|
| $ | produces the $ sign |
| $G | > |
| $L | < |
| $B | I (the vertical bar) |
| $Q | = |
| $_ | carriage return/line feed |

There is one more character which goes with PROMPT, and it is the most powerful of all: $E. This is the "escape" character which, as we shall see, generates the numerical value 27, and which tells the computer that what follows is a special sequence of commands, known as an "escape sequence".

# The great escape

Using $E, we can now play around with the cursor, the screen colours, and even the effect of pressing keys on the keyboard. One very important point to note first of all is that this aspect of prompt will only work with ECHO ON, so in a batch file, where you will probably have switched to ECHO OFF in the first line, you will have to put it back on for the duration of this PROMPT command, otherwise it won't generate the desired effects.

Let's start with a simple example of PROMPT with $E. I prefer to work with intense yellow on a blue background, so in my AUTOEXEC.BAT file I have included these two lines:

```
PROMPT $E[1;33;44m
PROMPT $P$G
```

Three points to note: First, although the "$E" is not case sensitive, the letter at the end of the escape sequence is, believe it or not. So in this instance, it must be "m", not "M". Secondly, the open square bracket after the "$E" is essential, as are the semicolon separators. Don't put commas by mistake, otherwise PROMPT will ignore you. The semicolons are only used between the numbers, not before the "m" or other letter which ends the sequence. Also, the dollar sign in front of the E is necessary.

So, if you just wanted to reset the screen to normal white on black, no semicolon would be needed:

```
PROMPT $E[0m
```

Point number three is that if you use PROMPT with "$E", always add after it the actual prompt line you want to appear on screen, otherwise you may well end up with no prompt at all, as the command has to double up, as it were, between supplying "A>", or whatever, and playing around with colours and cursors.

The "m" at the end of this particular sequence tells the trained eye that it is an SGR function, or to give it its full long-winded title, Set Graphics Rendition. Here is the full list of foreground and background colours and other attributes which you can use with "m":

| parameter | significance |
|---|---|
| 0 | normal black on white |
| 1 | bold (high intensity) |
| 4 | underline (monochrome display only) |
| 5 | blink on |
| 7 | reverse video |
| 8 | cancelled (invisible) |

Now for the actual colours:

| foreground | background | colour |
|---|---|---|
| 30 | 40 | black |
| 31 | 41 | red |
| 32 | 42 | green |
| 33 | 43 | yellow |
| 34 | 44 | blue |
| 35 | 45 | magenta |
| 36 | 46 | cyan |
| 37 | 47 | white |

# Getting in the MODE

It is also possible to use PROMPT to change the screen mode. Those of you with experience of the pioneering days of micros, either of the Sinclair Spectrum with the dead flesh keyboard, or the BBC micro with its massive 32K memory, will recall struggling to read fuzzy print on a TV screen, on which the 80 column mode of the BBC was all but illegible, particularly on a colour TV.

Most of the screen modes were forty characters wide to encourage legibility, and one of the features built in to MS-DOS which hardly gets a mention nowadays is the 40-column mode. The other is a cassette handling facility, which is now just about entirely obsolete. Try to create a designer-screen to open your menu batch file with, using something like this as the basis:

```
ECHO OFF
PROMPT $[0h
PROMPT $P$G
ECHO "This is big character mode..."
```

The second PROMPT is necessary to restore "normal service", and should be the PROMPT you normally work with. Oh yes, just in case you don't want to be stuck in Ladybird Book size lettering for ever, return to normal with:

```
PROMPT $E[3h
PROMPT $E[P$G
```

Strictly speaking, you should use 0h for 40x25 black and white, and 1h for 40x25 colour. And, for the 80x25 mode, 2h is for black and white. However, either seems to work on all the systems I've tried it out on, but I give them here for completeness.

Alternatively, you could use the external command MODE, which can have the following parameters in relation to the screen display:

```
MODE 40
MODE 80
```

– and in addition, the numbers may be prefaced by CO for colour, MO for monochrome.

If you wish to use MODE in batch files, ensure that there is a path to it. It may well suit your purpose to add MODE to the list of programs to copy to the RAM drive.

## All round the screen

Now, to complete the picture with PROMPT followed by escape sequences, the very important cursor control sequences. In what follows, a question mark stands for a number in the range 1-80 for the screen columns, or 1-25 for the rows on screen. If the number is omitted, the value of 1 is assumed. In other words:

```
$E[?A
```

– is the command to move the cursor up one or more rows. That means:

```
$E[A
```

– tells it to move up one row, and:

```
$E[13A
```

– tells it to move up 13 rows. In the case of this or any of the other cursor control commands, if you try and move the cursor off the screen, it won't go.

Next in the alphabet is B for down (don't ask me why A = up and B = down – probably for the same reason that C and D mean what they do!):

```
$E[?B
```

And a move to the right and left respectively are achieved by:

```
$E[?C
$E[?D
```

Now the most useful of all, the command to locate the cursor anywhere on the screen:

```
E$[?;?f
```

Perversely, the command is lower case, and even more perversely, you could replace it by "H". Again, don't blame me – I don't make them up, I just write about them.

Four more commands complete the cursor department. First, two to save the current cursor position and restore it:

```
$E[s
$E[u
```

And two to erase part or all of the screen:

```
$E[2J
```

– is the equivalent of the MS-DOS command CLS, clear the entire screen and return the cursor to the home position (column 1, row 1). And:

```
$E[K
```

– erases the rest of the current line.

## PROMPT corner

Now, armed with all that information, let's set about designing a statusful mega-prompt for a batch file incorporating as many of those features as we can cram into a 127 character line. If you run into an error message "Out of environment space", that will be explained in the chapter on SET and the environment. Only a relatively stingy amount of memory is set aside by default in memory for saving information like the current prompt. If you do run out of space, MS-DOS simply chops off the end of the prompt message, which may leave you high and dry with an odd-looking prompt line, especially if you are moving round the screen or changing colours – or both.

The following mouthful should be typed as a single line and carefully checked for errors:

```
PROMPT $e[s$e[1;45f$e[K$e[2;45f$e[7m$e[KTIME =
$t$h$h$h$h$h$h$e[3;45f$e[KDATE = $d$e[4;45f$e[KDIR =
$p$e[1;33;44m$e[u$p$g
```

If we work through it a bit at a time, you will see that the first escape sequence saves the current position of the cursor. Then comes the first of three moves to column 45:

```
$e[1;45$e[K
```

That pair of sequences moves the cursor to row 1, column 45 and clears to the end of the line. First time round, this will have no effect, but do remember that if your prompt and cursor are currently – as they usually are – at the bottom of the screen, every time you press Enter the screen scrolls up by at least one line, and that means that, if you have a box at the top righthand corner which starts on line 2, which is what we are after for a neat effect, the contents of line 2 will be copied up to line 1, leaving a mess.

Hence we need to clear line one, and also line 2, because the contents of line 3 will otherwise move up to line 2, possibly leaving garbage at the end of line 2. This is quite typical of the messy programming required for the PROMPT command.

Then the next three lines are printed out, with backspacing over the seconds part of the time, and then the date and current path, followed by the restoration of the cursor and of the $P$G prompt. The one limitation of this PROMPT comes if you are buried deep in a remote subdirectory with a path like:

```
C:\FRED\JOE\HARRY\SAM\CHARLIE
```

– at which point you start to wrap round to the next line.

You can switch wrap round off with $E[7h and back on with $E[7l (that's 7 plus a lower case l) – at which time you will almost inevitably get the message "Out of environment space" which, as I said, will be dealt with later. Alternatively, why not just rely on your normal prompt for the path, and delete that part of the PROMPT line altogether?

Finally, the original cursor position is restored and a prompt printed.

## A bar on the bottom

If you fancy a bar at the bottom of the screen containing the time and date, that too can be arranged:

```
PROMPT $_$e[K$_$e[s$e[25;1f$e[7m$t $d
$e[1;33;44m$e[u$e[4A$_$e[K$_$e[K$p$g
```

Again, type that as a single line and save it as a batch file. You will note that, as a side effect, if you type CLS followed by Enter a number of times, the prompt will move down the screen two rows at a time without leaving a copy behind. The convoluted sequence of new lines, erase lines and movement up of the cursor is to prevent the screen overwriting the last line, which contains the time and date.

The assumption is that you are using intense yellow on blue. If you are not, change this part of the string to suit your own needs:

```
$e[1;33;44m
```

If you include the path after the time and date, and the path is of any length, the trailing part of it will get dragged up the screen if you type DIR, leaving some garbage at the beginning of the DIR listing. I have failed miserably to overcome this problem; doubtless there is a budding genius out there somewhere who can produce a full bar across the bottom of the screen which does not migrate upwards under any conditions, and which does not have any other unfortunate side effects either.

## Angle brackets puzzle

In examining the full list of PROMPT escape sequences and parameters, something odd may have struck your attention. And that is, that there's a particular parameter for the ">" sign. You might reasonably suppose that, as PROMPT treats all the characters it doesn't recognise as "special" as ordinary text, there's no need for even the most bureaucratically-minded systems programmer to come up with a variation on just another ASCII character.

Unfortunately, computer software systems are extremely complicated beasts, and every now and again their very complexities cause a conflict between two different features of the system. One simple example is a problem which every dialect of BASIC has to face up to:

```
PRINT "Hello world!"
```

But what if you want to print a double quote itself – when the sole function of the double quote is to act as a delimiter? The answer in BASIC is usually to employ the CHR$ command. A similar problem arises with the ">" character in MS-DOS, because like its opposite number "<" it has a particular function in life which becomes all too clear if you try and include it in a PROMPT line. Type this:

```
PROMPT This is a prompt ===>
```

– and you will be on the receiving end of a rather surprising error message, namely:

```
File creation error.
```

Equally, if you create a one-line batch file with this line:

```
ECHO Please type in a number between 1 - 4 ===>
```

– the same baffling message pops up when you try and run the batch file. The chevron – or open or close angle bracket – is what MS-DOS calls a redirection operator, and its role in life is to intercept what normally would come to and from the keyboard and place the result in a file or take the input from a file. The only way to display it in an ECHO command is to surround it with double quotes.

This redirection operator is a tool with quite a lot of potential, as we shall see. It allows you, for example, to keep a record of who has used your batch files and when, and that can be useful information if things go wrong, or, indeed, if some unauthorised individual has accessed the system.

How do these redirection operators work? Let's try an experiment and then refine it a little. If you create a batch file containing this line:

```
ECHO This file has been accessed > LOG
```

– we have the beginnings of a watchdog which can be inserted at any point in the batch file, but it is a pretty toothless creature at the moment, since there is no indication of the date and time. More of them in a moment. There's a far more urgent problem to be overcome.

If you run the batch file, you'll indeed find that you have redirected the ECHO message to a file called LOG, but even if the message was loaded with specific information, it would be of no use when the batch file was next run, since it would simply overwrite the contents of LOG with the next set of information.

## Appending to a file

Fortunately, MS-DOS comes to the rescue with a double chevron:

```
ECHO This file has been accessed >> LOG
```

The result of this line is to append to the file LOG rather than overwriting its existing contents, and as you will find if you experiment, it is user-friendly enough to append to a new file, if you see what I mean. In other words, if the double chevron finds no file called LOG, it creates one and inserts the line, but if one exists already, it obligingly appends the line. Every now and then, MS-DOS is almost kind to us users.

Incidentally, you can achieve more or less the same effect with TYPE, but the command:

```
TYPE FRED >> JOE
```

– will only function properly if there is a file called FRED in existence which will then be appended to JOE.

## Dating MS-DOS

Now to the next item on the agenda: it would make a great deal more sense if we could note the date and time of access to the system when we create a log file and append to it. At this point, however, a snag raises its ugly head. There appears to be no easy way of getting hold of the time and date and appending them to a file. If you use PROMPT plus $T and $D, the redirection operator will not divert the output to a named file, so that idea falls smartly on its nose. It simply creates a file of zero length.

For some reason, even in batch files, MS-DOS doesn't pick up the angle bracket on a line containing PROMPT and redirect it for us, even though the existence of $G seems to indicate that there is a problem.

If you just type DATE and TIME from the MS-DOS prompt, you are asked to enter the new date and time, and if you then press Enter, you are back at the prompt. So one rather untidy way of coping with the problem is to simulate the pressing of the Enter key by creating a one-line file just containing carriage return and line feed, and using the redirection operator "<" to tell MS-DOS to use the file as input instead of the keyboard.

Let's see how that works in practice. First of all, type:

```
COPY CON INPUT
```

Then press Enter twice, followed by F6, then Enter again. Twice is important, because the COPY CON command will not create a blank file, and that's not what we want anyway – we are after a file consisting of carriage return and line feed characters.

We can now experiment directly from the MS-DOS prompt before inserting the commands in a batch file. Type:

```
DATE < INPUT
```

– and you will receive a message like:

```
Current date is Sun 20-05-1990
Enter new date (dd-mm-yy):
```

For the time, you get a less helpful message, at least as far as entering the new time is concerned:

```
Current time is 13:53:05.10
Enter new time:
```

You can, in fact, just enter the hour and the minute, or more if you insist.

The spurious second line is a bit of an irritant. There is one immediate way round the problem, and that is to use what's known as piping. This is a technique whereby the output from one program is fed straight into another program. The trouble with this example is that it requires the presence of two more external commands in your RAM drive, and it is not the most elegant of solutions:

```
ECHO | MORE | DATE | FIND "C" > LOG
```

That user-indifferent line means summon up the date, feed into it the MORE command which will produce the output:

```
Current date....
Enter new date
```

And then the FIND command looks for the line containing a C and redirects that to the LOG file in append mode. I hope you followed all that. To get that to work, you will need MORE.COM and FIND.COM readily accessible.

When you insert the DATE or TIME commands into your log file this can, of course, be done on one line, like this:

```
DATE < INPUT >> LOG
```

## Going nowhere

While we are on the subject of redirection, it is well worth considering the problem of screen clutter if you are a tidy-minded individual, or if you are writing a batch file for someone else to use, who might fly into a panic if they see mysterious messages popping up on screen like:

```
3 file(s) copied
```

This message can be suppressed by sending it "nowhere", in other words to the NUL device, which is usually given the splendid title of the bit bucket, the place where all unwanted output can be banished, a sort of computing black hole:

```
COPY A:*.WP C: > NUL
```

This will suppress both the file names and the message telling you how many files have been copied. It doesn't take more than a handful of files to clutter up the screen output unacceptably.

One of the niggling inconsistencies of error messages is that some are copied to the standard output device, others to the standard error device, so that NUL doesn't always work. Create a batch file with these two lines, and you will see what I mean:

```
DIR ZZZ > NUL
DRI > NUL
```

Assuming that you don't have a file called ZZZ, the message "File not found" is suppressed and sent to the NUL device, but the "Bad command or file name" message is sent to the standard error device, and pops up on screen.

To avoid this situation, you can switch off all messages by using an uncommon internal MS-DOS command, CTTY, which changes the input and output devices from keyboard and screen, which enables you to install your own device drivers, but which can also be used to switch off all error messages, like this, assuming ECHO OFF:

```
CTTY NUL
DIR ZZZ
DRI
CTTY CON
```

A word of warning: do not forget to reset the output device back to the screen, otherwise you will wonder why your PC appears to be refusing to talk to you.

## Making an ECHO

The trouble with ECHO OFF being the first line is that – if you get my drift – ECHO is ON by default, so the first line is echoed on to the screen, which again might frighten nervous users. There are two ways round the problem. The first is to type as the first two lines of every batch file:

```
ECHO OFF
CLS
```

which clears the screen, wiping off the offending message. Method number two only functions if you have Version 3.3 or above of MS-DOS, and that is to use the "@" sign which will suppress the display of the MS-DOS command:

```
@ECHO OFF
```

If you just type plain:

```
ECHO
```

it will tell you if it is OFF or ON. It won't generate a blank line, as you will recall.

Blank lines help to make the layout of your batch file more attractive if you are putting a menu together, as we shall be doing later on. If you want to use ECHO to achieve the effect, it all depends on which version of MS-DOS you possess. Under Version 2, type ECHO followed by a full stop followed by a space, and for Version 3, type ECHO immediately followed by a full stop. Other characters also work, but I won't bore you with a list of them.

This is not a very satisfactory state of affairs if you want to ensure that your batch file works with whatever version of the operating system is being used, so one way round the problem is to create files containing nothing but blank lines and call them one, two, three and so forth:

`COPY CON THREE`

Press Enter, and follow that by three times Enter, the F6 key, and Enter, and to generate three blank lines in a batch file, type:

`TYPE THREE`

As always in computing, there are two ways of dealing with a problem – you either solve it, as we have just done with our blank line files, or you avoid it. Here is a simple way of getting round the problem, which does have the advantage of not requiring you to remember to have in the same directory the files ONE, TWO, THREE, etc. Simply put a neat box round your entire text:

```
ECHO *************************************
ECHO *                                   *
ECHO * Message between blank lines       *
ECHO *                                   *
ECHO *************************************
```

Alternatively, just put an asterisk at the beginning of each line.

# 6

# *Directory Enquiries*

---

Now that we have become familiar with redirection operators, we can turn to the business of a more adventurous variation on DIR.

There is no problem in creating a little batch file to make DIR list a variety of different files in the same or different directories:

```
ECHO OFF
DEL TEMP
CLS
:OK
DIR %1 >> TEMP
SHIFT
IF NOT "%1" == "" GOTO OK
MORE < TEMP
DEL TEMP
```

This file accumulates directory listings by appending them to the file TEMP. I assume you don't have a permanent file called TEMP – if you are perverse enough to have one, I leave you to change the temporary file's name.

If you truly want to play safe, call the temporary file !ZZZZ or some other name that even you are unlikely to require – or, if you are really paranoid, check for the presence of the name you are going to use for the temporary file:

```
IF EXIST !ZZZZ GOTO TISTHERE
```

– and abandon the program with an appropriate error message. Or you could PAUSE the batch file with a message to the effect that if you don't abandon at this moment, you will now proceed to erase the existing file called TEMP or !ZZZZ or whatever.

The batch file first switches ECHO OFF, then erases the file TEMP, if you happen to have one hanging around. If it doesn't exist, MS-DOS will put up an error message to that effect – but that's soon banished from view, as the next command clears the screen. Next, a directory listing as specified in parameter one is appended to the file TEMP, which means, first time round, creating the file of that name.

If you have called the batch file without any parameters, the command is executed as if it were simply:

```
DIR > TEMP
```

Then SHIFT moves the parameter list one to the left, and a check occurs to see if parameter one is now empty. If not, a directory listing as specified is appended to the TEMP file, and we keep going round until the parameter list is exhausted.

# There's MORE

When the list is duly exhausted, this odd-looking line appears:

```
MORE < TEMP
```

This evokes the external command MORE.COM, which should be made accessible to the batch file. The best way is to store it in the RAM drive with a path open to it as we described earlier. MORE puts up text a screenful at a time, and then prints the message:

```
--More--
```

– at the bottom of the screen. It then sits waiting for a keypress. Full directory listings soon gobble up whole screenfuls at a time, not least because of the lines of information that DIR generates even if no files are found.

This batch file is particularly useful if you are trying to find out what files are in different subdirectories at one go, and if you call it CAT.BAT, you might invoke it like this:

```
CAT FRED\*.BAK JOE\*.BAK
```

If you are mainly concerned with a quick search you can, of course, compress the information by changing the DIR line in the batch file to:

```
DIR %1/W >> TEMP
```

As I said a moment ago, if you invoke the batch file without a parameter, it will behave just as if you had typed DIR, and if you just have one parameter, again it behaves as if you had typed, for example:

```
DIR *.BAK
```

So, the benefit of designing the batch file in this way is that it extends an existing command, while still behaving as if it was the original command if called in the conventional manner. The only problem is the one we encountered with our substitute DEL command, and that is that we have – so far – to invent a new name for it, because DIR is an internal command and, as we all know, that takes priority over everything else. But that little matter will be sorted out later.

# Seek and ye shall FIND

However, let us now be a little more adventurous and go for some options which I wish DIR had but hasn't. One of the least satisfactory aspects of DIR is that it is not possible directly to list the subdirectories within the current directory. Even on a floppy disk it can be a bit of a bore determining which are the subdirectories, and on a hard disk with a crowded root directory it is something of a nightmare. You can whittle down the listing by typing:

```
DIR *.
```

– which lists files without extensions, and that will include directory names, but you will also find the listing cluttered up with all the "real" files without extensions. So it would be nice to have a batch file which does the job directly. Part of the answer lies in an external MS-DOS filter command FIND, which like MORE should be made accessible to your batch file.

FIND looks for specified strings and also for the absence of specified strings in text files. Let me put some flesh on that remark. Say we sent a directory listing to the file TEMP:

```
DIR > TEMP
```

The result, as you will know, is to send the directory listing to the file TEMP rather than on to the screen. The contents of TEMP might look like this:

```
Volume in drive D is MS-RAMDRIVE
Directory of D:\
DEMO     BAK          28      18-05-90    8:23a
X                     11      18-05-90    8:23a
Y                     11      18-05-90    8:23a
Z                     11      18-05-90    8:23a
XXX                  755      18-05-90    9:10a
RPED     EXE        4612      14-07-86    3:37p
DEMO     BAT          33      18-05-90    8:24a
FRED          <DIR>          18-05-90    8:30a
JOE           <DIR>          18-05-90    8:30a
HARRY         <DIR>          18-05-90    8:30a
TEMP                   0      18-05-90   10:02a
X        BAT         254      18-05-90    9:51a
X        BAK         245      18-05-90    9:51a
        13 File(s) 115712 bytes free
```

Note that, perversely, the file TEMP is opened at the time of the directory listing, but that the data has not been copied into it at the time at which DIR is called! You will find when you use the MS-DOS filter commands that there is quite often a temporary file, usually generated by the system with some strange name, located in the listing.

Now let us apply FIND to the contents of TEMP. First, the simplest application of FIND is to ask for a list of lines containing the string "DIR", like this:

```
FIND  "<DIR>" TEMP > TEMP1
```

The output in this case is redirected to another temporary file. It could equally well appear on screen. Note that I have retained the angle brackets round DIR, because you might have a file in your directory called:

`REDIR.BAT`

– or some such other name, containing the letters "DIR", which would then appear as an unwanted item in the list which should look like this:

```
---------- temp
FRED      <DIR>    18-05-90 8:30a
JOE       <DIR>    18-05-90 8:30a
HARRY     <DIR>    18-05-90 8:30a
```

Note that FIND strings are case sensitive, so "dir" would not work in this case. The rather scruffy-looking first line with the file name tagged on to the end is generated by MS-DOS and can be got rid of by applying the next most useful variation on FIND, looking for lines not containing the specified string. So if you type:

`FIND /V "---" TEMP1`

– the resultant list will be:

```
FRED      <DIR>    18-05-90 8:30a
JOE       <DIR>    18-05-90 8:30a
HARRY     <DIR>    18-05-90 8:30a
```

Using the vertical bar, or piping symbol as it is called, you can feed the output from one command into another, so here comes a mouthful which does it all at one go:

`DIR | FIND "<DIR>" | FIND /V "----" > TEMP`

What that unhelpful-looking collection states is this: take a full directory listing, pipe the output from that as input into the first FIND command, which creates a temporary file which contains subdirectories plus the garbage line, and that in turn is made into input to the second FIND. This generates a list of all the lines of the file not containing "----", and the result is dumped in TEMP.

# Taking the right direction

While you are still trying to unscramble that tangle of information, here's a word of warning about redirection. You'll have noticed that I redirected the input from TEMP to another file called TEMP1. In case you are tempted to redirect to the same file TEMP, don't. The result of such an endeavour is usually that MS-DOS goes round in ever-decreasing circles and you will have to reboot the machine.

Also, if you are appending to a file using the double chevron, do ensure that the double, rather than the single, angle bracket is there. As I indicated earlier, this line destroys the current contents of the file and replaces them by the text after ECHO:

`ECHO File %1 has been accessed > LOG`

But there is worse to come. If you were trying to copy file TEMP1 to TEMP, you might use TYPE like this:

`TYPE TEMP1 > TEMP`

No problem. But if you had a rush of blood to the head and keyed in:

```
TYPE TEMP > TEMP
```

– you would actually destroy the current contents of TEMP and create a file of zero length. Do, then, be very careful when using redirection to append to, or alter, existing files. If in doubt about this or any other aspect of MS-DOS, the best thing to do is to practise on files which are dispensible and see what happens.

Now perhaps we can get into business and add the new subdirectory listing facility to our CAT.BAT file. Trouble is, when we call the batch file, we can't specify as one of the parameters:

```
<DIR>
```

– for the simple reason that the two chevrons round DIR are, not surprisingly, treated by MS-DOS as redirection operators, and if you type one of the following:

```
CAT <DIR
CAT DIR>
CAT <DIR>
```

– it will just generate error messages, as MS-DOS will assume that you are trying to read from or create a non-existent file. So let's borrow the idea of a parameter preceded by a slash, like the /V after FIND which means "look for lines not containing the specified string", and create a pseudo-MS-DOS command:

```
CAT /S
```

That will be trained to look for subdirectories to the current directory if we add a command or two to the batch file along these lines:

```
ECHO OFF
DEL TEMP
CLS
:OK
IF "%1" == "/S" GOTO SUB
IF "%1" == "/s" GOTO SUB
DIR %1 >> TEMP
:CONTINUE
SHIFT
IF NOT "%1" == "" GOTO OK
MORE < TEMP
DEL TEMP
GOTO END
:SUB
DIR | FIND "<DIR>" | FIND /V "----" > TEMP
GOTO CONTINUE
:END
```

That allows for lower or upper case parameters. So the principle of FIND /V is easily adapted to list all the files in a directory which don't have, say, the .BAK extension:

```
DIR | FIND /V "BAK" > TEMP
```

And this idea can be extended more or less at will.

## Sorted directories

By using another filter program, SORT, we can also specify a directory listing which prints out the result in alphabetical order, or file size order, or date of creation/updating order. If you type:

```
DIR | SORT /+14 > TEMP
```

– the output will look something like this:

```
0A0B0F43                  0        18-05-90    10:11a
0A0B0F48                  0        18-05-90    10:11a
Y          BAT           10        18-05-90    10:10a
X                        11        18-05-90     8:23a
Y                        11        18-05-90     8:23a
Z                        11        18-05-90     8:23a
DEMO       BAK           28        18-05-90     8:23a
DEMO       BAT           33        18-05-90     8:24a
X          BAK          245        18-05-90     9:51a
X          BAT          254        18-05-90     9:51a
XXX                     755        18-05-90     9:10a
RPED       EXE         4612        14-07-86     3:37p
Directory of D:\
FRED              <DIR>            18-05-90     8:30a
JOE               <DIR>            18-05-90     8:30a
HARRY             <DIR>            18-05-90     8:30a

        22 File(s) 109056 bytes free
Volume in drive D is MS-RAMDRIVE
```

The first two files are temporary files with obscure names based on the current state of the internal clock. If you have Version 2 of MS-DOS, the names given are %PIPE1 and %PIPE2. As in the case of TEMP earlier, the temporary files are zero bytes in length, presumably because the actual listing of the directory takes place after the files have been opened for input purposes, but before they have been used.

The rest of the files are sorted in order of increasing size, with the odd side effect that subdirectories, which have a space in the column selected, come last in the list. The plus sign is essential in the parameter which specifies which column the sort begins. Don't ask me why.

Of course, you can sort on any column number you like, and the following commands sort the directory according to the specified criteria in brackets:

```
DIR | SORT      (file name)
DIR | SORT /+10 (extension name)
DIR | SORT /+14 (file size)
DIR | SORT /+24 (day - using UK format)
DIR | SORT /+27 (month)
DIR | SORT /+30 (year)
DIR | SORT /+34 (time)
```

To incorporate all that lot into our CAT.BAT file will involve two problems. The first is organisational; in other words, unless we take avoiding action, there will be a rash of GOTOs and labels all over the place, making the file a nightmare to develop and debug. Secondly, if we depend on parameters like /F, /E and so on, we are back with the old MS-DOS problem of having to know or remember them in advance, otherwise we won't be able to use them.

The best way round the problem is to use a menu system, and that we shall be able to do only if we find a means of making batch files interactive, so the time has finally come to examine the possibilities, first with a simple menu program and then back to our variations on DIR.

# 7

# *Interactive Batch Files*

---

Wouldn't it be nice if you could write a menu program which appeared automatically each time you loaded the system, and which enabled you to select a program or option, like a sorted directory listing, at the press of a button?

One of the many deficiencies of MS-DOS batch files is the absence of a built-in interaction with the keyboard. The only command which even begins to move in this direction is PAUSE, which can only really be used in circumstances like this:

```
ECHO OFF
...
ECHO Please load the data disk now...
PAUSE
```

This will cause the batch file to halt and to put up this message on screen, which we have come across already:

```
Strike a key when ready ...
```

But there is no way that striking different keys could result in the batch file jumping to different labels. I'm thinking in terms of something like this:

```
IF KEYHIT == A THEN GOTO DATABASE
IF KEYHIT == B THEN GOTO BASIC
```

and so on. The two lines above are pure fantasy, but they can be emulated with a bit of craft and guile, and that's what we are going to have a stab at in this section.

If the batch file commands are deficient in power and range, at least they allow us to incorporate operating system commands, like DIR and XCOPY, and our own home-grown commands, whether in BASIC or some other high level language, or indeed in assembler. That's the feature we are now going to exploit.

## The numbers game

First, let's assume that you have a disk, or subdirectory on hard disk which contains a number of games – all cerebral stuff of course, like chess and draughts, not a space invader or pacman in sight. The project we set ourselves is to devise a menu which will look something like this:

```
*** MY GAMES ***
Please select one of the following:
(A) Chess
(B) Draughts
(C) Scrabble
(D) Mastermind - or if no one is looking:
(E) Space invaders

Press a key between A and E, or X to exit to MS-DOS
```

As well as the games options, you should always give the user the opportunity to exit to the operating system. X is better than "E", since you may want to add another game or games at a later stage.

How do we persuade MS-DOS to load the chess program when we press A, the draughts when we press B, and so on? There is actually a brute force approach, but this involves exiting from the batch file with this line:

```
ECHO Press a key between A and E plus Enter ...
```

That concludes the batch file. Then you simply rename your chess program:

```
REN CHESS.COM A.COM
```

– and so on down the list. This means that when the batch file ends and returns you to the MS-DOS prompt, you type the appropriate letter, plus Enter, and the program you require is run. To ensure that you return back to the menu, you could instead create a series of mini-batch files, beginning with A.BAT, and leave your chess program name unchanged:

```
ECHO OFF
CLS
CHESS
MENU
```

– which runs the chess program and then, when you've finished, runs the menu batch file again, assuming you call it MENU.BAT.

There are two problems with this technique, though, apart from the proliferation of batch files. First, you have to press Enter after the letter selected. And if you press the wrong key, you end up in the operating system on the receiving end of an error message, which is not very helpful if you are trying to be user friendly.

So, we ought to put our thinking caps on and dream up something a little more sophisticated.

# Coping with ERRORLEVEL

If you dig in your MS-DOS manual, you will find – eventually – among the batch file commands a reference to the IF subcommand and one of the condition parameters, ERRORLEVEL, an extremely verbose and not very appropriately named subcommand. It really ought to be called EXITCODE, as you'll see.

The manual will tell you that ERRORLEVEL inspects the exit code of a previous program and takes the value true if that program had an exit code equal to the one which is specified or higher than that number. What that indigestible mouthful means we shall examine in a second, but here first is a typical ERRORLEVEL line:

```
IF ERRORLEVEL 65 GOTO CHESS
```

There's a catch in that line which will require us to do some patching and mending later on, but that's the general idea. The problem is, where do we get this "exit code" from? The answer is: From an assembler program designed to generate such a code.

When dealing with DEBUG we'll find out what the next few lines actually mean, but just take what follows on trust for the moment. It is a little assembler program which reads in letters, converts them to upper case and exits, leaving the ASCII value of that letter as the exit code.

First create a little file containing the following letters and hexadecimal numbers and call it UC:

```
COPY CON UC
E 100 B4 08 CD 21 24 DF B4 4C CD 21 CD 20
R CX
12
W
Q
```

Then press F6 and Enter. List the file on screen, as it is vital that you have it right, otherwise your computer could go into a permanent sulk and need resetting or switching off and starting all over again. Note that what you are typing in after the E in line two are numbers in hexadecimal, which is why they might appear odd if you are unfamiliar with them. All is explained in Appendix A.

You need to have DEBUG in the same drive, or accessible to the subdirectory you are in, for the next bit to work. Type:

```
DEBUG UC.COM < UC
```

– ignoring the message about "File not found". What you are doing is to run the DEBUG program not, as we shall do later, from the keyboard, but from the file UC, creating an assembler object code program in the file UC.COM. Now do a DIR, and you should find a little file UC.COM sitting there waiting for you to try it out.

So, let's create a short batch file to do just that:

```
COPY CON DEMO.BAT
UC
IF ERRORLEVEL 65 ECHO I did it!
```

– as usual, press F6 and Enter to save the file. Now type DEMO, and when the cursor is sitting waiting for you, press upper case A. You should see the message: I did it! If not, check back and try again. The 65 is the decimal ASCII value of upper case A.

What we have now achieved is a small assembler program just 12 bytes long which generates an exit code and acts on it. There is, however, a catch. If you run the batch file a few times, you will discover that you get the I did it! message if you type A, or B, or C, or in fact, any key with an ASCII value greater than or equal to 65. You have to make a modification to the IF command to ensure that it pinpoints just "A" and "a" and nothing else at all:

```
IF ERRORLEVEL 65 IF NOT ERRORLEVEL 66 ECHO I did it!
```

If you type in lower case "a" or any other letter, the program converts it for you to upper case using a technique you will find explained later when we deal with DEBUG.

Now we are ready to go into business with our menu batch file. It should look something like this:

```
ECHO OFF
:BEGIN
CLS
ECHO * *** MY GAMES ***
ECHO * Please select one of the following:
ECHO * (A) Chess
ECHO * (B) Draughts
ECHO * (C) Scrabble
ECHO * (D) Mastermind - or if no one is looking
ECHO * (E) Space invaders
ECHO *
ECHO * Press a key between A and E, or X to exit to MS-DOS
:TRYAGAIN
UC
IF ERRORLEVEL 65 IF NOT ERRORLEVEL 66 GOTO CHESS
IF ERRORLEVEL 66 IF NOT ERRORLEVEL 67 GOTO DRAUGHTS
IF ERRORLEVEL 67 IF NOT ERRORLEVEL 68 GOTO SCRABBLE
IF ERRORLEVEL 68 IF NOT ERRORLEVEL 69 GOTO MASTERMIND
IF ERRORLEVEL 88 IF NOT ERRORLEVEL 89 GOTO END
ECHO Please press a letter in range!
GOTO TRYAGAIN
```

Then you add the appropriate commands for chess, and so on. Here's what you key in for chess – assuming the program is called CHESS.COM – and for exiting from the batch file:

```
:CHESS
CHESS
GOTO BEGIN

:END
ECHO Thank you for using the games package.
ECHO Exiting to MS-DOS ...
```

To test out the program, replace the lines dealing with chess with something like:

```
ECHO Chess being played...
PAUSE
GOTO BEGIN
```

The one administrative detail to remember is that, if you copy this menu batch file across to another directory or disk, don't forget to take UC.COM along with you or have a PATH set up to it, otherwise with ECHO set to OFF, the batch file apparently goes into an infinite loop, until you press Ctrl+C.

# Back to directories

Now let's reconsider the CAT.BAT program in the light of our newly-acquired interactive facility, and see how we can improve the directory listings routine.

In extending the possibilities of our directory listing file, CAT.BAT, we need to make quite a few changes to the main batch file and we'll also need to introduce an additional, smaller file. Here are the listings first, explanations afterwards:

```
ECHO OFF
DEL TEMP
CLS
IF NOT "%1" == "" GOTO NOMENU
SHIFT
ECHO THE OPTIONS ARE AS FOLLOWS:
ECHO (A) SORT BY FILE NAME
ECHO (B) SORT BY EXTENSION NAME
ECHO (C) SORT BY FILE SIZE
ECHO (D) SORT BY DAY
ECHO (E) SORT BY MONTH
ECHO (F) SORT BY YEAR
ECHO (G) SORT BY TIME
ECHO (H) LIST SUBDIRECTORIES (OR USE /S PARAMETER IN CALL)
ECHO *****
ECHO Please type a letter A-H or Enter for a normal DIR listing
:READAGAIN
UC
IF ERRORLEVEL 65 IF NOT ERRORLEVEL 66 SORTDIR
IF ERRORLEVEL 66 IF NOT ERRORLEVEL 67 SORTDIR /+10
IF ERRORLEVEL 67 IF NOT ERRORLEVEL 68 SORTDIR /+14
IF ERRORLEVEL 68 IF NOT ERRORLEVEL 69 SORTDIR /+24
IF ERRORLEVEL 69 IF NOT ERRORLEVEL 70 SORTDIR /+27
IF ERRORLEVEL 70 IF NOT ERRORLEVEL 71 SORTDIR /+30
IF ERRORLEVEL 71 IF NOT ERRORLEVEL 72 SORTDIR /+34
IF ERRORLEVEL 72 IF NOT ERRORLEVEL 73 GOTO SUB
IF ERRORLEVEL 13 IF NOT ERRORLEVEL 14 GOTO NOMENU
ECHO PLEASE TYPE A LETTER IN RANGE OR ENTER
GOTO READAGAIN
:NOMENU
CLS
:OK
IF "%1" == "/S" GOTO SUB
IF "%1" == "/s" GOTO SUB
IF NOT "%1" == "" GOTO SFOR
```

```
ECHO DIRECTORY FULL LISTING > TEMP
GOTO JUMP
:SFOR
ECHO DIRECTORY LISTING SEARCH FOR %1: > TEMP
:JUMP
DIR %1 > TEMP
:CONTINUE
ECHO ********************************************* > TEMP
SHIFT
IF NOT "%1" == "" GOTO OK
MORE < TEMP
GOTO END
:SUB
ECHO DIRECTORY LISTING SEARCH FOR SUBDIRECTORIES > TEMP
DIR | FIND "<DIR>" | FIND /V "----" > TEMP
GOTO CONTINUE
:END
DEL TEMP
ECHO ********** END OF LISTING OF DIRECTORIES ********** > TEMP
```

Now for the smaller file:

```
ECHO OFF
CLS
ECHO SORTED DIRECTORY LISTING
DIR | SORT %1 | MORE
ECHO ************END OF SORTED DIRECTORY LISTING
```

In order to try and maintain a measure of compatibility with MS-DOS DIR, if you call the batch file without any parameters, it first puts up the menu, but if you just press Enter, it goes on to provide a normal full directory listing. Hence the SHIFT in the fifth line. The options are activated by the UC.COM program. If an appropriate letter between A-G is keyed in, the smaller batch file SORTDIR.BAT, as I've called it, is invoked with, where necessary, a parameter indicating the column number where the sort is to be based.

If H is entered a request for a listing of subdirectories is assumed, and if Enter (ASCII value 13) is keyed in the program provides a standard directory listing.

Apart from a few cosmetic additions, the rest of the file is more or less the same. The most important alteration is to tell the user what kind of directory listing has been requested. In the case of sorted listings, you could add a number of IF statements at the beginning of the file and after the CLS command like this example:

```
IF "%1" == "/+14" ECHO DIRECTORY SORTED BY SIZE > TEMP
```

That makes our variation on DIR just about as sophisticated as we can get it without allowing for accessing other directories using the sort facilities. Probably you might manage that, too, with a bit of ingenuity.

## Back to DELete

When we considered our variations on the DEL command earlier, I promised to upgrade the program to exploit interaction appropriately, in other words to allow the user to skip an item in the list without having to abandon the deleting process. So, in a case like this:

```
WIPE A*.* B* *.BAK
```

– if there are no files that match the template A*.*, the user will be able to skip to the next in the list, and if he or she doesn't wish to get rid of the files that match B*, he can similarly move on to the next item.

Here's the improved listing, which has a couple of other enhancements made to it:

```
ECHO OFF
CLS
IF "%1" == "" GOTO ERROR
:AGAIN
IF EXIST %1 GOTO FOUND
ECHO I cannot find any files called: %1
ECHO Press Q to quit, any other key to continue
UC
IF ERRORLEVEL 81 IF NOT ERRORLEVEL 82 GOTO FINISH
GOTO GETRID1
:FOUND
ECHO You have asked me to delete: %1
DIR %1/P
ECHO Are you sure you want to erase? Type Y or N ...
:INPUT
UC
IF ERRORLEVEL 89 IF NOT ERRORLEVEL 90 GOTO GETRID
IF ERRORLEVEL 78 IF NOT ERRORLEVEL 79 GOTO SAVE
ECHO Please type either Y or N
GOTO INPUT
:GETRID
DEL %1
ECHO I have deleted %1
GOTO GETRID1
:SAVE
ECHO I have not deleted %1
:GETRID1
SHIFT
IF "%1" == "" GOTO FINISH
GOTO AGAIN
:ERROR
ECHO You haven't specified a file name. Please try again.
:FINISH
ECHO Delete program finished...
```

As you will notice, IF EXIST can, fortunately, deal with wildcards in testing to see if there is a match for delete. I have also added a line immediately before the directory listing which should help in cases where DIR offers more information than the DEL command is trained to delete. In other words, if you ask to:

```
WIPE A*.
```

– only those matching files without an extension will be offered up for deletion, although the DIR listing will give all those that match this template:

```
DIR A*.*
```

There are two sets of questions to which the UC program captures the replies. The first comes after an absence of a match has been detected, and the second to ask – once a match has been found – if the user wants to erase the files that have been specified.

Note that in each case, and in the other examples using UC, I have always checked that the response matches the question. In other words, unless I have indicated that "any other key" can be pressed, I don't let a user get away with pressing a key other than, for example, Y or N. This is not a matter of computing bureaucracy, since they may have just hit the wrong key or, even worse, if I don't capture the wrong responses, I might be tempted to make a false assumption about what the user's intention was, with possibly disastrous results.

So, now we have at our disposal an extremely potent tool for batch files in the UC.COM program.

# 8

# *FOR Better or Worse*

One of the most user-hostile aspects of batch files is the FOR subcommand, which is described in manuals in inscrutable terms something like this:

```
FOR %%variable IN (set) DO command
```

What that mouth-watering morsel actually does isn't exactly lucidly revealed by the format of the command, although it is fairly self-evident that it has something to do with repeating. This is a simple example which should give you an idea of how to beef up the DIR command:

```
FOR %%A IN (*.WP *.BAK) DO DIR %%A
```

Here is an attempt to translate that line into something approaching plain English: Take a dummy parameter, which has to be one letter, and call it "%A". Given the fact that in batch files a single per cent sign refers to parameters of the batch file typed in when the file is called, we need two of the brutes to arrive at the required format of a per cent sign followed by a character. Then take the text inside the brackets one chunk at a time and perform the instruction after the DO, substituting for %A in our example *.WP and *.BAK.

That is a long-winded way of saying that the effect of the FOR command we have just instanced is to generate two directory listings:

```
DIR *.WP
```

```
DIR *.BAK
```

Do note that, while you can use any letter instead of A, the parameter is case sensitive, so %%A isn't the same as %%a, and if you mistype one for the other, you can end up with as baffling a bug as any program has ever been infested with.

Let me summarise, in case you still find the whole business a little baffling. The FOR command requires a dummy parameter in the form of a per cent sign plus a single letter. As MS-DOS batch files have already hijacked the single per cent sign for the purposes of parameter substitution when the file is invoked – using %1, %2, and so on – it is necessary to put two per cent signs to have the effect of generating one.

Then the FOR command sets up a list of one or more items inside brackets to be substituted in sequence for the dummy parameter and used in whatever comes after the DO command. Here are a couple more examples, which don't achieve very much, but which might help to make things (even) clearer.

First, imagine that for some reason best known to yourself you want to echo on screen Today is MONDAY, Today is TUESDAY, one after the other. You could do it like this:

```
FOR %%Z in (MONDAY TUESDAY WEDNESDAY) DO ECHO Today is %%Z
```

That should help to make the command a little less impenetrable. One more example:

```
FOR %%B IN (%1 %2) DO COPY %%B PRN
```

If this came in a batch file called PRINTF.BAT, invoked like this:

```
PRINTF FILEONE FILETWO
```

– the two files, if they exist, are printed on the PRN device, in other words, the printer, one after the other.

## Another kind of DIR

The FOR subcommand now means that you could create a different variation on the DIR command from MS-DOS which would effectively ask for selective DIR listings:

```
IF "%1" == "" GOTO NORMAL
:AGAIN
FOR %%A IN (%1) DO DIR %%A/P
SHIFT
IF "%1" == "" GOTO END
GOTO AGAIN
:NORMAL
DIR /P
:END
```

What the batch file means is this: The first line sees if you have called it without parameters, in which case it behaves just as if you had typed plain DIR. If not, a double substitution takes place, if you can follow the FOR command line. There is only one string in the brackets, so the command is executed just once.

The command DIR %%A takes the contents of the brackets – %1 – and substitutes that for %%A, and then a second substitution takes place – the contents of the first parameter of the file are used to qualify the directory listing. Then the parameters are shifted one to the left and the process repeated until we run out of parameters. I've included the /P parameter since, as you know, even with relatively short DIR listings you soon run off the top of the screen. A sample call of the file – let's call it CAT1 – would be:

```
CAT1 *.WP *.BAK
```

Once you have got the drift of the FOR command, you can turn it into quite a powerful tool, provided only that you remember that the command has to fit on a single line, with a maximum of 127 characters. Do remember that when the line is interpreted, all dummy parameters are expanded, so you might run into this restriction sooner than you think.

Here's another hoop you might like to jump through using FOR. In this example, you can check through two directories for matching file names and make backup copies if the second directory doesn't contain them. In the listing, I have created a subdirectory on the RAM drive – which for you, remember, will probably be C: or D: depending on whether you have a hard disk – and put a few short files in it.

In real life, the program would make more sense if, say, you were comparing the contents of a subdirectory on your hard disk or on one floppy disk and backing up as appropriate on to the backup floppy disk:

```
:AGAIN
FOR %%A IN (%1) DO IF EXIST D:\FRED\%%A IF NOT EXIST D:%%A COPY D:\FRED\%%A D:
SHIFT
IF NOT "%1"=="" GOTO AGAIN
```

If we name our file MATCH.BAT, it could be called with, say:

```
MATCH A B C D
```

– if you were specifically interested in the files A, B, C and D, or, if you were after all the files with the extensions .DAT and .WS, the file could be rewritten on one line as:

```
FOR %%A IN (*.DAT *.WS) DO IF EXIST D:\FRED\%%A IF NOT EXIST D:%%A COPY
D:\FRED\%%A D:
```

# Going inside out

You will have noticed that batch files aren't exactly God's gift to structured programming. Not only are they pretty verbose, with error-prone keywords for typists like ERRORLEVEL, but there also appears to be no way round the problems of hopping back and forth over labels, and if you forget to conclude one part of a batch file with a GOTO END command, with the appropriate :END label concluding the file, the result can be disastrous. Take this as an example of what not to do:

```
ECHO OFF
IF "%1" == "A" GOTO DOTHIS
IF "%1" == "B" GOTO DOTHAT
:DOTHIS
ECHO I'm doing this
:DOTHAT
ECHO I'm doing that
```

What happens is that MS-DOS checks for the first condition, and if it is true, executes the command after DOTHIS. And then, without as much as a by-your-leave, it falls straight through the next label and executes the command after DOTHAT.

Worse still, if the first parameter is neither A nor B, the batch file has the brass neck to execute both sets of commands. This is one of the commonest causes of errors in batch file design.

To get round the problem, you have to indulge in this kind of messy and accident-prone label-hopping:

```
ECHO OFF
IF "%1" == "A" GOTO DOTHIS
IF "%1" == "B" GOTO DOTHAT
GOTO FAIL
:DOTHIS
ECHO I'm doing this
GOTO END
:DOTHAT
ECHO I'm doing that
GOTO END
:FAIL
ECHO You didn't specify an option...
GOTO FINISH
:END
ECHO Program successfully completed.
:FINISH
```

Surely there is a way round this kind of mess? The answer is, you will be relieved to know, yes – there are at least two ways round the problem. The first is to simulate a block structure which would have the effect of carrying out the DOTHIS or the DOTHAT followed by the equivalent of a STOP command. This can easily be done by carving up the batch file into separate batch files.

If you take the commands after DOTHIS and put them in a separate file called DOTHIS.BAT, you will find that if you call one batch file from inside another, MS-DOS by default abandons the first batch file and lands you back at the MS-DOS prompt when it has finished executing the commands in the second batch file, and if that's what you intended, that makes life neater and easier.

So, the dog's breakfast above can now be rewritten – assuming the existence of batch files called DOTHIS.BAT and DOTHAT.BAT – in a way rather more fit for human consumption:

```
ECHO OFF
IF "%1" == "A" DOTHIS
IF "%1" == "B" DOTHAT
ECHO You didn't specify an option
```

That is a great improvement, as you can readily see. But what if you wanted to execute DOTHIS and then return to the calling batch file? The way in which it is achieved depends on whether or not you have Version 3.3 and above of MS-DOS. If not, it is a little more complicated to call a batch file from within a batch file, but not much.

Before Version 3.3, you have to use the COMMAND command, which loads a new version of the transient part of the command processor into the system, runs the batch file, and then returns control back to the previous command processor. This does take up memory, and it also means, if you are a floppies only person, that you have to have COMMAND.COM available to be able to load a copy of it into memory. This only takes up an additional 20K or so of memory.

If you are not completely put off by that explanation, here is an illustration of the COMMAND calling system at work. Assume that you have created a batch file called NEST.BAT, consisting of two lines:

```
ECHO OFF
ECHO This is the nested batch file
```

Create another batch file called OUTSIDE.BAT, or some other similarly inventive name:

```
ECHO OFF
ECHO This is the batch file which is about to call NEST
COMMAND /C NEST
ECHO And here we are back again in the OUTSIDE batch file
```

Do note two things: The first point is that the inner batch file does not inherit the ECHO OFF from the outer file unless you have Version 3.3, so it has to appear at the beginning of the file to avoid clutter. Secondly, you must use the /C parameter, which tells MS-DOS to load a temporary copy of the command processor.

If you are fortunate enough to have MS-DOS Version 3.3 or above, you will be relieved to know that there is a new subcommand which avoids all that messing about. Appropriately, it goes by the name of CALL:

```
ECHO OFF
ECHO This is OUTSIDE
CALL NEST
ECHO And here we are in OUTSIDE again.
```

Not only is it more convenient, it also "remembers" that ECHO is OFF in the outside file, so you do not have to repeat that line.

Going back to the FOR subcommand, you can create a really powerful structure with a command like the following, assuming that B1, B2, B3 and B4 are batch files you wish to call:

```
FOR %%A IN (B1 B2 B3 B4) DO COMMAND /C %%A
```

or, for Version 3.3 and above:

```
FOR %%A IN (B1 B2 B3 B4) DO CALL %%A
```

And, if you like to make life really complicated, you can call inner batch files using parameters, but do check first with dummy parameters that you are achieving what you actually want to do rather than what MS-DOS thinks you want to do.

## Jumping in

The techniques I have described so far help you get round some of the unstructured clumsiness of the batch file system, and here is a further simple trick which at the same time helps to overcome another infuriating aspect of batch files.

We saw earlier that the parameter with the double per cent sign after the FOR subcommand is case sensitive. In other words, %%A is not the same as %%a, and the same applies to any parameters you type in when calling a batch file, so the following are not identical when calling the batch file DAY.BAT:

```
DAY MONDAY
DAY monday
DAY Monday
```

– and so on. To test for each possible combination of upper and lower case letters would mean starting with:

```
IF "%1" == "MONDAY" GOTO MONFOUND
```

– and going on for more lines than my arithmetic can cope with. This means that you should, in theory, test for each and every one of the possible combinations of a parameter's name if it is to be tested in this way. File names, thank goodness, are converted to upper case so when you ask for:

```
COPY %1 D:
```

– it doesn't matter if the parameter you typed in when calling the batch file is upper or lower case. Once again, though, there is a way round this general problem. As far as its own commands and labels are concerned, batch files are not case sensitive, so the following are identical:

```
:FRED
:fred
:fRED
```

– and so on. This means that all you have to do to jump to a particular part of the batch file bearing this label is to type:

```
GOTO %1
```

– and your problems of case-sensitivity are solved – unless, of course, you mistype the label name as FERD, which will cause the program to exit with an error code! The moral of all this is that if you want to test for options, by far the best route to take is to use our interactive technique with UC.COM with a menu listing.

One of the things you can't do with a label is to use the parameters called to vary the name of the label. You can't say:

```
GOTO %1
...
:%1
```

I suspect this is because MS-DOS goes in for parameter substitution and using the redirection operators < > and so forth when it interprets a line, but when it scans down the file for a label matching a GOTO it doesn't do that. That causes a whole range of potentially crafty tricks with batch files to go straight out of the window.

# Label advice

While on the subject of labels, two points are worth recording. The first is that it doesn't matter if you don't call a label in a batch file, so you can use a label as a comment line, so long as you use in the first string of characters after the colon only those characters which are valid for file names:

```
:this is a comment
```

You could, if you wished, go to THIS.

Point number two is a little more problematic. Batch files are not compiled; they are interpreted, rather like many dialects of BASIC. The difference between a compiler and an interpreter is that, in the case of the compiler, a special program tries to make sense of the entire source code first, and converts it into object code in the form of machine code instructions. That makes a compiler much faster than an interpreter, which literally tries to "interpret" – or try and make sense of – each line at a time, and in the case of a loop, keeps on interpreting every time a line is encountered.

So, one difference between the two is that a compiler would spot a missing label or duplicate labels at compile time and flag an error, whereas an interpreter would only do so if a GOTO LABEL command was interpreted and no LABEL was found. Note that, when batch files are being executed, you usually get error messages if a command or file can't be found, and the batch file trundles on to the next command. The lack of a label, however, is regarded as a fatal error, and the batch file halts whenever this condition occurs.

One of the oddities of the interpreter is the way it handles labels, and in the case of the batch file the system starts looking from the beginning of the file every time, regardless of where it happens to be at the point where the GOTO occurs. So, you can have the same label as many times as you like in a batch file, as long as you take on board the fact that any GOTO will always pick up the first one in the file and studiously ignore the rest.

That is a rich potential source of bugs in batch files, particularly when you add to the brew the little-publicised fact that MS-DOS only looks at the first 8 characters of a label and ignores the rest. Precisely what happens when you try and GOTO an oversize label depends on which version of the operating system you have, but as you can imagine, you can easily end up in the wrong part of the batch file if you have labels like this:

```
:VERBOSITY1
:VERBOSITY2
```

Incidentally, it also depends on which version you have as to whether a line with leading spaces followed by a colon will be accepted – most versions require the colon to be the first character in the line. This and the other quirks of the batch file system should be borne in mind if you are writing for users who may have different brands of MS-DOS on their machines, and you should be particularly rigorous about this if you are writing for the commercial market.

# 9

## A Notepad for You

Now the time has come to stretch the batch file to its limit by creating an original notepad which will help you in the coming chapters to type in assembler code, as well as being an invaluable tool for everyday programming and electronic filofaxing on a small scale.

This is a cheeky little program which will be even more enhanced later when we get down to investigating DEBUG. This Mark One version will allow you to create a file up to 20 lines in length, and retype lines on screen until you are happy with it. You can edit the text in any order, and if you leave blank lines they will be ignored.

In order to run the routine, you require two batch files, the main one called NOTE.BAT, and a much smaller one called R.BAT. In addition, you will require the UC.COM program from the section on interactive batch files and a new 20-byte program called POS.COM.

Again, all the files are on the disk that accompanies this book, together with the completed version of the program which allows you to edit existing files, but it should not take you too long to type in these routines and get a unique facility up and running. First, here is the main batch file, followed by a detailed explanation of what it does:

```
ECHO OFF
IF "%1"=="M" GOTO SKIP
ECHO ON
PROMPT $E[13;13;10;26;13;10p
PROMPT
:SKIP
ECHO OFF
IF "%1"== "M" GOTO continue
CLS
POS F
ECHO Please press Enter to start the program..
COPY CON !A
CLS
ECHO ** *NOTE PAD*
```

```
ECHO **
ECHO **
ECHO **
:CONTINUE
POS @
ECHO ********************************************************************
ECHO **(a)
ECHO **(b)
ECHO **(c)
ECHO **(d)
ECHO **(e)
ECHO **(f)
ECHO **
:MORE
POS R
ECHO Please type a-f to enter/retype a line, z to finish
UC
REM line to be added here later to read-in of existing files
IF ERRORLEVEL 65 IF NOT ERRORLEVEL 66 R a
IF ERRORLEVEL 66 IF NOT ERRORLEVEL 67 R b
IF ERRORLEVEL 67 IF NOT ERRORLEVEL 68 R c
IF ERRORLEVEL 68 IF NOT ERRORLEVEL 69 R d
IF ERRORLEVEL 69 IF NOT ERRORLEVEL 70 R e
IF ERRORLEVEL 70 IF NOT ERRORLEVEL 71 R f
IF ERRORLEVEL 90 GOTO END
GOTO MORE
:END
CTTY NUL
FOR %%A IN (!B !C !D !E !F) DO IF EXIST %%A COPY !A + %%A !A
IF EXIST NOTE.TXT COPY NOTE.TXT NOTE.BAK
COPY !A NOTE.TXT
DEL !?.*
CTTY CON
ECHO ON
PROMPT $E[13;13p
PROMPT
```

The idea behind the program is that the main routine which I've just listed calls another batch file which deals with inputting a single line of text, and which then calls the main file again with the parameter M (standing for more, if you like).

If parameter %1 is not M – which it isn't when you first call the program by typing NOTE – a PROMPT command is called which alters the effect of pressing the Enter key on the keyboard:

```
PROMPT $E[13;13;10;26;13;10p
PROMPT
```

The "p" command at the end of the escape sequence, which must be in lower case, remember, tells MS-DOS to alter the value of one of the keyboard keys, the one which issues the value 13 (in other words, the Enter key). From now on in the program, if Enter is pressed, the result will be to issue the sequence listed between semicolons after the 13 (in other words, a carriage return line feed), followed by the value for Ctrl+Z, followed by another carriage return line feed.

What this means is that Enter has been converted into a single keypress which generates all the code necessary to terminate a one-line entry to a COPY CON routine, and this is how the notepad file is going to be built up, as a series of one-line files to be concatenated (stuck together) at the end of the program.

# A PROMPT return

As always, when PROMPT is used for an offbeat purpose like this, the normal PROMPT is restored afterwards. To ensure that you return at the end of the batch file to your own customised prompt if you have one, either replace the last line of the main batch file with your customised PROMPT command line, or save the prompt at the beginning of the file and restore it at the end, using the technique relating to %PROMPT%, as described later in the section of this book concerning the MS-DOS environment.

One important point to note is that if you interrupt this program at any point, the Enter key will be set up wrongly, so to restore it type:

```
PROMPT $E[13;13p
PROMPT
```

– to make Enter issue just 13 again, otherwise you will keep getting odd error messages. The last two lines of the batch file restore Enter to its former glory.

The next line is one of the most cunning parts of the program, and it will be explained in full when we get on to assembler proper. At this point, all you need to know is that:

```
POS f
```

– must have a space after the POS, but that the case of the parameter "f" is not significant. The reason that I have put it into lower case throughout will become clear in a second or two. The effect of the POS command is to place the cursor five characters in from the left on a specified line. The line specified by "a", for example, is line 6, which is where the line containing "(a)" is located. And those letters not only match the screen position of the line you type in, they correspond to the temporary file name that will hold the line of text.

To create the file, type DEBUG and key in the following lines, regardless of what messages appear on screen, pressing Enter at the end of each line:

```
DEBUG POS.COM
E 100 8A 36 82 00 80 E6 DF 80 EE 3C B4 02 B7 00 B2 07
E 110 CD 10 B4 09 BA 1B 01 CD 21 CD 20 1B 5B 4B 24
R CX
20
W
Q
```

Alternatively, if you prefer, you could follow the practice adopted with the UC.COM program. First create a file called POS using COPY CON POS and containing lines two onwards of the listing I have just given – especially not forgetting the Q in the last line. Then type:

```
DEBUG POS.COM < POS
```

– once again ignoring the File not found message.

As before, remember that the numbers on the lines which begin with E are hexadecimal. To check that the program works, type:

```
POS f
```

– and the cursor should move about halfway down the screen and a couple of columns in. If you have any information on the screen at that point, you will find that the program also erases to the end of the line, a factor which will come in useful when it comes to retyping a line of your notepad.

So the first time through, the Enter key is reset, the screen cleared for neatness' sake, and you are asked to press Enter to start the program. In fact, this creates a blank file called !A. If this file doesn't exist, the program will crash when it comes to putting all the minifiles together at the end.

The files are called !A, !B and so on, on the assumption that you don't have any files with names beginning with an exclamation mark. If you really must have files like that, either locate this routine in a separate subdirectory or rename them.

And finally, in the first call of the program NOTE.BAT, the screen is cleared and the note pad outline printed on screen. You will see that, in order to avoid a program listing that goes on for ever, I have just catered for five lines – you can type in up to twenty, and make the necessary additions to the ECHO ***(a) and so forth lines, as well as a couple more additions, to which I shall refer as we come to them.

Now comes the call:

```
POS r
```

– which places the cursor near the bottom of the screen, and the bottom of screen menu appears. It allows you to type a-f, and you will need to alter that message if you wish to have more lines, and you will also have to type in additional IF ERRORLEVEL lines with increasing numbers in them, and incrementing the letter at the end of the line. For example, to add "g":

```
IF ERRORLEVEL 71 IF NOT ERRORLEVEL 72 R g
```

What is the meaning of the mysterious two letters at the end of the line:

```
R a
```

– and so forth? They call the smaller file R.BAT with the parameter a, b, c, and so on. Here it is:

```
POS %1
COPY CON !%1 > nul
NOTE M
```

This locates the cursor next to the appropriate line, and allows you to type in a line to the appropriate file. Note that the program is not so sophisticated that it can cope with you running over the end of the line.

Note also the use of the redirection operator > which sends the message "1 File(s) copied" to the bit bucket after you have typed the line in. However, infuriatingly, it doesn't get rid of the ^Z character generated when you press our modified version of the Enter key at the end of typing the line.

That's why I have started each line with a double asterisk, because for that fraction of a second when the ^Z is echoed at the beginning of the next line before the main program is summoned again, it is lost among the asterisks and hardly noticed.

The call:

```
NOTE M
```

calls the main routine once more, with the M parameter which causes a jump to the line:

```
POS @
```

To cut a long story short, the ASCII value of "@" is one less than that of "A", so the cursor is placed just at the right spot before the ECHO **(a) line, and the string of asterisks is printed out, followed by as many lines as you have typed in, and wherever the ^Z occurs, it is overwritten by two asterisks. Note, therefore, that you need a final line of two asterisks after your last text line.

And so it goes on, round and round until you have completed keying in your text. If you opt for the same line twice, the original contents are cleared and you type in a complete new line.

When you have finished inputting, you type "z" to exit and that brings you to the END label. At this point, you will get a lot of screen clutter, so I have added the commands:

```
CTTY NUL
...
CTTY CON
```

– which redirect all input and output to NUL and then back to CON again. If you are at all nervous that you might hit the keyboard during this sequence and cause the system to hang, which it will do with CTTY set to NUL, just leave out the first CTTY and replace the second one with CLS. That will leave you with some garbage, but not too much.

Now to deal with the FOR %%A line:

```
FOR %%A IN (!B !C !D !E !F) DO IF EXIST %%A COPY !A + %%A !A
```

Remember that this must be typed as a single line, and that you will have to add !G and so on inside the round brackets if you opt for a longer file. What the command does is to look for each of the files (= lines of text) which you have typed in, and if they exist, append them to !A.

That's why we had to create !A right at the beginning, just in case some awkward so and so omitted to type anything on the first line. As the program is set up, all blank lines are ignored, unless you omit to type anything in !A, where there is a blank line put there at the beginning of the program.

So, if you wish to allow blank lines, place this command near the beginning of the NOTE.BAT file after the line:

```
COPY CON !A
```

– allowing for as many lines of text as you require:

```
FOR %%A IN (!B !C !D !E !F) DO COPY !A %%A
```

– which will set up the files with blank lines in them. The reason why I have not allowed for blank lines is that the main purpose for which you might be using the routine later in the book is for keying in assembler programs, and blank lines will have unpleasant side effects. So, you may like to create two versions, one for notes, another for assembler source programs.

The next line creates a back-up of your note file, if you have one – this is in preparation for later editing of existing files – and deletes all the !A, !B and so on temporary files.

Finally the prompt is reset, and with a sigh of relief it is all over.

You might like to add a call to another batch file at the end of NOTE.BAT if you want to use it extensively before we get to the more sophisticated version. Add this line to NOTE.BAT:

```
ECHO To rename your NOTE.BAT file, type: NEW followed by the name
```

Then you call the batch file NEW from the MS-DOS prompt:

```
IF "%1"=="". GOTO GOOF
IF EXIST %1 GOTO PROBLEMS
REN NOTE.BAT %1
ECHO File renamed to %1
GOTO END
:GOOF
ECHO You haven't specified a file. Please call NEW again.
GOTO END
:PROBLEMS
ECHO The file %1 exists already. Please call NEW again
:END
```

That is one very useful little routine, but as we shall see later it can be made even more user-friendly than it is at present.

# 10

# *Putting Batch All Together*

The batch file commands we have looked at are as follows:

```
CALL (MS-DOS 3.3)
ECHO
FOR
GOTO
IF (plus NOT, EXIST, ERRORLEVEL)
PAUSE
REM
SHIFT
```

These are all internal commands, so they should like all the other internal commands be regarded as reserved words. That is to say, don't try and create a .COM, .EXE or BAT file called ECHO, or REM, because MS-DOS looks first at its internal commands before going elsewhere, and your precious file will never be executed.

## Batch from the keyboard

As these are just like internal commands, it is possible to type them in straight from the MS-DOS prompt, although the GOTO and SHIFT commands don't make a great deal of sense outside a batch file.

So, for example, you can put a comment up on screen when you go off to lunch to remind yourself about something to do when you return:

```
REM Call Sales at 2.30
```

Of the other commands, IF and FOR are the most useful from the keyboard.

To make a check for the presence or absence of a file, you could type:

```
IF NOT EXIST C:\LETTERS\FRED ECHO It's not there
```

Or, to be a little more sophisticated:

```
FOR %A IN (SUB1 SUB2) DO IF EXIST C:\%A\FRED ECHO It's in %A
```

This will cause a search to take place in the subdirectories SUB1 and SUB2 for the file FRED, and the ECHO message will tell you which, if any, of the subdirectories, it is in. Note that from the MS-DOS prompt you only need one per cent sign before the single letter.

Another use of the FOR command is to persuade COPY to work on more than one set of files at a time. If you wanted to back up your .DAT files and your .WP files to drive B, try:

```
FOR %A IN (*.BAT *.WP) DO COPY %A B:
```

But the amount of time and anguish typing that little lot in could be much better spent in writing a batch file.

## Developing batch files

Finally, here are a couple of hints about developing batch files and a recap of the main pitfalls.

If you keep ECHO ON during development, you can watch what is going on, but there are two drawbacks to this situation. The first is that the batch file when running will tend to generate a great spaghetti-like list of echoed commands which will soon zoom off the top of the screen, usually including the very one you're most keen on examining again.

There are two particular ways of dealing with the problem. The first is to press Ctrl+P and list what is happening on your printer. Alternatively, if you can localise the bug you are trying to eradicate from the batch file, you can of course put ECHO ON at particular points in the file, rather than having it on all the way through.

The second drawback with ECHO is having to switch it on and off as you are developing a batch file, when you are alternating between debugging and watching it on screen to see if the layout is right and if the file is actually doing what it is supposed to do.

There is a simple technique to overcome the problem, and it is one which I borrowed from the old days of mainframe computers when I was writing programs in a language called ALGOL 60. One way of debugging then was to list the value of variables at certain points in the program, and it was always a pain having to enter and remove the checking lines, not least because you never know when you may have to go back, many moons later, to a supposedly bugless program and check it out again.

In ALGOL variables have to be declared at the beginning of the program, so I would always include this variable and set it to TRUE:

```
BOOLEAN test;
test := TRUE;
```

Statements in ALGOL end with a semicolon. The Boolean variable is nothing more frightening than another way of saying a variable which has the value true or false. Then, at a later stage in the program, I would insert a block of statements like this:

```
IF test THEN
BEGIN
.....
END;
```

When test was TRUE, the print statements in the block were executed, but when the program was in production mode, the statement was replaced by:

```
test:=FALSE;
```

That technique can readily be adapted when you are developing programs in BASIC or any other language, and for batch files we can even be a little more clever, in that we don't have to change a line in the file at all. The technique goes like this if you want to alternate ECHO ON and OFF. Start the program with these three lines:

```
ECHO OFF
IF "%1" == "*" ECHO ON
IF "%1" == "*" SHIFT
```

The assumption is that when you run the batch file, make the first parameter an asterisk if you want ECHO ON, and if you have other parameters you want to use simply put them second, third, and so on, and they will be shifted one to the left so that the rest of the program runs normally. The other assumption, in case there is someone out there insisting on using it, is that you don't ever want parameter %1 to be an asterisk in a production run. If you really can't live without that option, just use a different character or character combination.

There is another crafty aspect to this device, and that is you can retain the facility for selectively switching ECHO ON and OFF during the running of the batch file, to enable you to gloss over, say, a menu listing which doesn't need to be checked through every time the file is run. The only limitation to this approach is that you should not use SHIFT elsewhere in the batch file, otherwise the asterisk will disappear altogether. Here is a batch file which has no other useful function in life than to demonstrate how the idea works:

```
ECHO OFF
IF "%1" == "*" SHIFT
ECHO Line one
ECHO Line two
IF %0 == * ECHO ON
ECHO Line three
ECHO Line four
ECHO OFF
ECHO Line five
```

If the first parameter is an asterisk, the SHIFT command moves all the other parameters, if there are any, one to the left. This not only ensures that your first "real" parameter is in pole position, so to speak, but it also moves %1 to %0, which is the location normally taken up by the name of the batch file itself.

So, if the asterisk has taken over the spot belonging to the batch file name, ECHO goes ON at the appropriate point. Fortunately, MS-DOS doesn't mind ECHO OFF being called if ECHO is already OFF, and no error message is generated in the case where %0 is not an asterisk.

If you are wondering why I did not surround the %0 in quotes, the reason is that it is not likely that this parameter will ever be empty, and if it gets emptied by an excess of SHIFTing, you may well be grateful for an error message at that point.

If you really insist on using SHIFT and switching ECHO on and off in the middle of a file, you will have to set an environment variable to play that trick for you. That's something for a later chapter.

Another approach to debugging batch files under development, still using our asterisk, is to insert optional PAUSE commands at strategic points in the file:

```
IF %0 == * PAUSE
```

Also, if you have one or more CLS commands in a file, you will lose the command echo – unless you have your printer copying the output, that is. So, you could also include this variation on a plain CLS:

```
IF NOT %0 == * CLS
```

To check that you are actually turning up at a particular label, again the asterisk can come in useful:

```
:CONTINUE
IF %0 == * ECHO Got to label CONTINUE
```

## Final thoughts

Batch files are extremely verbose, and not too easy to debug. If you find that something mysterious is going wrong, first of all switch ECHO ON at the appropriate point.

IF is a bit of a pain. You can run a string of IFs one after another on a line, like this:

```
IF NOT EXIST Filea IF NOT EXIST Fileb GOTO CONTINUE
ECHO One of the files is missing
GOTO ERROR
:CONTINUE
```

But you won't get the right response from:

```
IF "%1" == "YES" GOTO MORE IF "%1" == "NO" GOTO EXIT
```

– even though both of the %1 occurrences are duly replaced with the parameter if you run that command with ECHO ON. You have to split the line into two separate commands for it to work properly.

Even though ECHO simply prints out what comes after it on screen, it still goes in for parameter substitution, which is useful, and as we noted earlier it also picks up > < and | and treats them as piping and redirection operators, but which can be a nuisance.

We all have our favourite errors in batch files, if favourite is the right word. One that caused me quite a lot of grief when I was less conversant with MS-DOS than I am now was this line:

```
:LABEL1 ECHO This is label 1
```

Nothing ECHOed. The reason is quite simple: Everything after the first space in a label is ignored by the batch file processor. The plus side of that is that you can use the text after a label – even a dummy label you don't intend to use in the program – as a comment line.

Labels are a particular source of error, not least if you duplicate a label name. Remember that the batch file processor always starts looking at the beginning of the file for a label, so the first occurrence of the label will be the one it always goes for. That's a bug which can take quite a deal of fixing.

A last word of advice: Try and write your batch files in a modular fashion, even though the limited command language more or less defies you to do so. If you have a batch file with GOTOs threading in and out of one another, that is a recipe for potential disaster. The batch file is, after all, just another programming language, this time the MS-DOS operating system itself.

The real problem is that the operating system is designed to perform specific individual tasks rather than groups of different activities, and there is no real concession made to structured programming. A common pattern for batch files is the menu program, which has the following general structure:

```
Menu options
Choose option
GOTO label depending on option
:LABEL1
option one
GOTO END
:LABEL2
option two
GOTO END
....
:END
```

This kind of hopping around, which can get quite messy and confusing, can be overcome in a number of ways. The first is to create a short batch file which contains the "closing down" message at the end of the run and call it at the point where GOTO END would otherwise be.

Here is a possible listing for such a batch file called MENU.BAT:

```
ECHO OFF
CLS
ECHO Thank you for using this program.
ECHO Do you want to return to the menu?
UC
IF ERRORLEVEL 89 IF NOT ERRORLEVEL 90 MENU
```

Point number one: When you load one batch file from inside another, ECHO is ON, unless you are using CALL from MS-DOS Version 3.3 and above. The UC refers to the little .COM program we wrote a chapter or two back.

Point number two: There is no problem in calling the original batch file from within the one it called. In fact, you can call a batch file from within itself, if you get my meaning. Imagine a menu where there are four or five options. If the user types an incorrect option, instead of having to GOTO a label you could simply type:

```
%0
```

– unless, that is, you have been taking all my clever advice about using the %1 parameter as a switch for ECHO ON during batch file development!

Another shortcoming in batch files as far as structured programming is concerned is the lack of an ELSE feature in an IF command. It would make life so much easier. Instead of typing a mythical line like this:

```
IF EXISTS FRED GOTO A ELSE IF NOT EXISTS JOE GOTO B
```

– we are reduced to two-liners like:

```
IF EXISTS FRED GOTO A
IF NOT EXISTS JOE GOTO B
```

That has the same effect, but is nowhere near as neat and easy to follow.

One final point: Part of the concept of structured programming, when it isn't being too academic and doctrinaire, is to make programs more readable. One straightforward way of achieving this is to dispense with a scruffy-looking series of ECHO commands for a menu listing, or something of the sort, and put all the menu lines into a file. The bonuses from this approach are first, that there is no problem about blank lines, and second, that you simply issue one neat command from inside the batch file:

```
TYPE MENULIST
```

After all that has been said, though, it is quite a sense of achievement getting one of the beasts up and running, and in the long term batch files are an excellent way of optimising your use of the PC, especially when it comes to frequently-repeated tasks like an opening menu to give you a list of working options, or housekeeping back ups of files currently in use.

# *11*

# *Assembly Time with DEBUG*

In the next few chapters, we shall find out how to persuade a batch file to beep, play around with the size of the cursor, switch the Caps and Num Locks on and off from within a program, play a guessing game with the computer, create a loop counter for batch files, and devise a much-improved directory listing with additional information not normally available. All this and more will be achieved with the help of DEBUG, and by the end of the proceedings you will also have learned more than a little about the mysteries of 8086 assembly language programming. You'll find a complete description of DEBUG and its commands in Appendix B at the end of the book. At the end of each chapter on DEBUG, you will find a summary of the material covered and additional things for you to explore.

## How to DEBUG

One of the most important programs supplied on your MS-DOS disk – or in some cases your supplementary disk – goes by the name of "DEBUG.COM". As we shall see, it not only allows you to explore the memory of your PC as well as the contents of data files and programs, it has the additional bonus of letting you write your own assembler programs, and we shall be dipping our toes gently into 8086 assembler later on.

First things first, though. Why call it "DEBUG" at all? The main reason is that it is designed as a programming tool to allow the machine code programmer to iron out so-called bugs in programs. The actual term "bug", so the story goes, reaches back to the early days of computing, to 1945. One of the first ladies of computing, a certain Grace Hopper, was trying to cure a hardware fault on an early machine at Harvard University. When the fault was finally traced it was discovered that the cause of the trouble was a dead moth stuck in a relay. Hence the term "bug" was born. The joke has continued, even to the wittily named equivalent program for CP/M micros, called "DDT", the Dynamic Debugging Tool, which sounds just about ideal for a kind of computing insecticide.

Anyway, let's turn to our version of DEBUG for the PC. To load the program, insert your MS-DOS disk in drive A, or from the root directory on your hard disk just type:

```
DEBUG
```

After a second's pause, a rather unhelpful minus sign appears as a prompt. This is not a comment on your skills as a programmer, just DEBUG's way of telling you that it is sitting there politely waiting for you to do something. So oblige it by typing:

```
Q
```

for Quit, and you will find yourself back at the MS-DOS prompt. That's about as simple and mindless as a DEBUG session can get, but it is vital that you should know that this is the one and only escape route out of DEBUG short of rebooting the computer. Now let's try something a little more demanding.

Create a two-line file like this:

```
COPY CON FRED
```

And type in this text:

```
This is a demo file
```

– followed by Enter twice. This is to give us a couple of extra bytes to play around with in a moment. Next, press the F6 function key, which puts "^Z" – the end of file marker – up on the screen, and when you press Enter again you will find yourself back at the MS-DOS prompt. Now check that it is there by asking for it to be typed on the screen:

```
TYPE FRED
```

Let's examine the contents of FRED using DEBUG. There are two ways of telling DEBUG that we want to look at this particular file. Here's the easy way:

```
DEBUG FRED
```

The more complicated approach involves using the N and L commands, and we shall be meeting them later when we create programs from within DEBUG itself. Now the program is loaded, and it is also obligingly loaded FRED into memory ready for us to examine it. DEBUG works with a total of nineteen one-letter commands, of which we've already met Q, and which may or may not have numbers and/or letters after them. DEBUG doesn't mind if you work in upper or lower case, but I am sticking to upper case for the sake of clarity. The command to use now is:

```
D
```

– which asks the program to Dump a portion of memory on the screen. The output display should look something like this:

```
53AA:0100   54 68 69 73 20 69 73 20-61 20 64 65 6D 6F 20 66   This is a demo f
53AA:0110   69 6C 65 0D 0A 0D 0A 00-00 00 00 00 00 00 00 00   ile.............
```

```
53AA:0120  00 00 00 00 00 00 00 00-00 00 00 00 00 00 00 00  ................
53AA:0130  00 00 00 00 00 00 00 00-00 00 00 00 00 00 00 00  ................
53AA:0140  00 00 00 00 00 00 00 00-00 00 00 00 00 00 00 00  ................
53AA:0150  00 00 00 00 00 00 00 00-00 00 00 00 00 00 00 00  ................
53AA:0160  00 00 00 00 00 00 00 00-00 00 00 00 00 00 00 00  ................
53AA:0170  00 00 00 00 00 00 00 00-00 00 00 00 00 00 00 00  ................
```

That's a pretty confusing slab of information at first sight, but it all makes very good sense, as you will see. First, think of the information as being in three blocks: The lefthand set of numbers divided by a colon refers to memory addresses (and don't worry if that number is different in your display); the second set of numbers refers to the values in those memory addresses; and the righthand block contains an attempt by DEBUG to convert where possible into ASCII values the corresponding numbers from the middle block.

One very important point to bear in mind is that all the values are in hexadecimal. If you are not familiar with hex and why it is so useful in the binary world of your micro, turn to Appendix A which offers a painless introduction to the subject.

Now let's examine those three blocks in more detail. On the left are the memory addresses, which consist of two parts, the segment number and the offset, as they are called. If we look at the easy bit first, the offset number, you will see that the addresses are divided up into convenient chunks of sixteen. The first line is 100-10F, the second 110-11F, and so on. This means, if you count along the central block of numbers, that address 103 contains the value 73, address 111 contains 6C, and so forth.

You may be wondering why DEBUG causes the addresses to start at location 100 rather than plain zero. That's all to do with the way programs are loaded in MS-DOS, and whenever DEBUG is asked to load a file, it assumes that it might be dealing with a program, so it starts at 100. What happens to the addresses 0-0FF we shall see later on when we come to take our first steps in programming proper.

Now to the lefthand side of the colon, the segment number. As I said, this will vary according to the current contents of the memory and a variety of other factors, but the question you will be asking yourself is why MS-DOS doesn't have a simple straightforward numbering system from 0-FFFF for memory addresses, instead of this complicated double number.

The answer lies in the value of FFFF in hex, which comes out at 65535 in decimal. Starting from zero, this would only allow you to refer to 65536 locations in memory, 64K, when most PC computers have at least 512K, and many have 640K and more. So, a method had to be devised for addressing the maximum of one megabyte of memory, a million or so address locations, and that is why the memory is divided up into 16 times 64K segments. The number to the right of the colon is referred to as the "offset".

The central block of numbers, containing the values in the addresses, is split into two manageable sections of eight each by the dash in the middle. And on the righthand side, you will see the ASCII equivalent of those values. Upper case T in ASCII is 54, lower case h = 68, and the next in sequence, lower case i = 69.

In between each word is the value 20, a space, and at the end of the text comes the sequence 0D 0A twice, control codes which generate the functions carriage return and line feed. As there is no printable ASCII equivalent for those two codes, DEBUG places a dot in those locations.

In case you were wondering what happened to the Ctrl+Z you typed in to end the file, the marker is not included as part of the file itself. For a discussion of the role of the end-of-file marker, see the Chapter on EDLIN.

If you load a file containing ASCII characters outside the normal range, such as the accented characters, mathematical Greek or box drawing characters, DEBUG can't cope with them and puts a dot where they occur, which is not particularly helpful unless you have a full ASCII chart in front of you for reference purposes.

## Doing more dumping

Having done a straightforward dump of the contents of a file, let us take things a little further. If you type:

```
D
```

again, you will be treated to the next 128 memory locations, and so on. That's what D does by default, it starts at 100 hex and ploughs on 128 decimal locations at a time. You can control D much more strictly than that, though, either by specifying the start address, the start address followed by the last address you want to see, or alternatively by specifying a range of addresses. So, try the following, and see what happens:

```
D 109
D 104 111
D 108,123
D 100 L 20
```

You can separate the values by either a space or a comma, and there's no need for a space after the D. If the mood takes you, you can even put a comma after the D. The fourth example means: Starting at address 100, for the length of 20 hex bytes do a dump on screen, in other words bytes 100-11F. You can use the same approaches with other commands, too.

That's all very fascinating, but what about altering the contents of the file and saving the new version to disk? Let's say we want to change the text to "That is a demo file". This can be achieved by using the E ( = Enter) command, which is a powerful means of changing the contents of memory, or of examining them and then altering them.

First, the simple method. To change memory locations 101 and 102 from "is" to "at", all you need to do is type:

```
E 101 "at"
D 100 10F
```

The D command is to enable you to check that you have made the alteration you require, and this time you have to tell D to start at location 100, as you have already used it once or twice in this DEBUG session. In fact, it is sensible practice always to specify a start address with DEBUG commands, to help to reduce the ever-present opportunities for error and confusion.

It is also vital never to make a correction "blind", as it were, without subsequently checking with D, or when we are actually programming, with U. An error of a single byte one way or another can be disastrous, especially in programming, since the computer will try and make sense of the mangled instructions that follow – with the likelihood that your code could be corrupted or that the whole computer will seize up and require rebooting.

Another useful tip with D is to limit the amount of listing which appears, which I did in the above example, by typing one of the following:

```
D 100 10F
D 100 L 10
```

– if you only want to examine a handful of bytes. Two default batches of D gobble up most of the screen, and it can be most annoying to "lose" information off the top of the screen which you may want to check back on.

Now for something a little trickier. Let's assume that we want to add a full stop at the end of the sentence. We can't just overwrite the 0D at location 113, we need to enter a full stop and then 0D plus 0A. No problem. E can cope with a mix of ASCII values and numbers, so you can type:

```
E 113 "." 0D 0A
```

– or, if the fancy takes you:

```
E 113 3E 0D 0A
```

As you can guess, 3E is the ASCII equivalent of full stop. Try a memory dump to ensure that you have achieved what you set out to do. You will find that the file ends with:

```
0D 0A 0A
```

– which has precisely the same effect as 0D 0A 0D 0A. Note that DEBUG is permanently in "overwrite" mode, and that to insert bytes whilst shunting subsequent bytes further along the memory requires a little mental gymnastics, some careful checking, and the use of the M command, which is described in detail in Appendix B.

There is an alternative way to use E, but it is a little trickier, and it requires some practice. If you just type:

```
E 100
```

– the contents of address 100 will appear on screen, followed by a full stop. You can now do one of three things. If you press the space bar, the contents of address 100 remain unchanged, and the contents of the next location will pop up on the screen.

If you press Enter, you return back to the DEBUG minus prompt. But, if you type in a new hex value within the permitted range of 0-FF, the contents of that location are altered. Then you either press the space bar to examine the next address, or you press Enter to return to the prompt.

When you use E in this mode, however, you can only type in two-digit hex values, not ASCII characters. It does require a little experimentation to get it right, so have a go with this command, checking what you have done with the D command each time. And when you are confident with E, have a go at one more trick. To advance one byte, as you now know, you press the space bar, but to go back one byte you press the minus key. That's a useful card to have up your sleeve.

# Saving the file

Now you've altered the file, you want to save it to disk. There's a one-letter command which will do just that:

```
W
```

When you type that, you'll get a message like this:

```
Writing 17 bytes
```

Remember, that value is in hex like all DEBUG values. That's all very well and good, but how does DEBUG know that it is supposed to be writing 17 bytes and not 3 or 5000? That is a question we shall be exploring a little later on, but first let's use our knowledge gained of DEBUG so far to make a batch file draw attention to itself.

# A batch file that beeps

Our interactive batch file from a previous Chapter asked the user to type a letter within a range, and printed out a message like this if the user hit the wrong key:

```
Please type a letter in range!
```

It would be rather nice if the PC could be persuaded to give a beep from its rather tinny speaker at this point to draw the user's attention to the error of his ways. Given our knowledge of DEBUG so far, this presents no problem.

Create a one-line file, using COPY CON DEMO.BAT, containing the following line:

```
ECHO Please type a letter in range!X
```

The purpose of the X will become clear when you now use DEBUG on your batch file. If the one-line batch file is called FRED.BAT, type:

```
DEBUG FRED.BAT
D 100 125
```

– and you should see this output on screen:

```
33AA:0100   45 43 48 4F 20 50 6C 65-61 73 65 20 74 79 70 65 ECHO Please type
33AA:0110   20 61 20 6C 65 74 74 65-72 20 69 6E 20 72 61 6E a letter in ran
33AA:0120   67 65 21 58 0D 0A 00 00-00 00 00 00 00 00 00 00 ge!X...........
```

Work out the location of the capital X and alter its value to 7 using E. In this case, it is location 123 hex:

```
E 123 7
```

You have now altered the X to the value 7 in ASCII, a control code which causes the bell to ring, or rather the speaker to beep. In the old days of teleprinters, it actually was a bell, and the purpose was to wake up the operator at the other end of the teleprinter line.

Use W to write the file back to disk, and then run by typing DEMO, to ensure that you have got the sound effect working properly. It may puzzle you at first that the bell rings twice in quick succession, but that is simply because we have not switched ECHO OFF at the beginning of the file. Note that the bell also rings if you simply use the TYPE command.

So, one additional way of having a bell ready to ring at any time is to create a little file with just the bell in it, and insert a TYPE command at the appropriate spot in your batch file. That's just one of many neat little tricks you can perform with DEBUG. Here's a much more powerful one, which involves bending the operating system of MS-DOS itself.

## A new version of DIR

In our exploration of batch files, we devised a much more user-friendly version of DIR, but we couldn't call it DIR, because you will recall that whenever you type something in at the keyboard, MS-DOS looks first at its "internal" commands, the ones like DIR, COPY, and so on which are loaded into memory when you boot the machine up, then at .COM and .EXE files, and only then at .BAT files. We also devised an improved DEL. It would be nice if you could customise DIR and DEL for your own use or for that of others.

Here's how it can be done. First, though, just to be on the safe side, make a copy of your MS-DOS disk on to a blank disk using DISKCOPY and work from that, in case you press the wrong buttons and make a mess of the most important file on the disk, namely COMMAND.COM.

This program contains the main part of the operating system, and is always sitting inside the memory of your PC, some of it at the top of the memory well out of harm's way. Occasionally, memory-greedy programs overwrite part of COM-MAND.COM and that's why floppy disk users sometimes get asked to reload the MS-DOS disk before exiting back to the prompt.

What we are going to do is to examine the innards of COMMAND.COM and alter three bytes to enable us to rename its version of DIR to XXX and use our own version – DIR.BAT – which calls the MS-DOS command under its own control. So, for starters, type:

```
DEBUG COMMAND.COM
```

To find out where the name DIR is located, we could type D and keep on pressing it until we stumbled across DIR on the righthand side of the display, but that's not a very elegant way of going about things, particularly as the bytes we are after are located a fair way into the program.

So let me introduce you to a very powerful command: S, for search. With S, you need to tell DEBUG where you are starting from and where you will finish – and, on top of that, what it is you are looking for. In the case of the string being searched for, you can either type in ASCII characters, hex values, or a cocktail of the two, just as with E.

The 64 dollar question is: How do we know where the search ought to finish? We know we must start at location 100 hex, but we must first find out how big the file is. The simplest way of all is to type:

```
DIR COMMAND.COM
```

at the MS-DOS prompt, and you will see against the file name a value in the region of 25000 bytes, according to which version of MS-DOS you are running. To be on the safe side, round that up to the nearest hex equivalent, 6200:

```
S 100 6200 "DIR"
```

The request is to search from locations 100 to 6200 in the current segment for the string inside the double quotes. That will generate a list of five numbers, indicating that the command has found five occurrences of "DIR" in the file. My Version 3.3 came up with these values:

```
33C1:5190
33C1:5484
33C1:5502
33C1:5511
33C1:5520
```

Incidentally, S for search is case sensitive when dealing with ASCII characters in quotes, so if you put lower case "dir" inside the quotes you would generate a different set of numbers. You might like to track them down and find out what's in those addresses. A clue: As "dir" is part of the word "directory", you might well expect to come across some of the error messages lurking inside COMMAND.COM.

What we need to find is which of the five numbers refers to the DIR we want to change. Using D, list the contents of the memory locations for the five numbers, starting sixteen bytes earlier in case the DIR is part of a word or the information immediately preceding it is important. So, for example, if your first number is 5190, type:

```
D 5180
```

## Sums in hex

Remember, if the number is 5000, we are working in hex and subtracting sixteen leaves you with 4FF0. If you get confused about this – and who doesn't? – help is at hand from DEBUG itself. It includes a command which does primitive hex calculations for you. If you type:

```
H 5000 10
```

– DEBUG will obligingly provide you with the sum and the difference of the two numbers:

```
5010 4FF0
```

## Finding DIR

If you now work through the areas of memory, you should find the following strings containing DIR:

```
<DIR>
DIR
CHDIR
MKDIR
RMDIR
```

In other words, we have found the string of characters which DIR uses to indicate a subdirectory in the on-screen display, the DIR command itself, and the three other internal DOS commands which involve directories. The first allows you to change directories, the second to make a new directory, and the third to remove an unwanted directory. Another search would reveal their shortened forms (CD, MD and RD respectively).

So, by a process of elimination, it is the second occurrence of DIR which we want to change. The exact address will vary according to the version of DOS which you have, but working from my machine which runs MS-DOS 3.3, the address is 5484, so I would type:

```
E 5484 "XXX"
```

Check that you have achieved the desired effect by using the D command. If you now save COMMAND.COM back to your disk using W and then reboot pressing Ctrl+Alt+Del in the usual way, you will find that the DIR command has gone missing, and in order to get a directory listing, you have to type:

```
XXX
```

That means that we have craftily created ourselves an opportunity to devise our own batch file called DIR.BAT in which we call up the actual DIR command by including the line XXX in the file.

This is indeed a powerful tool, but it should be used with caution and thoroughly checked out before you actually use it for real.

# Summary

The command DEBUG is loaded from the MS-DOS prompt either with or without a parameter. In the latter case, this should be the name of a file as in:

```
DEBUG COMMAND.COM
```

Remember that the only way to disentangle yourself from the clutches of DEBUG is to type:

```
Q
```

– for Quit. Alternatively, if you have got into a real mess and the system hangs, it is a case of pressing Ctrl+Alt+Del or, if things are really bad, a system reset – or if you don't have that option, switching off and starting all over again.

To display areas of memory, use this command:

```
D
```

– which by default will start at address 100 and dump hex 80 bytes on to the screen in the format segment:offset, followed by the first 10 hex bytes in hex, then an attempt by DEBUG to make ASCII sense of them. D can have three kinds of parameters:

```
D 220
D 230 24F
D 1000 L 20
```

The first simply specifies the start address and assumes you want 80 hex bytes dumped. The second specifies the start and end addresses for the dump – in which case be careful if you have specified a large number, or the information will simply scroll straight off the top of the screen.

The same applies to the third option, which tells DEBUG to start at a specified address and list the next 20 bytes in the case given above.

The E command is the least easy to master. It can be used in two ways, in the first case either to insert ASCII, strings, or both – like this:

```
E 100 "This is a string with carriage return line feed",0D,0A
```

– or by specifying an address:

```
E 100
```

– at which point E will show you the next byte and let you do one of the following:
  (1) Press Enter to conclude using E;
  (2) Press space bar to move to the next higher byte;
  (3) Press minus to move to the next lower byte;
  (4) Enter a new value for the byte, followed by (1), (2) or (3).

The S for search command is less fraught, and can be used with the same parameters as D and with the same mix of ASCII and strings as E. Remember that any string inside quotes is case sensitive.

When things go wrong, DEBUG tries to be helpful. It has one catch-all error message:

```
^ Error
```

– in which the carat is used as an arrow to point at where in the line things started to go amiss. Here are some examples explained:

```
S "DIR"
   ^ Error
```

Here, the objection is to the beginning of the string. DEBUG expects to find a number or sequence of numbers indicating the search boundaries first.

```
D 1000 999
       ^ Error
```

At first the marker appears to be in the wrong place, but what it is saying is that "I got as far as this in the second number, and expected to find another digit, since I can't dump backwards from a given address to a lower address".

```
E 1000 "unfinished string

           " Error
```

Here DEBUG can't find the closing quotes in the string.

Experiment with these commands, and deliberately make mistakes so that you can see what the error message is and how you can recover easily from them. Try loading another program into DEBUG – and why not try DEBUG itself:

```
DEBUG DEBUG.COM
```

Look for the string "Error" and you will see when you dump the memory around the first occurrence of the string that there are a couple of other error messages which DEBUG has up its sleeve.

The H for Hex, command needs treating with a little care, as it is something of a blunt instrument. It comes in most useful when you are trying to unscramble hex values, particularly as when 100 – 1 isn't 99:

```
H 100 1
0101 00FF
```

Remember that the first value is the product of the two numbers, and the second is the difference between them. When adding, of course, it doesn't matter which way round you enter the parameters to H, but when subtracting it is significant:

```
H 100 10
0110 00F0

H 10 100
0110 FF10
```

So, H isn't particularly bright at negative numbers, and the same problems will occur if you try adding or subtracting around the maximum value it can cope with, namely FFFF. Otherwise it is a valuable tool and a great help in coming to terms with the vagaries of hex. If only it had a hex to decimal converter and vice versa it would have been perfect.

# 12

# *Registers and Cursors*

## Calling the registers

A little while ago, I promised to explain just how it is that DEBUG knows how big a file is, and in order to get the answer we need to turn to examine the heart of the 8086 CPU (Central Processor Unit) which drives your PC, the registers, which in turn will give us a lead into writing a few lines of assembly language itself. If you type the following sequence of commands:

```
DEBUG COMMAND.COM
R
```

– you will be on the receiving end of a register listing which looks something like this, although many of the actual values will vary depending on circumstances:

```
AX=0000  BX=0000  CX=62DC  DX=0000 SP=FFEE BP=0000  SI=0000  DI=0000
DS=33C1  ES=33C1  SS=33C1  CS=33C1 IP=0100    NV UP EI PL NZ NA PO NC
33C1:0100 E92D0D          JMP       0E30
```

At first sight, this all looks just about as user friendly as a herd of charging rhino, but everything does make good sense, as we shall see when we gradually work our way through it. If you examine the first line and a half, you will see that there appear to be 13 hex numbers, each of four digits. Each hex value, you'll remember, corresponds to up to 1111 in binary, so these are 16-bit numbers, each with a two-letter name against them. In computer speak, a 16-bit value is called a word, and so each of these registers contains a word of memory.

For the moment, let us concentrate on the first four: AX, BX, CX and DX. These are registers inside the CPU where many of the key operations of the computer take place. For convenience, they can also be divided up into pairs of 8-bit registers, like this:

```
AH + AL = AX
BH + BL = BX
```

```
CH + CL = CX
DH + DL = DX
```

The "H" stands for the High byte, the "L" for the Low byte. The most important register of all is AX, where A = Accumulator, in which arithmetical operations take place. B = Base register, C = Count register, and D = Data register. More about the details of these as the occasion arises.

The other 16-bit registers refer to index, pointer and segment functions, and there is in fact a 14th register which is indicated by that jumble of pairs of letters in the latter half of the second row. That's the register holding the status flags, of which again more later.

For the moment, just look at the count register, CX. It contains the hex value 62DC (which may be more or less in the case of your version of MS-DOS), and that adds up to 25308 in decimal. That's the size of the COMMAND.COM program, and DEBUG uses the CX register to work out how many bytes to save to file. The BX register should be set to zero, because that's called into use when you create extra large files. Of course, these registers have many other uses in actual programming.

The third line of the listing generated by the R command tells us about the instruction which is next in line to be carried out by the computer, and in this case it is the first instruction in the program, as you can see by examining the value in the IP, or Instruction Pointer register, in the middle of the second line. It has the value 100, at which address all programs start.

The next line gives the full address of the program followed by the machine code generated by the instruction: JMP 0E30, which is a jump to the address 0E30. As we shall see soon, this information is vital to our adventure into assembly programming on which we are now going to embark, and the registers can be inspected and modified in a similar way to that which we use to examine and alter addresses in memory, using D and E.

The third area for inspecting and modifying is the actual program itself, and for this we use the commands A to assemble code into memory, and U to unassemble it into a mnemonic code which – more or less – makes sense on the screen. Normally, computer folk speak in terms of a disassembler, but presumably this was ruled out as the D command had already been taken up for Dumping areas of memory on screen.

## Bending the cursor

Now let's try and write our first program using DEBUG. It is only four lines long, but it does actually serve a useful purpose, and it will enable you to experiment and customise one aspect of your PC's screen. First, here is the listing which you type in after loading DEBUG and typing A (for Assemble) plus, as always, Enter. For the moment, ignore the rather odd-looking numbers separated by a colon on the left which appear as you key the instructions in. What you type is:

```
DEBUG
A
MOV AH, 01
MOV CX, 0004
INT 10
INT 20
```

Type those lines in (either upper or lower case will do), and follow them by a blank line which brings you back to the minus prompt of DEBUG. Note that this time DEBUG is typed without any parameter or file name. So, before I explain what the instructions mean, let me first show how you save the program. First, DEBUG needs to have a name for the program, so type:

```
N CURON.COM
```

The ".COM" extension tells the operating system that it is an actual executable program. Next, being rather stupid, DEBUG needs to know how big the program is. We can find that out by looking at the numbers which appeared as you were typing the program in. To review them, type the unassemble command:

```
U100
```

– and you should see something like this on your screen:

```
33C0:0100 B401      MOV AH,01
33C0:0102 B90400    MOV CX,0004
33C0:0105 CD10      INT 10
33C0:0107 CD20      INT 20
33C0:0109
```

That's followed by garbage, which is simply DEBUG trying to make sense of what happens to be in memory at that point. It is usually in the form of a horrendously complicated-looking instruction like:

```
ADD [BX+SI],AL
```

That does actually make sense, but for the moment let's keep to our relatively simple piece of code. Remember that the number on the left of the colon refers – in hex, of course – to the segment of memory which is being used by DEBUG, and that can vary from time to time and from one machine to another depending on what other memory requirements are currently in force.

What interests us is the number after the colon, which gives the actual count of the number of bytes being used. The first instruction in the program moves the value 01 into the AH register, the high byte of the AX register, and you can see from the next column of numbers that this instruction takes up two bytes. The first byte, B4, is the machine code for this particular instruction, and the 01, as you will have guessed, is the number to be moved.

The second instruction is two bytes further on starting at address 102. This time it takes up three bytes, the first being the machine code itself – B9 – and the rest being the number which is moved. No, your eyes don't deceive you: The number 0004 is the "wrong way round" in the machine code. More of that oddity later.

So, now we come to two "interrupt" instructions, both sharing the machine code value CD, but with different parameters. The second one is a standard way of halting a machine code program and passing control neatly and tidily back to MS-DOS. More about all this in a moment or two. The total number of bytes gobbled up is 9, and you can see that value at the beginning of the first "free" line of the disassembled code, since it points to address 109 – remember that programs start at 100.

Now, in order to be able to write this program to our named file we need to put the number of bytes to write into the CX register. As you remember, that's the count register where DEBUG looks for the number of bytes to save. The R, for Register, command can be used to alter the registers or flags by using the appropriate letters after it. So, we can examine and alter the CX register by typing:

R CX

and a number will appear, giving the current value of CX, plus a colon after which you type the digit 9 plus Enter. Type R again, and you will see the altered value of CX. Now just type:

W

– and DEBUG will politely tell you it has written 9 bytes.

The moment has at last arrived at which we can reveal all and demonstrate what the program does. Type:

G

– and the DEBUG should come up with the message "Program terminated normally". More than that, you will see that you have acquired a nasty big blob of a cursor instead of the neat little line which you are used to. The program demonstrates that it is possible to change the size of the cursor – but how do we go about restoring the standard cursor? First type:

Q

– to quit from DEBUG. It is a most important point to remember that you should never – repeat, never – try running the same program twice within a single DEBUG session. If you don't quit and reload, you will probably end up by causing your PC to go into a sulk from which it can only be rescued by pressing Ctrl+Alt+Del to reboot, or even switching off and starting again.

On the other side of the coin, don't forget to save any alterations to your program before you type Q – once you have quitted, it is too late to rescue the situation.

Now you can shortcut your way back to DEBUG by naming the program as the parameter to the command itself, like this:

DEBUG CURON.COM

Using the U, for unassemble, command, type:

U100

– just to check that the program is back again, and now let's examine it in a little more detail.

## Interrupts explained

We shall be using the word "interrupt" a great deal in future, so it deserves a word of explanation. The CPU of the computer needs to be kept in touch with the outside world – it needs to be told, for example, when data is coming in from a keyboard or port, or when something pretty disastrous occurs. The CPU also needs to be able to cope with different levels of priority, and to ensure that it deals with such events in a logical way.

Imagine you are reading the newspaper when the phone rings. You interrupt your reading to answer. As you are dealing with the call, the front door bell goes. "Let whoever it is wait a moment," you say to yourself and finish the call. But just as you are going to the front door to service that particular interrupt, to use the computing jargon, the chip pan in the kitchen which you left on by mistake at lunch time catches fire, filling the house with smoke. That's a non-maskable interrupt; one which takes priority over everything else.

The software interrupts called by INT are the commonest on the PC, and we shall mainly be using INT 21, which is concerned with input and output, dealing with files and records, directories, disk drives, and a number of other key functions, and INT 10, which manages the BIOS – Basic Input and Output – of the computer, from handling the keyboard and mouse to dealing with colours and, as in this case, the size of the cursor.

When an interrupt is handled by the computer, it expects to find the appropriate function number in the AH register, and sometimes also one or more other registers set to particular values. When the call is complete, a value or values may be returned in one or more registers.

In the case of our cursor program, the INT call is 10 in hex, the function is number 1, which sets the cursor type, and the shape of the cursor is determined by the two halves of the CX register. Remember that the AX, BX, CX and DX registers can be split into halves, a byte each. The CH value (0-4) gives the starting line, and the CL value (0-4) gives the ending line of the cursor. Clearly, if you start at 0 and end at 4 – as we did in our program – you are going to end up with the biggest cursor on offer, in other words a blob cursor.

You might think that to get back to our normal slender cursor at the bottom of the line you would change the value of CX to 0001. Let's try this out. There are two ways of modifying the code, the first being to assemble a new instruction at address 102:

```
A102
```

– plus Enter, then the new instruction:

```
MOV CX,0001
```

– followed by Enter twice. Alternatively, you could use the E command to enter new values for the individual bytes at 103 and 104.

Now save the program by using the W command, and just to make a change, type Q to quit and run the program from the MS-DOS prompt by typing:

```
CURON
```

MS-DOS looks for the file called "CURON.COM" to run, and if it finds it, executes it. At this point we see another example of computers being perverse, or rather, computer programmers.

Most thinking people might suppose that 0 = bottom of line and 4 = top of line.

But that's far too easy, and we see that the reverse is the case. We now have a cursor at the top of the line, believe it or not, and to get back to the MS-DOS default cursor we have to reload the program and change the second instruction to:

```
MOV CX, 0304
```

Setting the value to 0404 leaves a very skinny undernourished cursor indeed. In case you were wondering, the blink rate cannot be modified, because that is set by the hardware.

However, you can use the same function of interrupt 10 to switch the cursor off altogether. Here's a DEBUG session which will do that for you:

```
DEBUG CUROFF.COM
A
MOV AH, 01
MOV CH, 20
INT 10
INT 20
```

This effectively loads the cursor start register with a value out of range. Now press Enter twice, and then alter the value of the CX register to the value 8. Then use W to write the result to file and Q to quit. This will work with MDA, CGA and VGA displays. For others, you will have to use function 2 of INT 10 to set the cursor position off the screen.

If you incorporate your CURON and CUROFF programs into batch files you can get rid of a superfluous cursor while they are running, and then restore it when the batch file has finished.

A final word about INT 20: It is crucial to end every program with a call back to MS-DOS, otherwise you leave the computer to charge through memory, trying to interpret random data as if it was a program, almost inevitably causing the system to hang. So, never forget the INT 20 instruction at the end of every program – well, nearly every program. There is an alternate way of ending programs, and that relates to our interactive batch file program, which we shall be considering later.

## The bit before the program

Now let's write a general-purpose program which will set the cursor type to a specified value, if we typed in, say:

```
CURSOR 2 4
```

– or the really odd things that happen if you type:

```
CURSOR 9 0
```

The command CURSOR is followed in these two examples by what's called a "command tail". Quite often, MS-DOS commands have a tail of some kind or other, like:

```
DIR *.COM
XCOPY A: B:
```

But where does MS-DOS hide its tail? The answer lies in the PSP I briefly referred to earlier, the Program Segment Prefix which lies at the beginning of the segment from offset 0 to offset 0FF. To see what happens to the command tail, type:

```
DEBUG CURSOR.COM 2 4
D 0,0FF
```

Ignore the error message which says DEBUG can't find the file. The D command will display the contents of the program segment prefix, and if you inspect the odd-looking collection of numbers and letters, you'll see a couple of curious things.

The numbers 2 and 4 appear three times in this PSP area, as does a jumble of different bytes. A brief word of explanation: the first part of the PSP contains information to enable the program to function properly within its environment.

Starting at 5C two file control blocks, as they are called, are set up, and at 81 onwards the command tail of the program is stored, and this is also the default disk transfer area, the place where data on its way to and from disk is brought unless the programmer puts it somewhere else.

So, we can grab the information at 81 plus as data for our cursor juggling program:

```
33AA:0080 04 20 32 20 34 0D 6F 72-2E 63 6F 6D 20 32 20 34   . 2 4.or.com 2 4
```

If you examine the contents of those addresses starting at 81, you will see 20, the hex ASCII for space, followed by 32, then another space, then 34 and 0D, carriage return. If you quit from DEBUG and reload it, this time with two spaces between the parts of the command tail:

```
DEBUG CURSOR.COM 2    4
D 80 8F
```

This is faithfully reproduced in the memory locations starting at 81, byte for byte:

```
33AA:0000 06 20 20 32 20 20 34 0D-2E 63 6F 6D 20 20 32 20   . 2 4..com 2
```

This means that the program must be clever enough to pick up the parameters even if the user types in too many spaces. Incidentally, you will probably have gathered that the function of location 80 is to record the number of bytes in the command tail, not including the carriage return.

So now reload DEBUG and type the program in, using:

```
DEBUG CURSOR.COM
A
```

As in the case of all longish listings in the rest of this book, I have placed on the lefthand side of each instruction the offset address to help you check that you have keyed the program in correctly and as points of reference when the program is explained in detail. Do not type these numbers in yourself, of course:

```
0100 MOV SI,0081
0103 MOV AL,[SI]
0105 CMP AL,0D
0107 JZ 0129
```

```
0109 CMP AL, 20
010B JNZ 0110
010D INC SI
010E JMP 0103
0110 MOV CH, AL
0112 INC SI
0113 MOV AL, [SI]
0115 CMP AL, 0D
0117 JZ 0129
0119 CMP AL, 20
011B JZ 0112
011D MOV CL, AL
011F AND CX, 0F0F
0123 MOV AH, 01
0125 INT 10
0127 INT 20
0129 MOV AH, 02
012B MOV DL, 07
012D INT 21
012F INT 20
```

A few bytes extra saved to disk do no harm, so set CX to 100 and write the file to disk, then type:

```
U 100 12F
```

– which will disassemble what you have typed in so that you can check the location number for accuracy.

What this program does is to load into the SI (Source Index) register the address of the beginning of the command tail in the PSP. It doesn't have to be the SI register, the DI or BX will do just as well. Then, as the square brackets indicate, the contents of the address pointed to by the SI register are loaded into the AL register, the low byte of AX.

First time round that will be 20, a space, but first I have checked for a carriage return, which means that the user has failed to type any parameters at all. In that case, we jump to location 129, where a single byte is output, the familiar 7 to cause the bell to beep its disapproval.

The program loops round to 103 until it finds a non-space character and places it in the CH register, the starting point for the cursor. Then the process is repeated for the second parameter. First we check to see if there isn't one, and if so the error beep is invoked again. Then we loop until we find a non-space character and place it in CL.

We'll be dealing in detail with AND later on, but take it that the instruction:

```
AND CX, 0F0F
```

– converts the value in CX to one which will be recognised by the interrupt, which is now evoked.

If you run the program, you can manipulate the cursor, and if you put a larger value in the first parameter than in the second you may well find the cursor splitting into two, and producing an attention-grabbing effect. Try also with other keyboard values than just 0-9 to see what happens.

# Summary

Examining the registers is easy with the command:

```
R
```

To practise with it and the Assemble, Unassemble, Write and Go commands introduced in this chapter, type in this mini-program after loading DEBUG like this:

```
DEBUG WRITE.COM
```

Ignore the message telling you that DEBUG can't find the file. Of course it can't, you've just thought the name up, but despite the message DEBUG notes this as the file to write to later. Then type:

```
A 100
```

– before keying in these lines. It strictly doesn't matter about the 100, since DEBUG knows to start at 100 hex for all programs anyway:

```
MOV AL,02
MOV DL,07
INT 21
INT 20
```

Then press Enter twice to return to the prompt. To inspect the listing, type:

```
U100
```

And, while you are at it, try practising what happens when you make a mistake with U. DEBUG will take the start address you give it and try and make sense of the bytes which it is presented with. If all else fails and it can't come up with an instruction code of any kind, you will see a plaintive ?? in the listing, but its ingenuity knows few bounds.

If you typed:

```
U101
```

– in error, you would come up with a pretty impressive-looking couple of instructions, the first of which has probably never been used in the whole history of 8086 programming, though I am quite happy to stand corrected:

```
AND DH,[BP+SI+CD07]
AND BP,CX
```

If you try unassembling from the middle of an instruction, gobbledygook will probably be your reward.

Now to save the program. Remember first to set the CX register to an appropriate value, in this case 8 bytes:

```
R CX
```

– then, at the colon prompt, type 8 plus Enter. Then type:

```
W
Q
```

Always save before you quit if you have created a file or added to one.

If you are told that DEBUG hasn't got a file to write to; in other words, you loaded DEBUG without a parameter and created a new file, all is not lost. Use the N for Name command:

```
N FRED.COM
```

If you have loaded DEBUG without parameters and want to L for Load an existing file, you need two steps, first to name it – then load it:

```
N FRED.COM
L
```

For some reason, DEBUG won't let you give a parameter to L to load it directly, just to make life a little awkward.

As I mention later, there is a chance of disaster occurring when you try and write a file. If you receive a message telling you that there is insufficient disk space to save the file, pause for a moment. Do not – repeat not – quit from DEBUG.

This needs some explaining. The Write command looks not just at CX, but also at the lower end of the BX register, which means that if you have BX loaded with the value 000F and CX with the value 0008, DEBUG will try and write F0008 bytes and fail miserably, unless you are working from hard disk, in which case you will have created in decimal a file 983,048 bytes long!

That isn't the end of the story. If you had loaded your file FRED.COM and made a couple of changes to it, do not fondly think that all will be well if you just quit, because the old version of FRED.COM will still be there. It won't, as I discovered the hard way. DEBUG, when overwriting an existing file and finding that the disk space is too small, works in such a way that the file is actually deleted altogether.

That can also happen when you are working with "sensible" values and the disk or RAM drive just happens to fill up, so beware.

If BX contains a silly value, you must alter the BX register down to zero using:

```
R BX
```

– and then have another go at writing. Otherwise, you will have to pray that you have a recent backup, or alternatively, there is nothing to stop you writing to a different drive:

```
N B:PANIC.COM
W
```

That should save your proverbial bacon.

Now back to the program. Load it and run it using G, and you will find you have created an alternative method of getting the bell to ring. Function 2 of INT 21 outputs the character in the DL register.

Quit from DEBUG – remember never to try running a program more than once with DEBUG loaded – and reload. This time use A with the appropriate address number to change 07 to 41, and watch what happens. Try a few more times with the exotic end of the PC's character set, values in the range 80-FE to familiarise yourself with the processes involved.

One final point: You will notice again the garbage which the command U generates at the end of a listing. This is because the memory area is filled with spaces and the space character, hex 20, just happens to output this oddball instruction.

To avoid, or at least minimise, this screen clutter, specify a second parameter to U, for example:

```
U 100 110
```

Or, if you like you can use a new command, F, to fill an area of RAM with the hex value 90:

```
F 100 2000 90
```

Why 90? That – curiously – is the NOP or do nothing instruction.

# 13

# *Putting on Masks and Locks*

We turn now to a little unfinished business from the batch file chapter, and that relates to explaining the two programs you typed in to make your batch files interactive and to move the cursor to a given position on the screen. You were asked to type in a rather baffling sequence of letters and hex digits and take them on trust.

## The interactive program

The first program we put together created a file called UC.COM. If you now load that using DEBUG:

```
DEBUG UC.COM
```

– and unassemble it with the U command, you should see this sequence of instructions before you:

```
MOV AH,08
INT 21
AND AL,DF
MOV AH,4C
INT 21
INT 20
```

Of all the interrupts used by the PC, INT 21 is the one most widely used and with the biggest repertoire. Here we see it in action with function 8, which says: Wait until a key on the keyboard is depressed, and then read it without echoing it on the screen. If you wanted to echo the character on the screen, you would use function 1 instead, but in this case it would just be generating unwanted clutter.

The next call of INT 21 involves function 4C, which is an alternative to INT 20. This terminates the program, but in addition to that, it returns the contents of AL as the termination code, or what we called in the batch file chapter the "exit code". This is the alternative way of terminating a program which I referred to earlier. The call to INT 20 is pure habit on my part – if you are writing in assembler and fail to return to the calling program, usually MS-DOS, then interesting but disastrous things can happen, so I always include this instruction at the end as belt and braces just in case I forget the 4C call or mistype it.

Now to the instruction I have omitted to mention so far:

```
AND AL,DF
```

The DF after the comma is a hexadecimal value, equivalent to decimal 223, although it is the pattern which the hex represents which is important, as we shall see in a moment.

This AND instruction is similar to the instruction in the cursor manipulation program in the previous section which I also omitted to explain:

```
AND CX,0F0F
```

In order to find out exactly what is going on with the AND instruction, the best technique is to single step through the program using the two DEBUG commands T and P. The difference between them is rather important.

If you type R for the contents of the registers, you will see that the IP (instruction Pointer) is set to 0100, the beginning of the program, and that the MOV instruction is about to be carried out.

Type:

```
T
```

– and that instruction will be executed, and as an added bonus you obtain a free listing of all the registers and the next instruction, as if you had typed R. One important point to note is that the IP has not advanced to 101, as you might at first have suspected, but to 102. So, the IP is not an instruction counter, starting with instruction number one, and so on, but an instruction pointer.

The reason for this distinction is that each instruction or op code may take up a different number of bytes in memory. If you examine the MOV AH,08 instruction (type U100 to list the entire program again) you will see that the machine code equivalent to the left of the disassembled instruction takes up two bytes:

```
B408
```

The computer, being rather stupid, needs to know where the next instruction starts – this is worked out automatically – and in this case it is at location 102. If the IP pointed at 101, it would be pointing at part of the previous instruction, with catastrophic results. As machine code is simply a collection of hex numbers, muddled up with addresses and values, it is vital that there is some means of ensuring that the machine knows which are which, and that is why the IP is advanced at execution time to point precisely to the beginning of each new instruction in turn.

So, to recap: Typing T advances the program from the current instruction to the next instruction, in other words, it traces one instruction at a time – and prints out the contents of the registers for our delectation each time, too.

Now that we've come to the INT 21 instruction, though, we do not want to type T, because each of the interrupts in machine code sends the program off on a long sequence of built-in instructions which carry out step by step what you have asked it to do. If you did type T, you would not only get involved in a wild goose chase all over the computer memory, including parts that even the famous lager advert can't reach, but you'll probably end up crashing your program as well, so we need here to type:

```
P
```

– which tells the debugger to proceed to carry out the subroutine, interrupt or whatever is to be found at the current position of the IP. The program pauses, waiting for you to input a single character. If at this point you type in a lower case "a", the contents of the AX register will be:

```
AX=0861
```

The AH register still contains the value 08 from the INT 21 call, and the AL register now holds the value 61, the ASCII for lower case "a". Now use T to single step past the AND AL,DF instruction and you will see that the contents of AL have changed:

```
AX=0841
```

AL now contains the ASCII value for upper case A. To explain this little piece of apparent electronic magic, we need to refer to the binary equivalents of the ASCII codes. Full details of hex and binary are to be found in Appendix A, remember. The binary equivalents we need to consider are:

```
a = 01100001
A = 01000001
DF = 11011111
```

If you examine those strings of zeroes and ones carefully, you will recognise that the difference between "a" and "A" is just one bit, and that bit is represented by a zero at the corresponding location in the value DF. The instruction AND tells the computer to compare two values, in this case the contents of AL and the hex value DF, and if the appropriate bit is set in each case, that bit is retained, otherwise it is set to zero.

As the binary for A-Z are the same as the binary for a-z, except for that one bit in the middle, using AND DF on any lower case value will convert it to upper case. Try it out by running the program through DEBUG a few times, but do remember to quit from DEBUG on each occasion – never try to run a program more than once in a single DEBUG session, or disaster may attend.

This conversion is an extremely useful timesaver, otherwise you would have to write twice as many lines in your batch file to find out what the exit code is. It avoids having to type in the wordy IF ERRORLEVEL .. IF NOT ERRORLEVEL command twice for each letter, once for lower case, once for upper case.

This technique is called "bit masking" using the logical operators, and for those of you who insist on working the other way round, from upper case to lower case, a different operator is required. Use the COPY command to make another version of UC.COM:

```
COPY UC.COM LC.COM
```

– load DEBUG with LC.COM and use the A command to change the program as follows:

```
A 104
OR AL,20
```

– followed by Enter twice. The OR command has the exact opposite effect of the AND, so if you typed in upper case A:

```
a = 01100001
A = 01000001
20 = 00100000
```

– ORing the two means setting the bit only if the values are different, so when comparing "A" and hex 20, 0 + 1 gives 1, but 1 + 1 yields 0. And you will see that hex 20 is the mirror image, so to speak, of DF. It just has one bit set where DF had a bit left out. By this means, the missing bit in the middle in upper case A is inserted and converts it to lower case. It's simple when you know, but the whole business appears pretty mysterious if you don't.

So now we can make sense of the instruction:

```
AND CX,0F0F
```

This has the effect of zeroising the first four bits of each byte, or nibble as four bits are actually called in the jargon. This is to ensure that the interrupt is fed a meaningful number in the range 0-F for the start and end values of the cursor. The binary for 0F0F is:

```
00110011
```

# Getting into position

The second of the programs which you typed in "blind" located the cursor at a given point on screen depending on the value of the command tail:

```
POS a
```

– set the cursor to the appropriate point at the beginning of the first line of the notepad. It also involves a simple use of a mask, so it is appropriate to give it a brief glance at this point. If you feed the program into DEBUG:

```
DEBUG POS.COM
```

– and type:

```
U
```

– this should be the result, and this time I include the offset numbers and machine code, for reasons which will be clear in a moment:

```
0100 8A368200      MOV DH, [0082]
0104 80E6DF        AND DH, DF
0107 80EE3C        SUB DH, 3C
010A B402          MOV AH, 02
010C B700          MOV BH, 00
010E B207          MOV DL, 07
0110 CD10          INT 10
0112 B409          MOV AH, 09
0114 BA1B01        MOV DX, 011B
0117 CD21          INT 21
0119 CD20          INT 20
011B 1B5B4B        SBB BX, [BP+DI+4B]
011E 2420          AND AL, 20
```

As you already know, location 82 in the program segment prefix should be the address where the beginning of the command tail will be found if one space is keyed in after the program name, so as a reminder, POS f should have these values in locations 80 and following:

```
02 20 66 0D
```

The first value is the length of the tail, two bytes, the second is the space, and the third is lower case f. The carriage return character terminates the string but isn't included in the byte count.

The contents of location 82, then, are loaded into the DH register. But why the DH register? All will be clear in a second. First, the value is ANDed with DF to convert it to upper case, then 3C is subtracted from it.

At the end of that process (46 – 3C) we arrive at the answer A in hex, 10 in decimal. Then DL is loaded with 7, so the value in the whole of the DX register is now:

```
0A07
```

Register AH is loaded with the function number 2, and then INT 10 is called. What that interrupt does is to move the cursor to a particular location on the screen, which is determined – you guessed it – by the values in the DH and DL registers, which correspond to the row and column respectively.

The contents of BH are zeroised to tell the operating system that we are dealing with the current display page.

So, the cursor is moved to row 10, column 7 on the screen, which is designed to match the line beginning:

```
**(f)
```

– on our notepad template. So, with a little tinkering, you could modify the program to point to any location on screen, by using two parameters in the command tail and modifying each accordingly.

Next, function 9 of INT 21 is called, and that outputs a string terminated by the dollar sign (24 hex). Normally, we would locate text strings well out of the way of the program itself, but on this occasion I placed it immediately after the INT 20 which terminates the program so as to allow you to type program and data in all at once using just a couple of lines beginning with the E, for Enter, command.

That's why I included the addresses and machine code equivalents in the program listing. If you examine the address loaded into the DX register, 011B, you will see that it comes immediately after the end of the program and DEBUG has a valiant attempt at interpreting the bytes located there into a couple of programming instructions, the first of which is a pretty baroque and unlikely combination of registers and values.

If you look at the code on the left of the two instructions, though, all becomes clear:

```
1B 5B 4B 24 20
```

This, as you will recognise from our exploration of PROMPT, is an escape sequence, starting with the escape character and hotly pursued by an open bracket. Ignoring the trailing 20 at the end which just happens to be there as part of DEBUG's heroic efforts to interpret the bytes as instructions, the sequence is equivalent to this PROMPT command tail:

```
$E [K
```

– which erases from the cursor position to the end of the current line, and that was the second objective of the POS program, to clear the line for re-editing where needed.

This demonstrates that you can use the print string function 9 of INT 21 to issue the equivalent of all the PROMPT commands, replacing the "$E" by the actual ASCII escape character, 1B – and then terminating the sequence with 24, hex for dollars.

# Picking the locks

Let us explore this masking technique a little further with some valuable mini-programs to deal with the Lock keys on the PC. The AT clone I'm writing this book on has the annoying habit of booting up with the NumLock key switched on, because it has a separate keypad with its own Pg Up and similar keys.

Although there are alternate PgUp and PgDn keys, I always hit the ones on the numeric pad by sheer force of habit, with irritating results. That's why I include a short program in the AUTOEXEC.BAT file which switches off the NumLock. And when I run assembly programs, I like to have the CapsLock switched on for me, so another little program performs that task.

Do note that if you are running the programs I shall be describing in this and the next chapter from a PC, rather than an AT or above, the instructions you give will indeed change the status of the locks, switching Caps Lock and the others on and off, but, annoyingly, the LED light on your keyboard will not change. This is because it was only with the AT that the user was given control over the actual LEDs themselves.

Still, it is important to follow through the flashing lights program that comes later on, as it contains some important new ideas for your knowledge of assembler, not least in the way it shows you how to move the bit mask up and down.

How control over the locks can be achieved requires a little detective work. Load DEBUG without any parameters, ensure that your Caps Lock, NumLock and Scroll

Lock keys are all off, in other words, the LEDs are not switched on, and then type:

```
D0040:0017 17
```

That simply dumps from location 17 to location 17, in other words, just one byte in segment 40, way down in the bargain basement of the PC's RAM. This is part of the area of memory reserved for the BIOS (Basic Input Output System), and 0040:0017 is the first of two bytes dealing with keyboard control of the lock keys, and also with the Alt, Ctrl, Shift and SysReq keys. You should find that the value returned at this location is zero.

Now let's try an experiment. Put the Caps Lock key on, and dump the same byte on screen again. Remember, you don't have to type the D command all over again – just pressing the F3 key plus Enter always – well, nearly always – duplicates the last command you typed on screen. Then try with various combinations of the Caps Lock, Num Lock and Scroll Lock keys to see what happens. The result should be something like this (all values in hex, of course):

```
All locks off           00
Scroll Lock on          10
Num Lock on             20
Scroll + Num Lock on    30
Caps Lock on            40
Scroll + Caps Lock on   50
Num + Caps Lock on      60
All 3 locks on          70
```

As you will have guessed from your knowledge of the relationship between hex and binary, what is happening here is that different bits in the byte at address 0040:0017 are being set and unset according to the combination of locks on or off at any given time.

Let's follow the Num Lock in more detail. The value 20 in hex is equivalent to this value in binary:

```
00100000
```

This means that in every case in which the Num Lock is on the fifth bit should be set (bits are counted from the least significant on the right, which is called bit 0), and it turns out to be true if you examine the values 30, 60 and 70, each of which involves setting the Num Lock:

```
30 = 00110000
60 = 01100000
70 = 01110000
```

– and as you can see, the fifth bit is set in each case. So, if we want to write a program which knocks out the fifth bit whilst leaving all the rest intact, we need to AND the contents of 0040:0017 with a value which has a hole in it at the fifth bit, so to speak, and by pure coincidence we are back with our old friend DF.

If all three locks are set and we AND the byte with DF, you can see what happens from the following:

```
70      = 01110000
DF      = 11011111
```
_____
```
result = 01010000
```

That result is 50 hex, which leaves the Scroll and Caps locks on whilst switching off the Num Lock.

Now for a program which achieves this result. First, though, you will have noticed that the address is way down at the bottom of the memory, in segment 0040, which means that we are going to have to change the data segment register in order to address the right byte. This has to be done in two stages, for reasons best known to the 8086 processor. First the DX register is loaded with the value, then it is transferred across:

```
MOV DX,0040
MOV DS,DX
```

Next we have to move into the AL register the contents of the address, and to do that we put the address offset number in square brackets:

```
MOV AL,[0017]
```

This means: Move into AL the contents of the address referenced by DS:DX, in other words 0040:0017, then we AND it with the value we require, and finally move it back into the same address. The full program can be written like this:

```
DEBUG NUMAWAY.COM
A
MOV DX,40
MOV DS,DX
MOV AL,[0017]
AND AL,DF
MOV [0017],AL
INT 20
```

Now Enter twice, then set the CX register to 0F, write the program to disk, and quit from DEBUG. A reminder – use this command to set up the CX register for altering:

```
R CX
```

Then switch your Num Lock on and run the program to ensure that all is well. To switch the Caps Lock off, change the AND instruction operand to BF. I'll leave you to work out the other values.

# Summary

To experiment further with some of the material covered in this chapter, create a four-line program called PRINTME.COM:

```
MOV AH,09
MOV DX,1000
```

```
INT 21
INT 20
```

You will need to save about 1200 bytes worth. Then in the area specified by DX, in other words starting at address 1000 (do remember the third zero, otherwise you will overwrite the program, like I did when I was trying it out for you!), type:

```
E1000 1B,"[2J",1B,"[s",1B,"[14;19f Right in the middle!",1B,"[u$"
```

If you now save that and run it, you should get the screen cleared, the message printed in the middle of the screen, and the saved cursor position unsaved, leaving you near the top of the screen.

As you can see, the escape sequences are almost the same as with PROMPT, except that $E ends up as 1B. Practise with a few more like that – try, for example, getting a message at each corner of the screen.

On the subject of T and P, it is always better to know how to dig yourself out of a hole just in case you fall in. If you reload DEBUG with the PRINTME program and trace it up to the INT 21 instruction, all will be well, but if instead of hopping over the interrupt with P you type T, here is how to extricate yourself from the situation. If you try it, you will be greeted with something like this display:

```
0274:1460 2E          CS
0274:1461 3A26FF0D     CMP AH,[0DFF]
```

To get back to where you were, you can't simply type:

```
U100
```

– and find out how to get back to the next instruction. As you can see, the segment number has changed, in my case to 0274, one of the areas where the BIOS routines live and have their being. Turn instead to the second line of the register display, and the segment registers in particular:

```
DS=33C0 ES=33C0 SS=33C0 CS=0274
```

Now the current instruction is defined as being in the CS, or code segment, and you can see that it is 0274. When we started off the program we made no changes to the default segments, so all the other segment registers, the data segment, extra segment and stack segment all still contain the original value. In my case, it is 33C0. It doesn't actually matter what figure is there, since you can reference it like this:

```
U DS:100
```

– and there you will find your main program, and if you have typed it in exactly as above, you would be able to return to it by typing:

```
G DS:107
```

– go to instruction 107, in this case INT 20, but the point remains the same. You have managed to overcome what could otherwise be a rather nasty little problem.

# 14

## Bells and Whistles

---

Now for something lighthearted to relax with after all that effort devoted to meaningful activities. Let's write a program which rings the bell and flashes the key LEDs on and off in sequence to draw your attention to the fact that the computer requires you to input something. At the same time, a number of important new ideas will be introduced.

This program will work even if you have a PC, not an AT, but the lights themselves will stay at their current values. First type this program into DEBUG and save it (with a .COM extension, of course). I've added in the address numbers on the left which should appear - don't type them in, they are simply there to allow you to check and for me to refer to them when working through the program:

```
0100 MOV DX, 0040
0103 MOV DS, DX
0105 MOV AL, 00
0107 MOV CX, 0007
010A ADD AL, 10
010C MOV [0017], AL
010F PUSH AX
0110 MOV AH, 0B
0112 INT 21
0114 CMP AL, 00
0116 JNZ 012C
0118 MOV BX, FFFF
011B DEC BX
011C CMP BX, 00
011F JNZ 11B
0121 MOV DL, 07
0123 MOV AH, 02
0125 INT 21
0127 POP AX
0128 LOOP 010A
012A JMP 0105
```
*- program continues on the next page -*

```
012C POP AX
012D MOV AL,00
012F MOV [0017],AL
0132 INT 20
0134
```

This means that you should allocate at least 34 bytes to the file. I tend to overestimate by several hundred bytes (a) because space is hardly that critical and (b) one of my favourite errors is to add program instructions to an existing file and then unthinkingly write it without upgrading the value in CX.

Assembler buffs may notice that there are other, possibly better, ways of writing this program but they shouldn't be reading this anyway, and I am using the program to demonstrate various techniques, not as a vehicle for showing off my programming virtuosity. A subset of the 8086 instruction set is being used in order to make the learning curve as easy as possible and also to show more clearly how things work.

Once you have got the program up and running and had some fun with it, you might like to take a closer look at it, single stepping with T and P to the accompaniment of this explanation of what is going on.

## The program details

The first two lines are familiar - they renumber the DS register, and you can watch that happen. At 105, I zeroise AL in preparation for incrementing it in steps of 10 from 10 to 70, switching on each of the combinations of locks in turn, and in the next instruction the value 07 is placed in the CX - count - register. If you cast your eye down to 128, you will see a LOOP instruction. Using DEBUG, we have to refer to actual addresses in memory, rather than symbolic labels as in, say, BASIC, so the actual address we loop back to is 010A, which adds 10 to the AL register as a preliminary to saving the new value of AL in 0040:0017 and thereby changing the pattern of lights and the settings of the locks.

LOOP is one of those neat 8086 instructions which achieves a great deal in a short space: It first decrements the CX register, then compares the contents with zero, and if they are not zero, a jump to the address takes place. As you step through the program, watch the contents of CX decrease and those of AL increase.

When CX is zero (at which point AL = 70), the instruction at 128 is executed - we jump back to 105, AL and CX are zeroised, and looping takes place all over again.

In a moment we shall discover how we extract ourselves from what appears to be an infinite double loop, but first consider one of the big log jam problems in writing any kind of program in assembly language. Throughout the looping, we need to increment AL and save it (at 10C) in the appropriate location, but as you can see there are two calls of INT 21 in the loop, both of which require the AH register and one of which actually changes the contents of the AL register.

So, a means must be found of putting AX into temporary storage, and the means used here is to PUSH AX on to the top of the stack. If you single step as far as 10F and then use T to trace that instruction, watch as you do so the contents of the SP register. It drops by 2 to FFFC, and this needs more than a word of explanation.

The stack is a special area of memory in which information can be stored a word at a time. By default, it grows downwards from the top of the current code segment, as you can see from the SS, or Stack Segment r33egister. This can be changed if the program is likely to grow so big that it will swamp the stack. Every time you PUSH something on to the stack, the SP is decremented by two and the word which is PUSHed ends up on the stack.

As we have altered the DS register, it is necessary to prefix the dump request for the stack contents with the current code segment. So, in order to inspect what has happened to the stack - now pointing to FFFC - you need to type:

```
D SS:FFFC FFFD
```

We have to specify the stack segment, remember, as we have changed segments to poke around with the locks. This can easily be done by typing SS: - there's no need to key in the actual value of the stack segment register, but you can easily obtain it by asking for a display of the current register contents. Surprisingly, the result is not 0010 but the reverse, 0100. As we saw earlier, for perverse reasons of its own, the 8086 stores addresses and register contents "back to front", with the low byte first, and the high byte second.

There are two other important aspects of the stack worthy of mention: First, it is used as the "return address" whenever you call a subroutine. In other words, the stack is given the next instruction address to hold temporarily and when you return from the subroutine, it pops it back into the instruction pointer, so that you can carry on your merry way. Secondly, the stack is a LIFO stack, in other words, it follows the good trades union practice of last in, first out. So, if you type:

```
PUSH AX
PUSH CX
PUSH DI
```

- it is rather like shunting three goods trucks marked AX, CX, and DI into a sidings. You have to extract them in reverse order if you want to avoid disaster:

```
POP DI
POP CX
POP AX
```

Failure to do so may be amusing to the computer, but it will cause havoc to your program.

Finally, with the stack, for every PUSH there must be a POP, which sounds rather like something Confucius said, otherwise you will end up with the stack in a mess and the computer in a sulk.

Moving further down the program listing, INT 21 function 0B is a useful little item which we shall be using in the next section to generate a pseudo-random number of sorts in a simple assembler game. What it does is to check to see if a key on the keyboard has been depressed, if not AL is set to zero, otherwise it is set to FF if at least one character is available. How it is possible for more than one character to be available when just one key is pressed we shall see in the chapter on the keyboard, when we deal with the question of extended ASCII.

If the keyboard has not been touched, the program moves on to the four instructions starting at 0118. They should be more or less self-explanatory - what is happening here is that I have built in a delay. The BX register is filled and allowed to decrement to zero. If you find this too slow, try putting a smaller value for BX. If you find it too fast, you could either repeat the loop or use the LOOP command, first setting the CX register to the appropriate value.

The three instructions at 0121 and following call function 2 of INT 21, which outputs the character in the DL register, and in this case the character is 07, which causes the bell to ring. That's familiar ground which has been covered already.

Finally, when a key on the keyboard has been pressed, I've switched off all the locks at 12D and 12F to return things to normality.

# Summary

Remember in relation to PUSH and POP, as in just about everything else with DEBUG, that it is possible to observe in detail what is going on inside the machine.

In the case of stack operations, you need to refer to the SS. I don't mean that rather dubious military organisation in Germany before and during World War Two, but the stack segment register. Unless you set it otherwise, the SS register bears the same number as the other segment registers at the beginning of the program.

Data, code and stack all share the same 64K segment, but if for any reason you want one or more of these to grow substantially, you are at liberty to move them elsewhere, provided that you are not treading outside the RAM available for user programs.

The code grows upwards from location 100 in the segment, and the stack "grows" downwards from locations FFFE and FFFF in pairs of bytes, or words. It is important to remember that the program uses the stack when you CALL a subroutine. Let's see what happens with this rather mindless example:

```
MOV AX,1234
PUSH AX
CALL 500
POP AX
INT 20
```

Use A 500 to put the instruction RET at that address, and then use T to single step through the instructions. The stack pointer starts off at FFEE, and when you PUSH the contents of AX on to the stack, it points to FFEC, two less.

At this point, do note one of the important principles of computing. A write operation is destructive, in other words, the previous contents of an address written to are lost, but a read operation is not. So when the contents of AX are read on to the top of the stack, AX itself still contains the same value. It is not a move operation.

Then when we call our one-line subroutine at 500, the pointer has stepped down to FFEA, and if you interrogate its contents, this is what should occur:

```
D FFEA FFFF
07 01 34 12 00 00
```

The "top" of the stack, as it is called despite the fact that the wretched thing grows downwards, contains the value 0107 - stored backwards way on, in 8086 fashion. Where that comes from is clear when you examine the address of the next instruction after the call of the subroutine:

```
0107 POP AX
```

In other words, what technically occurs with a CALL is that the IP (Instruction

Pointer) holding the address of the next instruction is pushed on to the stack and the IP is loaded with the operand to the CALL, in this case 500.

You will see that the 1234, again stored backwards, is now second in line on the stack. After the return from the subroutine, when the word on the top of the stack is popped into the IP and that leaves 1234 on the top of the stack ready to be popped back into AX.

Now for a demonstration of the LOOP instruction, coupled with an escape sequence or two. Here is a program which can be adapted for livening up your batch file displays. Again, the address numbers of the instructions are given for checking purposes:

```
0100 MOV AH,09
0102 MOV DX,1000
0105 INT 21
0107 MOV CX,0017
010A MOV DX,1010
010D MOV AH,09
010F INT 21
0111 MOV AL,[1013]
0114 INC AL
0116 CMP AL,3A
0118 JNZ 12A
011A MOV AL,30
011C MOV AH,[1012]
0120 INC AH
0122 MOV [1012],AH
0126 MOV [1015],AH
012A MOV [1013],AL
012D MOV [1016],AL
0130 PUSH CX
0131 MOV CX,FFFF
0134 LOOP 0134
0136 POP CX
0137 LOOP 010A
0139 INT 20
```

Then two small items of data:

```
E 1000 1B,"2J$"
E 1010 1B,"[01;01fHere we are$"
```

This program stripes the message down the screen, and if you make three different versions of it, each with a higher value at 1012-3, you can get your message striped three times down the screen.

The serious part involves the double use of CX. First, the screen is cleared, and then a loop of 23 decimal is set up at 107. The message at 1010 is printed on the screen, and the escape sequence is incremented. The digits are each incremented, and if the total reaches 3A (one more than ASCII for 9), the values are zeroised and the tens digit is incremented.

You can work all that out by single-stepping through the statements beginning at 116. Then at 130 CX is temporarily saved and a loop set up which does nothing; in other words, it just adds a fractional delay between each printing of the message on screen. If the delay is too long, reduce the number to taste.

Then the old value of CX is restored and the program loops back to 10A where the message is printed again, one column further across and one row further down until the loop is exhausted.

# 15

# *Think of a Letter*

To illustrate text string handling and other forms of input and output, I have concocted a variation on one of the simplest games you can play with the computer, the "Think of a number" game, and in this case I have made life a little simpler by making it a letter of the alphabet. I've stacked the odds in such a way that you should beat the computer on roughly two out of three occasions, but you will soon work out how to make things either easier or harder for yourself.

In order to get the game to work, the program is going to have to begin by asking you something like this:

```
Press any key to start the game ...
```

This is to enable a pseudo-random letter to be generated between A-Z. The string is going to have to be stored somewhere in memory, and as we are using DEBUG and absolute addresses, let's start at location 1000, far enough away in the memory not to be overwritten by our program. And while we are at it, we might as well make the display tidy by first clearing the screen and then displaying the text neatly in the middle.

This can be done using functions of INT 10, but I am going to use a different technique, which I find tends to generate less in the way of spaghetti programs. It's done with the escape sequences we met earlier with PROMPT, and if you start the program off like this, you will see how easy it is. You will note that as I build the program up, I always add INT 20 at the end of the current state of the program, to ensure that I am returned to the DEBUG prompt in good condition. I've given the address values which appear when you type in these instructions, so that you can see that the jump instructions make sense, but don't type them in yourself, of course:

```
DEBUG GAME1.COM
A
0100 MOV AH,09
0102 MOV DX,1000
```

```
0105 INT 21
0107 MOV CX,0019
010A MOV AH,0B
010C INT 21
010E CMP AL,00
0110 JNZ 116
0112 LOOP 010A
0114 JMP 1017
0116 INT 20
```
Then type:

```
E 1000 1B,"[2J",1B,"[12;12fPress any key to start the game ... $"
```

Set CX to 1500, which is more than enough for this program, and write the file to disk. When you run it, the first escape sequence clears the screen, and the second locates the string at column 12, row 12. The dollar sign, remember, is used by function 9 of INT 21 as a terminator. If you miss it off, the program goes on printing garbage until it chances across the value 24 hex somewhere in memory or crashes into the buffers at the end of memory.

Now to explain how we arrive at a letter for the player to guess at. Random number generation on a computer is not as easy as it might seem, especially in those cases – unlike here – where you are after a sequence of such numbers. The best way I've found to generate a random letter to set the game off is to tell the user to press a key to start, and in the time while the computer is waiting, a counter whizzes round and round and stops at the moment at which the key is pressed.

How is this done? If you look at the instruction at location 107, you will see that the value 19 is read into the CX – count – register. The number 19 is equivalent to decimal 25, so we are organising a countdown from 25-0, which can be stopped at any time and converted into an ASCII value in the range 41-5A, in other words A-Z.

Now for the crafty bit. Function 0B of INT 21, which we met in the bells and whistles program, "listens" to the keyboard, and if a key has been pressed, AL is set to FF, otherwise it is returned as zero. As you will see in the full program listing in a moment or two, it is then necessary to use function 08 of INT 21 to flush the keyboard of that incoming character, just to keep things tidy.

If no key has been depressed, the program toddles down to the LOOP instruction. This says something on these lines: Take the current value of the CX register and subtract 1 from it. If the answer is greater than zero, loop to the address which appears as the operand in the LOOP instruction, in this case location 10A, where we listen in again to see if a key has been pressed.

If the value of CX is zero, the next instruction in sequence is executed, in this case a jump to 107, where CX is reset to 19 all over again, and round and round it goes until the end of the world, the electricity supply gives up, or you press a key, whichever comes the sooner.

## How the game works

The game itself is organised like this: You are given 5 attempts at guessing the letter which the program has chosen, which balances the odds neatly between you and the computer, slightly in favour of the former, and at each attempt you are informed if you are too high or too low, and how many attempts you have left. If you guess correctly, you get a congratulatory message, and if you run out of tries you are given the right answer. Finally, you are given the option of having another go and a tally is kept of who is winning and who is losing.

Here is a complete listing of the program with the address numbers against each instruction so that you can check for accuracy and I can refer to them when explaining new material in a moment. Again, obviously, do not key in the address numbers.

If you are daunted by a program this length and fearful of making errors requiring lengthy re-typing, you could either buy the disk which accompanies this book, or type the program into a file first, using one of the techniques we discussed earlier, calling it something like PROGFILE, including the A and E commands with their respective line numbers, and adding the following lines at the end:

```
N GAME.COM
R CX
1500
Q
```

The Q is vital, remember, otherwise DEBUG goes into an infinite loop. Then type:

```
DEBUG < PROGFILE
```

– and the chevron redirection operator tells MS-DOS to regard PROGFILE as the input for DEBUG. That's why the Q is so important, otherwise DEBUG will never know when it is to quit.

## Listing the program

Here now is the first part of the listing, including the lines we have already keyed in. To continue from where you left off, type:

```
A116
```

Line numbers are added as usual for orientation purposes:

```
0100 MOV AH,09
0102 MOV DX,1000
0105 INT 21
0107 MOV CX,0019
010A MOV AH,0B
010C INT 21
010E CMP AL,00
0110 JNZ 116
0112 LOOP 010A
0114 JMP 0107
0116 MOV AH,08
0118 INT 21
011A ADD CL,41
011D MOV CH,06
011F CALL 0500
```
*–Program continues on next page*

```
0122 CMP CH, 00
0125 JZ 019C
0127 MOV AH, 09
0129 MOV DX, 1040
012C INT 21
012E MOV AH, 01
0130 INT 21
0132 AND AL, DF
0134 CMP AL, 41
0136 JL 0127
0138 CMP AL, 5A
013A JG 0127
013C MOV [0999], AL
013F CMP AL, CL
0141 JZ 0157
0143 JG 014E
0145 MOV AH, 09
0147 MOV DX, 10A0
014A INT 21
014C JMP 011F
014E MOV AH, 09
0150 MOV DX, 1080
0153 INT 21
0155 JMP 011F
0157 MOV AH, 09
0159 MOV DX, 10C0
015C INT 21
015E CMP [0999], CL
0162 JZ 169
0164 MOV SI, 0013
0167 JMP 016C
0169 MOV SI, 001D
016C MOV BX, [SI+1140]
0170 INC BH
0172 CMP BH, 3A
0175 JNZ 017B
0177 MOV BH, 30
0179 INC BL
017B MOV [SI+1140], BX
017F MOV AH, 09
0181 MOV DX, 1140
0184 INT 21
0186 MOV AH, 09
0188 MOV DX, 1120
018B INT 021
018D MOV AH, 08
018F INT 21
0191 AND AL, DF
0193 CMP AL, 59
0195 JNZ 019A
0197 JMP 0100
019A INT 20
019C MOV AH, 09
```
*– Program continues on next page*

```
019E MOV DX,10E0
01A1 INT 21
01A3 MOV DL,CL
01A5 MOV AH,02
01A7 INT 21
01A9 JMP 015B
```

Then type in these few lines starting at address 500 (the command is A 500):

```
0500 DEC CH
0502 MOV AH,09
0504 MOV DX,1100
0507 INT 21
0509 MOV DL,CH
050B ADD DL,30
050E MOV AH,02
0510 INT 21
0512 MOV AH,02
0514 MOV DL,07
0516 INT 21
0518 RET
```

Finally come the messages starting at address 1000. They are keyed in using the E command – and don't forget the dollar terminator in each case:

```
E1000 1B,"[2J",1B,"[12;12fPress any key to start the game ... $"
E1040 1B,"[12;12fPlease type a letter between A and Z ===> $"
E1080 1B,"[15;20f Too high!!! $"
E10A0 1B,"[15;20f Too low!!! $"
E10C0 1B,"[15;20f Correct!!! $"
E10E0 1B,"[15;20f The answer was $"
E1100 1B,"[18;20f No. of tries left = $"
E1120 0D,0A,0A,"Another go (Y/N)? $"
E1140 1b "[22;50fSCORE: Me 00 You 00$"
```

Note that the number of spaces in the last line are critical: "Me" is followed by two spaces, two zeroes, three spaces, "You", and then two spaces, then two more zeroes.

That completes the listing. Now for an explanation of what's going on. After the opening message on line 100, function 09 of INT 21, the random number generator we devised earlier gets into operation in the range A-Z. At 11A 41 is added to the value of CX to convert it into an ASCII character.

Now at 11D I move 6 into CH. That indicates the number of attempts allowed plus one, and that value can be varied up or down to make the game harder or easier. Then comes a CALL to a subroutine at line 11F. This is rather like the BASIC command GOSUB. If you single step through the program using T or P as appropriate, you will see the SP register is double decremented to FFFC, and you can use D to check that the return address from this subroutine is indeed to 122, to the next instruction in the main program.

The reason for the double decrement is that each address within the current segment is referenced by two bytes ( = a word), which again are stored backwards way on. Note that when you CALL a subroutine it doesn't have to be adjacent to the rest of the program, and you will see in the rest of these DEBUG chapters that I tend to use addresses like 500, 600 and so on, to ensure that each subroutine is well away from the next and, in turn, from the main program.

There is no rule as to where you put each part of your program plus data; you could in fact scatter it all over the available memory if the fancy takes you, so long as you access it correctly and don't try jumping to or calling addresses containing random values. If you are consistent, it helps greatly in debugging programs. All the programs in these chapters start – fairly obviously – at address 100, and call subroutines starting at whole hundreds from address 500.

Data is stored starting at 1000 and in tens – or more if a string is longer – intervals thereafter.

Back to our subroutine, which decrements the count in CH, copies the value across to the DL register, adds 30 to it to make it a value in the ASCII range 6-0, and prints it out with the appropriate message. Then the bell is rung and the RET pops the word on the top of the stack (122) back into the IP register and away we go. If your bell is noisy, just cut out the offending lines, or replace them with NOP (do nothing) instructions.

## Working out the attempts

If CH is zero, in other words, if we have used up all our attempts, the program jumps to 19C where the answer is given, and then via a further jump you are asked if you want another go. If it is not zero, input from the user is first ANDed to make it upper case, then checked to see if it is in the range A-Z, and next compared to the answer in CL.

If it is too high or low, a message to that effect is printed out, and if you guess correctly the appropriate congratulatory message appears.

No good game is complete without score-keeping, and this masterpiece in miniature is no exception. One of the infuriating aspects of computing is that there is a world of difference between the absolute value of numbers and their ASCII equivalent. In a language like BASIC, numbers are handled for us, but in assembler, we have to do the dirty work for ourselves.

What I mean is this: If you have a value 0 in the AL register, we have to add 30 to it to make the ASCII character "0" appear on screen, and even worse than that, if you increment 0 until it has the value 0A, you can't simply add 30 in hex to it to get 10 in decimal on the screen; you'll end up with a colon on the screen and egg on your face.

There are other fancy ways round the problem, but here is a simpleminded conversion routine which depends on the two sets of double zeroes in ASCII in the memory locations after 1140. The way in which the incrementation works is this. First, the last answer typed in is temporarily stored in location 999 by the instruction at 13C.

This location is just before the data area, and isn't being used for anything in this program. Then, at 15E, it is examined to see if the answer was correct or not. Let us follow what happens if the answer is – as is more likely than not when I am playing the game – wrong and I have run out of goes. At 164, the value 13 is added to the SI (Source Index) register.

This is the first of the two bytes containing zeroes which refer to the computer's score so far. Now comes the tricky bit. As you will recall, our machine code insists on loading these memory locations backwards way on into registers, so the instruction:

```
MOV BX, [SI+1140]
```

loads into the BX register the "wrong way round" the contents of the location 1140 plus SI, in other words 3030 first time round. If you are still with me, this means that the units value is in BH and the tens, if any, in BL. We then increment BH at 170, and if it is greater than 39, we zeroise it and increment BL. In other words, this is a simple way of counting up to 9 and when we get to 9 + 1, we set BH to zero and BL to 1 and then send the ASCII characters 10 back to the appropriate memory location.

You can work this through if you single step through the program, but that can be painfully slow, so here is an alternative technique. Run the program under DEBUG by typing:

```
G 169
```

– which tells the program to run until it gets to the instruction at address 169. So, keep pressing the same letter of the alphabet, which gives you a 26:1 chance of being wrong (or is it 25:1?), and the program will stop at the crucial point. Single step for the next three or four instructions using T, watching the contents of the register carefully, and inspecting 1140 plus using D. Then you can watch the next number being added in by typing:

```
G 169
```

once again.

## Listing the character set

To finish off the main section of this chapter, here is a little program demonstrating the use of function 2, together with loops and much pushing and popping. What it does is to provide you with a neat instant display of the characters between 80-FE, the exotic end of the PC's character set, together with their hex equivalents.

Program first, brief explanations next. Here is the main program:

```
0100 MOV SI,1020
0103 MOV BX,1008
0106 MOV [SI],BX
0108 MOV BX,1000
010B MOV [SI+02],BX
010E MOV CX,007F
0111 MOV DL,80
0113 PUSH DX
0114 CALL 0500
0117 POP DX
0118 MOV AH,02
011A INT 21
011C INC DL
011E PUSH CX
011F PUSH DX
0120 MOV CX,002
```
*– Program continues on next page*

```
0123 MOV AH,02
0125 MOV DL,20
0127 INT 21
0129 LOOP 123
012B POP DX
012C POP CX
012D LOOP 113
012F INT 20
```

Now the subroutine at 500:

```
0500 MOV SI,[1020]
0504 MOV DI,[1022]
0508 MOV DL,[SI]
050A MOV AH,02
050C INT 21
050E MOV DL,[DI]
0510 MOV AH,02
0512 INT 21
0514 INC DI
0515 MOV [1022],DI
0519 CMP DI,1010
051D JNZ 052B
051F MOV DI,1000
0522 MOV [1022],DI
0526 INC SI
0527 MOV [1020],SI
052B PUSH CX
052C MOV CX,0005
052F MOV AH,02
0531 MOV DL,20
0533 INT 21
0535 LOOP 052F
0537 POP CX
0538 RET
```

Finally, one line of data at 1000:

```
E 1000 "0123456789ABCDEF"
```

The program starts by storing two words at addresses 1020-1 and 1022-3. The first is 1008; the second is 1000. If that puzzles you, look along the data you have keyed in. 1008 points to 8, and 1000 points to 0. Those are our starting values in hex and also correspond to the initial value set in DL at 111.

What happens is that the value in DL is pushed on to the stack, and the subroutine prints out the ASCII of the addresses pointed to in 1021-2 and 1022-3. Then the latter address is incremented, to 1001 first time round, in time for the second value in the list. When incrementing it causes it to fall off the end of the list and point to 1010, it is reset to zero, and the address in 1020-1 is incremented to 1009.

You may find this use of pointers a bit tricky to begin with, but single step through the program and you will see it all working out for you. The purpose of the inner loops at 120 and 52C – which involve pushing the main value of CX which controls output from 80-7F on to the stack – is to print a number of spaces in order to pretty up the display and make it more intelligible.

You will also find it fun following the various values that are pushed and popped in the course of the program. Check that you have got them all matching properly, or strange things can happen, as when I was developing this program and at 12B popped CX before DX.

This is an extremely useful program, and you can create another parallel version for the values 0-7F by making these simple alterations:

```
0103 MOV BX,1000
```

```
0111 MOV DL,00
```

This will print out values in the lower range, but be prepared for the bell to ring and odd things to happen around the backspace (ASCII 8), carriage return and line feed part of the listing.

# Summary

This is an appropriate point to summarise the INT 21 functions which have to do with console input and output; in other words, writing in from the keyboard and printing out on the screen.

## Function 1

Character input with echo. This is used when you want to echo on the screen the character you key in. The character to be input is expected in the AL register.

## Function 2

Outputs a single character in DL to the screen.

## Function 5

Not mentioned so far, this prints a single character to the "standard list device", a fancy way of saying the printer. The program in the previous section can be adapted for listing the 80 – FF characters simply by replacing the MOV AH,02 with:

```
MOV AH,05
```

## Function 8

Character input without echo. Quite often, there is no point in cluttering up the screen with a response to a menu list or in other such circumstances. The character to be input is expected in the AL register.

## Function 9

Display a string. The first character of the string is in DX, and remember that the string must end with a dollar sign. The string can contain ASCII codes, so long as they are separated by commas from text, which should be in double quotes. Here is an example, which also illustrates how to output double quotes. This is the main program:

```
MOV AH,09
MOV DX,1000
INT 21
INT 20
```
Then type in this line:

```
E 1000 "This string has",22,"double quotes",22,24
```

If you must insist on outputting a dollars sign in the middle of a string, you will have to split the string into two and use function 2 in the middle to output the hex character 24.

# Function 0A

Buffered keyboard input. This is a little bit messy until you get used to it. First define the starting point of a buffer in RAM. Let's assume it is address 1000. The first byte should contain the maximum number of characters; the second will contain the number of characters which have been typed in, and the third byte onwards will contain the actual characters, terminated by 0D, the carriage return character.

When you have typed in the maximum number of characters minus one and try and type one more, the computer will squeal at you and not let you go further. When typing a line of text in, you can treat it exactly as if you were typing in at the MS-DOS prompt. All the editing function keys behave in the same way. Pressing Enter concludes the typing in.

Here is an example of what the contents of the buffer are when you have typed "Here I am", plus Enter. Asssume that the buffer is at 1000 and that it is set to accept 10 hex characters, on exiting from the function the values would be like this:

```
33C0:1000 10 0A 48 65 72 65 20 49-20 61 6D 21 0D 00 00   ..Here I am!..
```

The value at 1001 indicates that in decimal 10 characters have been keyed into the buffer.

# *16*

# *What Day Is It?*

Now for a routine which will enable you to key in the day, month and year you require, and in return you will be given the day of the week for that date. We shall be using the get date and set date functions of INT 21, and that not only involves some fancy computing footwork, it also implies some limitations to our program.

The valid dates as far as MS-DOS is concerned are from 1980 to 2099, so nothing outside that range will work. It also gives us an insight into the presumed life expectancy of MS-DOS itself!

To get hold of the date is quite straightforward. All you need to do is to key in these lines:

```
MOV AH,2A
INT 21
INT 20
```

If you load DEBUG and run that program by typing:

```
G104
```

– the contents of the relevant registers would look like this:

```
AL = 00
DH = 04
DL = 01
CX = 07C6
```

AL gives the day of the week. 00 = Sunday, 01 = Monday, and so on through the week. DH gives the month, in the range 1-12, and DL gives the day of the month in the range 1-31 (or less, where appropriate). Finally, the year is contained in CX, and the decimal value of 7C6 is 1990.

So, the date on which I wrote this section was April Fool's Day, 1990, and just goes to prove that authors have to work on a Sunday, poor April Fools. That all looks pretty straightforward, but when we come to examine the way in which MS-DOS actually stores the date and time when it comes to information about files, you will begin to wonder whether it would not have been more advisable to take up hang gliding over Vesuvius as a pastime.

Let's now assume that we need to know which day of the week Christmas Day was in 1989. The first task is to get the current date, save it somewhere, reset the date to 25th December, 1989, get that date and inspect the contents of the AL register.

Then we print out the day corresponding to the date, and finally reset the system date to what it was before we started to run the program. Do note, if you are a midnight oil burner, that it would not be wise to run this program at 23.59 hours 59 seconds as the current date is stored for the duration of the program run time, and you may end up with the date one day behind!

Before we look at the listing in detail, there is one fiddly technical problem to solve. As you can see from the register contents of the Get Date function, the values are plain numbers, not their ASCII equivalent, but when we key in numbers to the computer, they are in the form of an ASCII string.

If, for example, we use INT 21 function 0A, which sets up buffered keyboard input, what happens is that you are invited to type characters into a buffer which you set up in advance. Assume that the buffer is sitting at location 1000. The first byte will contain the maximum permissible length of the input buffer, the second byte will contain the actual number of characters typed in, and the third byte onwards will hold the string, followed by 0D, the carriage return character.

The beauty of this method is that it is exactly like typing in from the keyboard – you can use the Delete key to rub out errors, and the buffer length allows you to ensure that the user keeps within whatever limits you set. Note that the maximum is 126 characters, and in order to allow for the 0D character, the computer will beep at you if you try and key in one less than the number of characters you specify. We shall see soon how this is exploited in our program, but first comes the business of typing it all in – then come the explanations.

Here, then, comes the full program listing with explanations, a little at a time. First the main program, which is mercifully short:

```
0100 MOV AH,2A
0102 INT 21
0104 PUSH AX
0105 PUSH CX
0106 PUSH DX
0107 MOV AL,05
0109 MOV [10C0],AL
010C CALL 0500
010F POP DX
0110 POP CX
0111 POP AX
0112 MOV AH,2B
0114 INT 21
0116 INT 20
```

Short, but quite a lot appears to be going on. There are two unfamiliar functions of INT 21 called in this sequence, the first at 102, the second at 114. These are the get date and set date functions respectively, and in both cases three registers are involved.

When you get the date from MS-DOS using function 2A it arrives fairly neatly packaged in the following registers:

AL – contains the day of the week (0 = Sunday, 1 = Monday, and so on).

CX – contains the year.

DX – holds the month (1-12) in DH, and the day of the month (1-31) in DL.

This is mercifully matched by the information required by the set date function, 2B.

What happens in the main program is that the current date is obtained, and then the information is saved on the stack by PUSHing the AX, CX and DX registers. Single step through this part of the program to watch the stack register change in value, and use D to inspect the contents of the stack area.

Incidentally, a good technique when typing in a program like this, or indeed developing your own program, is to get the main program working first, and at the locations where you CALL subroutines, just put the single statement:

```
RET
```

That will enable you to test out, in part at least, the main module before working on the subroutines.

After the values have been preserved for posterity, the value 5 is located in 10C0, the beginning of a buffer which will allow the user to key in up to 4 characters, in other words, the length of a year like 1990 or 2010 or whatever.

The subroutine at 500, which itself calls a further routine at 600, is where the user is asked to key in the date for which he wishes to know the day of the week. Here comes the devilishly cunning bit: We then set the computer's date to the date the user has selected and if it is valid, we pick up the value in AL which returns the day of the week.

This we print out on the screen, and back we return to 010F. All that now remains for us is to restore the real date by POPping the three registers containing that information and calling the set date function. And then it is all over.

Now for the first of the two subroutines which itself contains some moderately fancy footwork:

```
0500 MOV CX, 0003
0503 MOV DX, 0FE0
0506 ADD DX, +20
0509 MOV AH, 09
050B INT 21
050D PUSH DX
050E PUSH CX
050F MOV AH, 0A
0511 MOV DX, 10C0
0514 INT 21
0516 CALL 0600
0519 POP CX
051A POP DX
051B MOV DI, DX
051D MOV [DI-2], BX
0520 LOOP 0506
0522 MOV AH, 2B
0524 MOV DL, [0FFE]
```

*– Program continued on next page –*

```
0528 MOV DH,[101E]
052C MOV CX,[103E]
0530 INT 21
0532 CMP AL,00
0534 JZ 053E
0536 MOV AH,09
0538 MOV DX,10A0
053B INT 21
053D RET
053E MOV DX,1060
0541 MOV AH,09
0543 INT 21
0545 MOV AH,2A
0547 INT 21
0549 XOR AH,AH
054B MOV BX,0003
054E MUL BX
0550 MOV DI,1080
0553 ADD DI,AX
0555 MOV CX,0003
0558 MOV AH,02
055A MOV DL,[DI]
055C INT 21
055E INC DI
055F LOOP 0558
0561 RET
```

That concludes the first of the two subroutines. Now there is a little matter of data areas to enter before that little lot is explained:

```
E 1000 "Please type the day $"
E 1020 0D,0A,"Please type the month $"
E 1040 0D,0A,"Please type the year $"
E 1060 0D,0A,"The day of the week is $"
E 1080 "SunMonTueWedThuFriSat"
E 10A0 0D,0A,"Not a valid date...$"
```

In the subroutine beginning at 500, I have gone overboard for loops, using the technique we have encountered before of setting up the CX register and LOOPing back, decrementing the value in the register by one until it is zero.

The first loop runs to 520. First, a count of 3 is established in CX, and then the apparently odd address of 0FE0 in DX, which points nowhere in particular, unless you take into account the next instruction which adds 20 in hex to DX first time round. The result is:

```
DX = 1000
```

– lo and behold, the address of the string requesting the first piece of information from the user. Each time round the loop, 20 more is added, so the addresses 1040 and 1060 become the starting points in turn for the interrupt call with function 09, which outputs a string terminated by a dollar sign.

The only penalty for this neat piece of programming – at least, I hope you think it is not too clumsy – is that you have to save the values in DX and CX by performing a double PUSH before the subroutine at 600 is called, which does the really dirty work of reading in the data and converting it to a form suitable for MS-DOS to treat it as parameters for setting a new date.

Once the day, month and year have been read in and duly converted, the converted values supplied by the user are used to set the date for which he wants to know the day of the week. How does this come about?

To answer this particular riddle, we need to go back to two so far unmentioned instructions which appear after the CALL 600:

```
051B MOV DI,DX
051D MOV [DI-2],BX
```

When the routine at 600 has finished its conversion task each time round, it deposits the result in BX, and I have found it a temporary home in the word immediately preceding the address of the string which asked for it. This cannot be done directly with the DX register, so to work through the procedure first time round, DX contains 1000, and that is moved to the DI register.

Then the value in BX is stored in the word pointed at by DI-2, in other words FFFE.

Single step this part of the program through if you are even less sure of what is going on than I was when I came back to the program a few weeks after having written it in order to try and put this explanation together.

Now comes the crunch. The day, month and year are loaded into the appropriate registers at 524, 528 and 52C. Then we try and set the computer's date to match. If the user has asked for an invalid date, we return from the function call with AL=FF, which is the reason for the test at 532. As you can see, if the date is invalid for any reason, a message – which starts at 10A0 – is put up on screen and the program returns to the main module.

If the date is valid, the day of the week is lodged in the DL register as a digit in the range 0-6. Starting at 1080, you will see that I have given the abbreviated form of the days of the week as three-character strings.

So, what we have to do now is to take the value in AL, get it to point to the appropriate offset from 1080 and output the three characters corresponding to the day. First AL is cleared, so that we can refer to the value as being in the whole of the AX register. The reason for this is that we are about to move 1080 into DI and add the day of the week value.

8086 assembler won't let you add half a register to a whole one, AL to DI, for example, hence the need to zeroise AH and add AX to DI at 550. Now DI points to the first letter in the three-character sequence.

Once more our doughty programmer sees an opportunity, however spurious, for setting up a loop, and instead of using a simple brute force method like:

```
MOV DL,[DI]
MOV DL,[DI][1]
MOV DL,[DI][2]
```

– and outputting them using function 2 of INT 21, we go through this loopy sequence of setting CX to 3, moving the address pointed to by DI into DL, outputting the character, incrementing DL and going round again. I was, after all, brought up to program in assembler in the 1960s when elegance and space-saving was all the rage. And I still really can't get used to the sinful waste of valuable RAM that the younger generation of programmer gets away with.

However, even after that slip into my anecdotage, we are not finished yet. The longish routine at 600 has yet to be typed in; but fear not, there's one more loop to be looped:

```
0600 XOR  CX,CX
0602 MOV  [10D0],CX
0606 MOV  [10D2],CX
060A MOV  CL,[10C1]
060E MOV  SI,10C1
0611 ADD  SI,CX
0613 MOV  DI,10D3
0616 STD
0617 REPZ
0618 MOVSB
0619 MOV  AX,0F0F
061C AND  [10D0],AX
0620 AND  [10D2],AX
0624 XOR  AX,AX
0626 MOV  AL,[10D0]
0629 MOV  BX,03E8
062C MUL  BX
062E PUSH AX
062F XOR  AX,AX
0631 MOV  AL,[10D1]
0634 MOV  BX,0064
0637 MUL  BX
0639 PUSH AX
063A XOR  AX,AX
063C MOV  AL,[10D2]
063F MOV  BX,000A
0642 MUL  BX
0644 XOR  BX,BX
0646 MOV  BL,[10D3]
064A ADD  BX,AX
064C MOV  CX,0002
064F POP  AX
0650 ADD  BX,AX
0652 LOOP 64F
0654 RET
```

And that, thankfully, is that as far as typing in goes. The problem comes with explaining what is going on, particularly with that rather weird-looking instruction at 616 which looks for all the world like a long-distance call instruction to a modem.

## Converting the numbers

I had to make a break at this point, to give myself the chance of working through the subroutine and making sure (a) that it worked and (b) that I comprehended what was going on. Here goes, based on an attempt to find out what day of the week was 25 December 1983. To spoil it all for you, it was a Sunday.

When the 25 has been input, using function 0A at 514 and with 10C0 as the start of the buffer, the state of the buffer is as follows, as you will find if you load the program using DEBUG and the command:

```
G 600
D 10C0
```

The values you should find there are:

```
05 02 32 35 0D
```

The 05 was inserted at the beginning of the buffer way back at the instruction located at 107 in the main module of the program. That, as you will remember, is the maximum length of the buffer minus one, since the length includes the 0D terminator.

The second byte of the buffer contains the length of the string – minus the concluding carriage return character – and as you can see, that is 02. Next, at long last, comes the string itself, two ASCII hex values 32 and 35 corresponding to the 2 and 5 keyed in by yourself.

What happens at 600 is that CX is cleared using the XOR instruction which clears every bit set – it is no more than a rather upmarket way of typing:

```
MOV CX,0
```

Then that zero is deposited in the four locations starting at address 10D0, which I am using as a workspace to convert the number to MS-DOS readable form, at least as far as the date goes.

Now we have to deposit the digits typed into this buffer starting at 10D0. The idea goes like this: The thousands are stored in 10D0, the hundreds in 10D1, the tens in 10D2 and the units in 10D3. The current value is two digits long, but it could be anything from one digit to four for the year.

What I have done is to devise a single conversion routine which will cope with that range of possibilities, so if you are following me down this particular thorny path, if there are two digits in the number currently to be converted, we want to end up with 10D0-10D3 looking like this:

```
00 00 32 35
```

– ready for conversion. The only sensible way to do this is backwards, starting from the units and working upwards as necessary to tens, hundreds and thousands.

That is why the instruction at 611 points the SI register at the last character in the string. Into the zeroised CX register the number of characters in the string are deposited by:

```
MOV CL,[10C1]
```

The DI register is set up with the address of the last byte in the four-byte address we zeroised and now comes that oddly telephonic-looking instruction:

```
STD
```

If you examine the flags on the righthand side of the register display, and step through this instruction, you will see one of them changing value, from UP to DN. Normally, when the computer is moving data around the memory, the assumption is that this happens in ever-increasing address values, and if you are a paranoid programmer you can ensure that this happens by clearing the direction flag, as it is called, with:

CLD

In this situation, however, we want to move down the memory for between one and four addresses, so this flag is now set to DN which it does not take an advanced cryptographer to establish means down.

The next two instructions, which you can type into DEBUG as a single line, separated by a space:

REPZ MOVSB

– but which it insists on putting on separate lines, is another splendid shorthand instruction, or rather duet of instructions. What it tells the assembler is to MOVSB; in other words, move a single byte, and REPZ, repeat until the CX register is zero.

However, it does a little more than that, as it wouldn't make a very great deal of sense to move the same single byte, and that is why we have set the direction flag. What happens is this: A single byte is taken from the address pointed to by the SI, the source index, and deposited in the address pointed to by the DI, or destination index.

Then the processor looks at the state of the direction flag, and in our present case, seeing that it is set to DN, decrements SI and DI as well as decrementing the CX register, and loops round until CX is exhausted.

In this present case, round we go twice and 10D0 is loaded with the values we listed a moment ago. But they aren't meaningful as far as the date function is concerned. Next comes a couple of AND instructions which clip off the 3 in 32 and 35, leaving plain vanilla numbers:

00 00 02 05

Now these numbers have to be converted into a single value, and this defied my attempts to devise a suitable loop without getting myself terminally confused. What happens next, then, is a piece of unashamed spaghetti programming. I'll take the most complicated example, if you would use a combination of G and T (not gin and tonic, I hasten to add) to get to the point at which you have inputted the year.

As a reminder, when you run the program under DEBUG, type:

G600

Then just type:

T

– to get one instruction past 600, and then repeat the G instruction until you have keyed in the year.

In order to generate a single hex value for 1, 9, 8, 3 input as ASCII – the target

number is 76F – which can then be used in the set and get date routines, we start off
with these values duly ANDed in 10D0:

```
01 09 08 03
```

What we need to do now is to multiply the 01 by 1000, the 09 by 100, the 08 by 10
and add them all together plus the 03 – the only slight problem being that this all has
to be done in hex.

If you wish to avert your gaze for the next few paragraphs and take what happens
for granted, I will not exactly blame you, but if you do want to stick with it, you will
gain a little extra buzz from seeing a complicated conversion actually working.

First, then, the value in 10D0, is moved into AL at 626 (the whole register has
been zeroised by the previous instruction) and it is now multiplied by hex 03E8,
which is 1000 in decimal. To store it temporarily, I have PUSHed it on to the stack.

The same procedure happens with the hundreds value which, like the thousands,
will be zero in two out of the three operations each time the program is run. As you
will have guessed, 64 hex at 634 is 100 in decimal. Then the tens value is added and
the result, left in AX as in the previous two cases, is added straight off to the units
value.

This leaves in BX the tens plus the units. Now we have to POP two values off the
top of the stack, the hundreds and the thousands, and add them in too. This is done –
you guessed again – by a loop, why not. It is set up at 64C: AX is POPped twice, and
the value is added to BX, then with RET control is handed back to the calling routine
at 519 which, as we said earlier, deposits that computed value in the word preceding
the string which asked for it in the first place.

This has been quite a difficult piece of programming to follow, and I hope you
have managed to make sense of my explanations. It demonstrates that, while
programming in assembler may seem unduly finicky to the programmer brought up
on BASIC, for example, it does show that, using assembler, you have complete
control over the computer, or as near to complete control as any mere mortal can get
to have over the mighty micro.

Next in line for discussion is an enhancement of batch files which will add a great
deal of power to your programming.

# Summary

These are the main instructions to do with simple arithmetic in assembler. If you
think they are a bit complicated, thank your lucky stars that you are not dealing with
any of the more primitive assemblers which don't have multiplication or division.
You just have to make up routines yourself. At least be grateful for small mercies.

## Adding

This uses the instruction ADD, which allows you to add two values together. It is
quite flexible, as these examples show:

```
ADD CH,99
ADD AX,DX
ADD CX,[1000]
```

## Subtracting

Similar flexibility is shown by SUB:

```
SUB AX,DX
SUB AL,BL
SUB AX,[1000]
```

## Multiplying

MUL comes in two sizes. It can either deal with bytes or words. It assumes in the first case that the contents of the AL register are multiplied by the operand. Here's a simple example:

```
MUL BL
```

Bigger size MUL multiplies the operand by the value in AX. It can tell the difference depending on the operand, so it will work out for you what to do:

```
MUL CX
```

Note that the result is stored in DX:AX, thus allowing for large numbers. If you are working in values over FFFF, ensure that DX doesn't contain a value you need somewhere else in the program.

## Dividing

This behaves similarly to MUL but the other way round, if you see what I mean. DIV looks to see if the operand is a byte or a word. If it is a byte – like AL, for example – it divides AX by the byte, stores the result in AL and the remainder in AH.

If we are dealing in words, DX:AX is divided by the operand, the answer goes to AX and the remainder to DX:

```
DIV BX
```

The contents of DX:AX are divided by whatever is in BX.

```
DIV [1000]
```

Here the divisor is at location 1000.

To check on the exact result of using these instructions, try them out using DEBUG. In all these cases, we are dealing with unsigned binary values. For more advanced arithmetic, particularly when using carry, check one of the books recommended in the bibliography.

# 17

## Looping the Loop

---

One of the more significant gaps in the batch file commands is one which would allow you to loop a given number of times. The equivalent in BASIC would be something like:

```
X = 20
WHILE X <> 0 DO
PRINT something
X= X - 1
WEND
```

If only we had a simple way of emulating this in MS-DOS batch files, we should be more than one ahead of the system. What we need is a command which can either set up a loop, or increment or decrement a value.

That's what our little program called COUNT is going to do. For the sake of programming simplicity, you will have to know your ASCII values for counts over nine if you want to check the count as it increases, but if you have survived so far in this book, that should be no great hardship to you.

Before giving the program listing, here is an indication of how the program works. I have called it COUNT.COM and when it is called it creates a one-byte file called CBIT which contains the current value of the count. To enable you to test the value, COUNT exits with a return code that can be inspected by ERRORLEVEL. It runs in the range 30 hex upwards, in other words from 0-9, and then up through the ASCII characters : ; < = > ? @ and then the letters A-Z and, if you must, right through to 255 decimal.

Here are a couple of examples of calling the program. If CBIT does not exist, one of these two calls will set it up:

```
COUNT
COUNT 8
```

In the first case, COUNT is set up with a default value of 30 hex, the minimum allowed, and in the second case with 38 hex. That number can then be manipulated in one of the following ways:

```
COUNT
COUNT +
COUNT -
COUNT 4
```

The default is to assume an increment of one, as in the first case. In other cases, note that there must be one space preceding the + ,– or ASCII value. The plus sign also generates an increment which is not checked within the program, so you could go on incrementing for ever, although every time you reached FF you would be returned to zero. The decrement halts at 30 and stays there. And there is, as you can see, no bar to resetting COUNT whenever you want.

To increment or decrement by two, just call COUNT twice in succession with the appropriate parameters.

So a typical loop might look like this:

```
COUNT 9
:LOOP
REM Do something
COUNT -
IF ERRORLEVEL 31 GOTO LOOP
REM Looping finished at this point
```

The coding for the program is broken up into three sections, each reasonably small, and there is also a small data section starting at 1000 hex. If you single step through the program you will notice that the saving and reloading of the file handle is not strictly necessary, but it is always safer, especially in a potentially messy program like this, to save and load information which might just get wiped out by additional program lines you may wish to key in at a later date.

The first part of the program goes like this:

```
0100  MOV AH,3D02
0103 MOV DX,1000
0106 INT 21
0108 JB 010F
010A MOV [1050],AX
010D JMP 0112
010F JMP 0200
0112 MOV AH,3F
0114 MOV BX,[1050]
0118 MOV CX,0001
011B MOV DX,1040
011E INT 21
0120 MOV AH,[0080]
0124 CMP AH,00
0127 JNZ 012F
0129 MOV AH,2B
012B MOV [0082],AH
012F MOV AH,[0082]
```
*– Program continued on next page –*

```
0133 CMP AH,2B
0136 JNZ 0145
0138 MOV AH,[1040]
013C INC AH
013E MOV [1040],AH
0142 JMP 0500
0145 CMP AH,2D
0148 JNZ 0158
014A MOV AH,[1040]
014E CMP AH,30
0151 JNZ 0156
0153 JMP 0500
0156 DEC AH
0158 MOV [1040],AH
015C JMP 0500
```

First, the program attempts to open the file CBIT using function 3D of INT 21, and if it fails to do so, carry is set.

In order to find out if a file already exists, a standard technique is to use this function of INT 21 to try and open it. If it is there, you can use it straight away; otherwise you simply call the create file function 3C to bring it into being.

## Jumping about a bit

So, in the absence of the file CBIT, the program jumps at 108 first to 10F and then to 200. The reason for this hop, step and jump approach is that I carved the program up into three distinct sections in different parts of memory, as it took me some time to get my thoughts unscrambled and the order of the program sorted out. In a situation like this, it is always best to keep the different parts of the program separated, in the same way that we kept CALLs to subroutines apart in earlier programs.

The reason for a double jump becomes clear if you examine the machine code for the two jump instructions:

```
0108 7205 JC 010F
...
010F E9EE00 JMP 0200
```

A JB, JNZ or similar instruction normally has just one byte after it, which allows a relative jump forward or back by around FF bytes. A JMP, on the other hand, has a two-byte word to allow it to hop all over the current segment. The issue is clouded with other notions, but I've tried to keep it simple and the advice is that if you are liable to jump a good way, make it a plain JMP instruction, so instead of, say:

```
JC 700
```

– try a JC to the next but one instruction and a JMP to the 700 location.

If you get an Error message when you are keying in a JC, JNZ or similar instruction, DEBUG is trying to tell you that you are trying to take a leap too far.

The address 1050 has been chosen for the file handle, of which more in a moment, and 1040 for the byte in the file CBIT. The name of CBIT plus a zero is located at 1000. I had intended using 1010 plus for an error message if you keyed in COUNT without parameters, but while the program was being developed it occurred to me that it was user-friendlier to permit assumed values, so the error message never materialised.

It is always a difficult path to tread between hurling a fusillade of Error This and Error That messages at a user and either trying to make sense of what has been keyed in or asking nicely for missing parameters if they are essential.

If you use an operating system like MS-DOS which presumes a lot of knowledge on the part of the user, then you might well yearn for a windows environment which does it all for you, but the irony is that if you want to make fast and serious progress, you are far better off working from the chilly environment of the MS-DOS prompt than from the claustrophobic confines of a windows or similar system.

That's my prejudice, anyway, and I am sticking to it.

The only data area you need to set up is for the file name:

```
E 1000 "CBIT",0
```

Under Version 1 of MS-DOS, opening a file was a bit of a bureaucratic nightmare. I'll spare you the gory details, and let us be thankful that Version 2 and above accepts what's called an ASCIIZ string when we wish to refer to a file name. That's an ASCII string terminated by a zero, as you can see from what you have just typed in.

That will allow MS-DOS to go off in search of a file by this name, whether for opening, closing, reading, creating, deleting or whatever.

If carry is set – in other words, if the file isn't found, we jump to address 200 where CBIT is created. If CBIT is duly found, function 3F of INT 21 at address 112 reads the single byte of the file (referenced by CX) into the address 1040 (referenced by DX).

## Handling a file

When a file is opened for business, the operating system doesn't want to be bothered with it by name, so it creates a unique number, or handle as it is called, to refer to the file by for the rest of the program. We need to store that handle for future use in the program, and if you single step to the point at which CBIT is successfully opened, you will find that the handle number is 5.

The reason for this apparently odd number – in both senses of the word – is that MS-DOS reserves handles 0-4 for the five standard input and output devices, screen, keyboard, printer and the rest. The maximum number of files you can have opened at any one time is 20, which is conditioned by the buffer space in the program segment prefix, and the actual number you allow is set by the FILES command in your CONFIG.SYS file, the maximum obviously being:

```
FILES=20
```

Of course, as soon as you close or delete a file within a program, that handle is released for further use.

There is one odd side effect of the handle which can cause a baffling error and one which you can't try and DEBUG because it causes the system to hang. As I said, every time you reference a file once you have opened or created it, you need the handle to tell MS-DOS which file you are after. The number of the handle is placed in the BX register, and if you try and close a file without loading the BX register, you could be in deep trouble.

If the BX register happens to be zero and you apply function 3E, the close file function of INT 21, you are telling the system to close down the standard input device, the keyboard, and the computer just goes into a permanent sulk! So do watch out for that nasty little pitfall. But back to our program and the counting mechanism.

Now we take advantage of the command tail, which we have exploited before and which starts at address 80. The byte at this address tells you how long the command tail is, and this is being checked at 120. If the command tail is zero length, in other words, if you have typed in plain vanilla COUNT without a tail, then the program has to make assumptions for you.

It assumes that you meant to type:

COUNT +

– and that is why at 129 the value 2B (the plus sign) is moved to address 82, where it would be expected to be found if you had typed it in instead of being lazy.

Now, at 12F and following, the contents of address 82 are examined. They can either be a plus sign (supplied by the user or by the program), a minus sign, or an ASCII value to set or reset the starting point for the counter.

If we find a plus, the value at address 1040 is incremented; if a minus it is decremented unless – hence the check for 30 at 14E – the value is already 30, otherwise the ASCII number found is loaded into 1040.

Now to consider what happens if CBIT doesn't exist and we have to create it. These instructions start at 200, so you need to preface your typing in, remember, with A 200:

```
0200 MOV AH,3C
0202 XOR CX,CX
0204 MOV DX,1000
0207 INT 21
0209 MOV [1050],AX
020C MOV AH,[0080]
0210 CMP AH,00
0213 JNZ 021B
0215 MOV AH,30
0217 MOV [0082],AH
021B MOV AH,[0082]
021F MOV [1040],AH
0223 JMP 50C
```

The routine checks to see if you have offered an initialising value, and if you haven't, it assumes a starting value of 30.

The appropriate value is loaded into address 1040, and a jump occurs to 50C where it is written to file.

So, now comes the final part of the program, which begins at address 500:

```
0500 MOV AH,3C
0502 XOR CX,CX
0504 MOV DX,1000
0507 INT 21
0509 MOV [1050],AX
```
*–Program continued on next page–*

```
050C MOV AH,40
050E MOV BX,[1050]
0512 MOV CX,0001
0515 MOV DX,1040
0518 INT 21
051A MOV AH,3E
051C MOV BX,[1050]
0520 INT 21
0522 MOV AL,[1040]
0525 MOV AH,4C
0527 INT 21
```

At 500, function 3C sets the file CBIT to zero length and prepares it for being written to. Then at 50C, one byte is duly written, and at 51A – this is strictly superfluous, but it is better to be safe – the file is closed. Finally, at 522 the current value of CBIT is loaded into AL preparatory to calling function 4C of INT 21 which exits from the program leaving a return code for IF ERRORLEVEL to examine.

There is an intriguing example of the COUNT program in use in the chapter dealing with box drawing, and it shows how you can actually put the magic of animation into your batch files.

# Summary
This is an appropriate point at which to examine the main functions of INT 21 which have to do with file handling.

## Function 3C
Create a file. This function requires the file attribute to be in CX. Normally you set this register to plain zero, but bits can be set to make it a read-only, hidden, system or other type of file. The address pointed to in DX expects an ASCIIZ string; in other words, the file name followed by a zero. Here is a typical call:

```
MOV AH,3C
MOV CX,0
MOV DX,1000
INT 21
```

And at 1000:

```
E 1000 "NEWFILE",0
```

If the call is successful, the handle value is returned in AX. For the first file you open the value is 5, and so on up to the limit of 20, depending on what you have set the FILES line to in CONFIG.SYS. The best thing to do with the handle is to save it as a word – I usually put it just before the filename, so:

```
MOV [0FFE],AX
```

Then it can simply be loaded into BX, which is the register the other functions that deal with files require, in a simple command:

```
MOV BX, [OFFE]
```

If the function fails, AX is set to the error code and carry is set. So, to test if something has gone wrong, put immediately after the INT 21:

```
JNC <address>
CALL 800
```

– where <address> is the location after the CALL, where the program continues normally, and the CALL – for the sake of illustration, to address 800 – deals with the error by printing out a message and halting the program.

Note that in the case of this and other calls, if you do not trap errors, the program blunders on regardless, and you will have to face the consequences.

## Function 3D

Open file. This call normally takes the form:

```
MOV AX,3D00
MOV DX,1000
INT 21
```

The function number is in AH, as usual. AL is set to zero for read access, to 1 for write access, and to 2 for read and write access. Again, the handle is returned in AX – but if carry is set, an error code is left in AX. DX contains the address of the start of the ASCIIZ string.

## Function 3E

Close file. Here you need just the handle in BX:

```
MOV AH,3E
MOV BX,OFFE
INT 21
```

That assumes the handle number has been previously saved at 0FFE. Once more, carry is set and a message is placed in AX if things go amiss. At the risk of becoming a bore, please remember again that if you inadvertently call this function with BX = 0000, you are more or less switching off your computer, because that closes down the keyboard!

## Function 3F

Read file. This function is called with these instructions:

```
MOV AH,3F
MOV BX,OFFE
MOV CX,1000
MOV DX,1050
INT 21
```

The values in BX, CX and DX are only by way of illustration. BX contains the file handle, CX the number of bytes you want to transfer and DX the start of the buffer to which you want to transfer.

Carry is set and AX contains the error code if things go wrong. If things go right, there is plenty of information for you. First, if AX is zero and carry not set, this means you have already read past the end of the file.

Secondly, if carry is not set but the value of AX is less than that of CX, you have probably read to the end of the file. If the two values are equal, you have read the required number of bytes and there is probably more of the file to come.

As this can be messy, I would try if I were you to read in the whole of a file at one go, unless you are dealing with a very large file indeed. If necessary, change the DS register – increment it by one, say – and save the data in a segment all by itself.

## Function 40

Write file. This is similar to the read file function:

```
MOV AH,40
MOV BH,0FFE
MOV CX,1000
MOV DX,1050
INT 21
```

Once again, the values in BH, CX and DX are for demonstration purposes. In this case, DX is the start address to write from. If after the function has been called, carry is not set but AX does not equal CX, you are probably trying to write to a full disk.

## Function 41

Delete file. This only requires an ASCIIZ file name in the buffer starting at DX:

```
MOV AH,41
MOV DX,1000
INT 21
```

Errors result if you try deleting a non-existent file or if the file is read only. Note that this function can only delete one file at a time; wild cards are not allowed.

## Turning the handle

If you consider functions 2 and 5 of INT 21, they deal with the standard screen device, with handle number 1, and the standard list device, with handle number 2, and they have the great disadvantage of dealing with one character at a time. There is nothing to stop you changing the handle numbers to suit yourself, and that is all that happens when you use redirection operators, and that allows you access to a function which can move large numbers of characters.

Here's an example using function 40, the write file or device function of INT 21. This function is normally used to write a specified number of characters from an area in memory to a file which has successfully been opened. Instead of using the handle of an open file, use 1, the value of the standard output device, the screen:

```
MOV AH,40
MOV BX,1
MOV CX,10
```

```
MOV DX,1000
INT 21
INT 20
```

And for data, something like:

**E 1000 "This command prints out the first 16 characters of this message"**

So, this is in effect an additional way round the dollar sign problem in outputting strings. As the number of characters output depends on the value in CX, this function will print out whatever is in the buffer, dollar sign included.

# *18*

# *Directory Enquiries*

---

As our exploration of DEBUG and assembler comes towards an end, I thought it would be interesting, to say the least, to try in this chapter and the one that follows to provide you with two more enhancements of the DIR program. This time, it will involve some fairly tricky programming, but I think we have come far enough down the line to cope with it.

The first mountain we are going to climb relates to listings of directories based on the date of creation or update of a file. Quite often, in a long directory, you are only interested in those files which have been created most recently, so that you can back them up for security purposes, or print the contents out.

There is no real way of achieving this in MS-DOS without either printing out the whole directory and going through it by hand or by a fairly messy procedure using FIND, which can only really pick out one specific date anyway. I'm interested in files created or updated on or after a user-specified date.

Incidentally, do not assume that the directory listing is roughly in date order. This would only be true if you were adding files to a disk or directory on hard disk without removing or updating any of them. MS-DOS uses a fairly complex formula for deciding where to put a file on a partially filled disk, and it is not impossible to find it popping up near the beginning of the listing, especially if there have been a large number of deletions on the disk.

The technique I am going to show you is to list the directory, or part of it, to a file, and then set to work on it with a small assembler program which in turn can be patched to perform different tricks. First we need to wrap our program up in a batch file. Let's call the batch file DDIR.BAT, and the program NEWDIR.COM. Later, I'll show you how to patch this program and the even more tricky one in the next chapter into the CAT.BAT program, which as you recall you may have renamed DIR.BAT using the technique described in Chapter 11. Here is what the batch file might look like:

```
ECHO OFF
DIR %1 > FRED
NEWDIR
DEL FRED
```

This will allow you to call the batch file either without parameters, in which case all of the current directory will be assumed, or with parameters corresponding to the normal command tail for DIR, in other words subdirectories, wild cards, and so on.

Using the redirection operator > the directory listing is written to the file FRED, and our program will be trained to pick up FRED and look for files and subdirectories created on or after a specific date.

There is one slight snag to directory listings, and that is that the file names don't always begin at the same number of bytes into the file. It all depends how much information there is in the first couple of lines about the drive, directory and volume label, if any.

That means we are going to have to train our program to sniff out where the file names begin. Fortunately, that isn't too difficult, because any directory listing contains a double carriage return line feed after the introductory information, followed by a single carriage return line feed, and then away we go to the file names proper.

So, we must incorporate this electronic sniffer dog routine at the beginning of the program to detect this double carriage return line feed. Working on the assumption that this program is between ourselves, I haven't incorporated sophisticated error trapping and messages and other checks, but by now you should be practised enough to write them in yourself at the appropriate junctures if you want to adapt this program for general use.

## Asking for a date

Here is the first part of the listing, which picks up FRED, reads it into a buffer, asks the user for the date, and then calls the subroutine which does the searching and printing:

```
0100 MOV AX,3D00
0103 MOV DX,1000
0106 INT 21
0108 JNB 010C
010A INT 20
010C MOV BX,AX
010E MOV AH,3F
0110 MOV CX,5000
0113 MOV DX,2000
0116 INT 21
0118 PUSH AX
0119 MOV AH,09
011B MOV DX,1010
011E INT 21
0120 MOV AL,09
0122 MOV [1050],AL
0125 MOV AH,0A
```

*- Program continued on next page -*

```
0127 MOV DX,1050
012A INT 21
012C MOV AL,[1052]
012F CMP AL,30
0131 JNZ 0138
0133 MOV AL,20
0135 MOV [1052],AL
0138 MOV DL,0D
013A MOV AH,02
013C INT 21
013E MOV DL,0A
0140 MOV AH,02
0142 INT 21
0144 POP AX
0145 ADD AX,2000
0148 MOV DX,AX
014A CALL 0500
014D INT 20
```

The first interrupt opens the file FRED, and if it can't be found the program terminates. This is one point where you could put an error message. Incidentally, the easiest way of doing that is not by painstakingly putting in extra code in the program, but by changing the INT 20 to an INT 21 using function 4C, ensuring that there is a value in AL which you can pick up in the batch file using ERRORLEVEL and issue the appropriate message from within the batch file.

At 10C the file handle, which should normally have the value 5, is swapped over to the BX register where it is needed for us to read the contents of the file. The CX register is set to 5000 - in hex, remember - which should be more than enough for most man-size directories, although you could increase the number if by some remote possibility you find it necessary. Now type:

```
E1000 "fred", 0
E1010 "Please give the date in this format : dd-mm-yy: $"
```

The contents of the file FRED are loaded starting at location 2000. One of the advantages of a little assembler program like this is that the actual program will take up just over 1000 bytes, but you can load vast quantities of data just about where you want within reason without increasing the size of the program itself, and therefore the amount of space it takes up on the disk.

At location 118, we have read in FRED. When function 3F of INT 21 is called, the AX register contains on exit the number of bytes transferred. This means, as you may remember, that you can load small amounts of file into a buffer and if on exit AX is the same as CX, it means that there is more to come from the file, but in our case AX will be less than CX and equal to the total length of the file.

That information is needed later, so we PUSH it away for the moment. Next up comes a message asking for the date in the format: dd-mm-yy. If your system doesn't have the English form of the date, swap it round by checking on how to alter the date format in your manual. It may mean adding a line to CONFIG.SYS, for example.

If the date isn't in English format, this program won't work - not without some fairly straightforward tweaking. When the date you give is compared with the date in the file, you will see that only the digits are compared, which means that you can actually use the format dd/mm/yy, or any other delimiter that takes your fancy. That's a small user-friendly bonus, as I for one can never remember which delimiters go with what.

## Keeping down the spaghetti

Note that you have to write 01-09-90 with leading zeroes, which is to avoid having to type in a raft of extra instructions which would make the program too spaghetti-like. Again, if you fancy your chances at improving my version to accommodate 1-9-90 as a format, that's up to you. I suggest that you put in an additional subroutine call just before CALL 500 to, say, 700, where you examine what the user has keyed in and expand it with zeroes if necessary to make it acceptable to the program.

If you key in a daft date format, the results are unpredictable, but again if you want to check that no one has more than 31 days in a month, you can feel free to wander into that murky territory, leap years and all. The best approach might be to run the program but to issue a warning that the results may not be what you intended.

Now for 120 and following, where I load the value 9 into address 1050, which is where the user's date is to be located, starting at 1052. This uses the function 0A, which we have come across before, and which reads from the keyboard into a buffer. The first byte of the buffer should be set to one more than the maximum permitted character - in this case 9 - and on exit the second byte will contain the number of characters typed in.

That would be a good starting point if you fancied adding a subroutine to modify the date format, since if the user keyed in less than 8 characters, it is a clear sign that something might be wrong. You could also allow for a user to key in no characters at all, and make the default either all the files in the directory, or those with today's date, but that would cause quite a lot of fiddly conversion using the get date function of INT 21, function number 2A.

After the date has been read in, I next check at locations 12C and following to see if there is a leading zero in the day part of the date. The reason for this is that the directory listing converts that leading zero to a space, at least on my system, so check to see if the same happens on yours. If you get a zero, then leave this part of the program out. Remember, if you remove any part of a program and want to keep the address numbering consistent with what I have given, just fill it out with NOP - do nothing - instructions.

Note that the month, bless its heart, does have a leading zero where needed in the DIR listing, just to make life interesting and varied. Never let it be said that MS-DOS makes things dull by being consistent.

So, the leading zero is converted to a space to match up with DIR, otherwise it won't pick up the date properly, and I issue a carriage return line feed to ensure that any output starts on the following line.

Now AX is popped out of retirement - that's the number of bytes in the file FRED, remember - and we add to it 2000 which, if luck is on our side, means that it is pointing to the end of the file, so that it can serve as a marker to stop us falling off the end of the file and wandering off into infinity.

We turn now to CALL 500, but as the first thing this subroutine does is to call another one at 600, let's type that in first. This is the routine which sniffs out the first line of the file containing the first directory entry:

```
0600 MOV SI,2020
0603 MOV AX,[SI]
0605 CMP AX,0A0D
0608 JZ 060D
060A INC SI
060B JMP 0603
060D ADD SI,+02
0610 MOV AX,[SI]
0612 CMP AX,0A0D
0615 JNZ 060A
0617 MOV BX,SI
0619 SUB BX,0A
061C RET
```

First an address near the beginning of the buffer containing FRED is loaded into SI, and then we look for the sequence 0D0A - remember that any pair of bytes loaded from memory is loaded backwards way on, and that is why the CMP instructions are looking for the sequence 0A0D. When two in a row - a double carriage return line feed - have been found, we then skip to the next single carriage return line feed, move the value into BX and subtract an initial amount which sets the register up for looking through the rest of the file.

Now for the main loop, which searches for dates and tries to compare them with what the user has keyed in. My grasp on logic is pretty tenuous, and it took me several attempts to work out exactly how to cope with matching two dates in this kind of format:

**29-11-89 (typed in by user)**
**03-09-90 (in the file FRED)**

The solution I finally came up with is to undertake three searches, starting with the tens digit of the year. This, incidentally, is the point at which you can juggle things round if the date is in US or any other odd format.

If the user's digit is less than the digit in FRED, then we have found a matching file at the first attempt, one which is of a later date than the starting date the user requested. The above pair fulfils that requirement.

If the user's tens digit for the year is greater than that in FRED, the search has failed at the first attempt. If they are equal, we look at the units digits and perform a simple comparison.

The same process is repeated with the month digits, and finally, if necessary, with the days, in both cases starting with the tens and moving if necessary to the units digits. If only I had paid more attention in maths classes at school, I'd probably have worked out a better method in five minutes flat.

Here now comes the listing for addresses 500 and following:

```
0500 CALL 0600
0503 ADD BX,+29
0506 CMP BX,DX
0508 JL 50B
050A RET
050B MOV SI,BX
```

*- Program continued on next page -*

```
050D MOV DI,1058
0510 MOV CX,0003
0513 MOV AH,[SI]
0515 MOV AL,[DI]
0517 CMP AH,AL
0519 JL 0503
051B JG 0531
051D MOV AH,[SI+01]
0520 MOV AL,[DI+01]
0523 CMP AH,AL
0525 JL 0503
0527 JG 0531
0529 SUB SI,+03
052C SUB DI,+03
052F LOOP 0513
0531 MOV SI,BX
0533 SUB SI,+1D
0536 MOV AH,02
0538 MOV DL,[SI]
053A INT 21
053C INC SI
053D CMP DL,0A
0540 JNZ 536
0542 JMP 0503
0544 INT 21
0546 INC SI
0547 CMP AL,0A
0549 JNZ 0534
054B JMP 0503
```

After the call to 600 to determine the starting point for the search, 29 (in hex, as always) is added to BX. This causes BX to point either to the tens digit of the year of the next directory entry, in which case we proceed to compare it, or it has fallen off the end of the file, as the comparison with DX might show, in which case the program is terminated.

The SI register is set up for the comparison to take place, and the DI register is also set up with the tens digit of the year part of the date which the user entered. The next part of the routine undertakes the comparisons two bytes at a time, as I explained earlier.

The subtractions at 529 and 52C move SI and DI to point to the tens digit of the month, and then, if necessary, the day. The comparisons are carried out three times, as established by the CX register, set to 3, and the LOOP instruction at 52F which, as you will recall, decrements CX each time it is executed and stops functioning when CX is zero.

If a match is found we end up at location 531. After a bit of judicious juggling to get to the beginning of the current record, the file entry is duly printed out, and back we go to repeat the process starting from 503.

Now that the program is in place, it is no great hardship to modify it to produce directory entries on or before a given date, or entries only on a given date. You can even bend the program to home in on files below or above a given size. In such cases, it is easier to copy the program and make new versions from the copy, running them from a menu.

# Summary

One of the subjects which arose in this and previous chapters is that of how to deal with a list, or table, of items. In this case, we have been moving a fixed number of bytes down the file containing a directory listing, and homing in on the tens digit of the year in which each file is created.

That's a relatively simple matter as, you may recall, was the program which told us which day of the week a particular date fell on. In that case, the date was stored as:

```
SunMonTueWedThurFriSat
```

- and a simple piece of mathematical juggling enabled us to take the base address, the value of the day of the week as returned from function 2A of INT 21 multiplied by three, and a loop to print out the next three characters from that location onwards.

So, as a memory-jogger, if the day of the week was day 4 returned in the AL register, the part of the program which found and printed out the three-character abbreviation went like this:

```
0549 XOR AH,AH
054B MOV BX,0003
054E MUL BX
0550 MOV DI,1080
0553 ADD DI,AX
0555 MOV CX,0003
0558 MOV AH,02
055A MOV DL,[DI]
055C INT 21
055E INC DI
055F LOOP 0558
```

But things are not as simple as that if you want to print out the days of the week in full, because they don't happen to be all the same length - and in such cases the best technique is to set up a table.

Assume that the days of the week are stored at 1000 in this format:

```
Sunday$Monday$Tuesday$Wednesday$Thursday$Friday$Saturday$
```

The dollar sign acts as a convenient terminator if we use function 9 to print out a string, but the problem is knowing where each day of the week starts. One rather hamfisted method would be to take the value in AL -0 for Sunday, 1 for Monday and so on - and look for that number of occurrences of the dollar sign, move to the next byte, and use that for the starting point of a call of function 9.

There is a much better way, and that is to set up a table of start addresses and access the appropriate element of the table. Here is a little program which demonstrates the technique:

```
0100 MOV SI,1000
```

```
0103 MOV DI,1050
0106 MOV CX,0007
0109 MOV [DI],SI
010B INC SI
010C MOV AL,[SI]
010E CMP AL,24
0110 JNZ 010B
0112 INC SI
0113 ADD DI,+02
0116 LOOP 0109
0118 MOV AH,2A
011A INT 21
011C MOV BL,02
011E MUL BL
0120 AND,AX,00FF
0123 MOV SI,AX
0125 MOV DX,[SI+1050]
0129 MOV AH,09
     INT 21
     INT 20
```

The days of the week are stored starting at 1000. The table starts at 1050. Now, in order to point to a particular location, we need a word (two bytes) stored backwards way on in true 8086 fashion - and the easiest way of achieving that objective is to get the program to do it for you.

That's what the first few lines up to 116 do. Let me talk you through step by step, as some people find the idea of pointers rather confusing. I must confess that I did when I first came into computing, and spent many an unhappy hour drawing boxes on pieces of paper and trying to debug assembler programs sorting text into alphabetical order and performing similar tricks requiring tables.

First, SI is loaded with the start of the list of days of the week and DI with the start address of the table. CX is loaded with the value seven, as we shall need seven entries in the table, one to point to each day of the week.

At 109, the word in SI is loaded into the address which is contained in DI. In other words, first time round the address 1000 is loaded into address 1050. Then the program looks along the string for the first dollar sign, and skips one past it to point to the beginning of Monday. At this point two is added to DI (result: 1052), and we loop back to 109, where the address in DI - 1052 - is loaded with the contents of SI, which point to the beginning of the word Monday.

And so it goes on through the rest of the week. If you find it at all hard to follow, single step through the program and keep checking on the contents of addresses 1000 onwards. At the end of the proceedings, when the program has exhausted the loop and dropped through to 118, the contents of 1050 onwards should be:

```
00 10 07 10 0E 10 16 10 20 10 29 10 30 10
```

To check on that, take the second last word in the list and unscramble it back into "normal" order: 1029. At address 1029 you will find the F of Friday, so it works.

And to prove that it really does, the rest of the program uses function 2A to get the date, multiply the value returned in AL by 2, switch that across to SI, and at 125 access the address pointing to the beginning of the appropriate word. Then the word is printed out.

When you have run the program under DEBUG and are happy with it, you can test it out either by temporarily changing the system date by tinkering with the MS-DOS command DATE, or by reloading DEBUG and typing:

```
G 120
```

Then change the contents of the AL register to any value between 0-7 by typing:

```
R AX
```

- and keying in the appropriate value. Then watch the right day for the value popping up on screen.

## Jumping tables

A more advanced application of tables comes with what are known as jump tables, and you might care to experiment with them with a due measure of caution. The idea goes like this: Say the program gives you a choice of four options, and you key in the appropriate number.

That number can be used to point to an element in a table just like the one we have designed, but with the crucial difference that the table doesn't contain data, but jump instructions to different areas of memory where different sets of instructions are carried out. So, you may have a table at address 1000 like this:

```
JMP 1050
JMP 2000
JMP 3000
```

- and so on. As you will have gathered, tables of various kinds are a very powerful tool indeed, but do check carefully before letting them loose on an unsuspecting user.

# 19

# Dating the Directory

As a kind of grand finale to our exploration of DEBUG and assembler, I offer you a much improved variation on DIR which I find suits my needs better than the home-grown MS-DOS variety when I am checking up on details of individual files.

It gives the size, date and time in more detail than DIR does, and on top of that it tells you what attributes are active for the file in question. It is also quite an interesting exercise in how to squeeze the most out of DEBUG.

Let's look at the problem. A directory listing of files only – I'm not wanting to clutter it up with subdirectories or volume labels – requires first of all a means of knowing whether the user wants the lot thrown at him or whether a selective listing is required. The best way of achieving that is to use the command tail, in just the same way as DIR does. If there is no command tail, we shall assume:

```
DIR *.*
```

Otherwise, we shall pick up the information at address 82 in the PSP and use that as our mask for selecting the required entries.

But how do we go about finding, not just one file, but a whole list of them? The answer lies in functions 4E and 4F of INT 21. They are, respectively, the "find first file" and "find next file" functions. In other words, MS-DOS has been nice to us and put together a duet of functions which look for the first file to match a particular name with or without wild cards, and then goes on to find the next one, and the one after that, until the list is exhausted.

There is one snag which can soon be ironed out. And that is that the DTA – Disk Transfer Address – has to be altered, because the default DTA at address 80 onwards in the PSP contains the command tail of the program which we are using as the name of the file or files to match. That is no problem, since function 1A of INT 21 allows us to locate our own DTA wherever the fancy takes us.

The real challenge is that the date and time are encoded, and also that every figure we receive, whether date, time or file size, is in hex, and will require us to convert it to an ASCII string.

In many respects, that's the trickiest problem of all, so let me show you how I tried to tackle it. Consider the date. It is stored as a value relative to the year 1980, and once we have winkled it out of the word (two bytes) into which it is packed, and added the hex for 1980 to it, we end up with a value in the AX register for the year 1990 which is 7C6.

When the subroutine picks up this value it assumes three things. First, that the amount to be converted is in the AX register. Second, that the number of bytes to be dealt with is in CX, so that we can cope with a four byte year as well as two bytes for the month and days of the month. And, finally, the DI register contains the start address into which the outcome in decimal is to be deposited.

If you are still following me after all that, let's look at the subroutine, which you should type in at address 800, which copes with this particular problem:

```
0800 XOR DX,DX
0802 MOV BX,000A
0805 DIV BX
0807 ADD DX,30
080A MOV [DI],DL
080C DEC DI
080D XOR DX,DX
080F LOOP 0805
0811 MOV DL,[DI]
0813 CMP DL,00
0816 JNZ 081C
0818 MOV DL,20
081A MOV [DI],DL
081C RET
```

First, the DX register is cleared, then the divisor 0A (= 10 in plain old decimal) is placed in BX. That clears the way for BX to be divided by the contents of AX. The remainder has 30 added to it to turn it into an ASCII value, and that value is deposited into the address which DI is pointing to.

As we are working backwards from units to tens and so on, the next task is to decrement DI and clear DX again, ready for the next division bell to ring, so to speak. At 80F we loop back to 805 until the number is exhausted and all the digits deposited into the appropriate address.

In case you are as confused as I was when I started putting all this together, let me work through the routine using the example of the year 7C6, or 1989, if you want to go decimal. When this value is first divided by 0A, the result of the division in the relevant registers is as follows:

```
AX=00C6 BX=000A CX=0004 DX=0009
```

When a division using BX takes place, the assumption is that the number to be divided is in the DX and AX registers, and that is why DX is zeroised initially. After the calculation, the result is left in AX, and the remainder (the bit we are currently interested in) in DX. Add 30 to that value, and we have 39, the hex ASCII equivalent of the digit 9.

Now we go round once again, decrementing CX and this time ending up with these values:

```
AX=0013 BX=000A CX=0003 DX=0008
```

That calculation provides the tens digit of the year, which is duly scaled up to the ASCII character value 38. And so the loop goes round, until all four digits representing 1989 are deposited in successive addresses to which DI points.

That's problem number one dealt with. Unfortunately, as we have discovered all too often in these pages, life is not easy for the hard-working programmer. The date and time are indeed sewn up into one word each, 16 bytes of information, but they are not placed there in a straightforward way. Before a holiday, it is the packing which always causes problems, but in computing, it's the other way round. Unpacking a neatly packaged value throws up a couple of awkward problems which have to be faced head on.

First of all, we need to type in the rest of the program, starting with the main module, which we shall look at before the routine which does all the messy business:

```
0100 XOR BX,BX
0102 MOV BL,[0080]
0106 MOV AL,0
0108 MOV [BX+0081],AL
010C CMP BL,00
010F JNZ 011F
0111 MOV BX,2E2A
0114 MOV,[0082],BX
0118 MOV BX,002A
011B MOV [0084],BX
011F MOV DX,1030
0122 MOV AH,09
0124 INT 21
0126 MOV AH,1A
0128 MOV DX,1000
012B INT 21
012D MOV [0990],AL
0130 MOV AH,4E
0312 XOR CX,CX
1034 MOV DX,0082
0137 INT 21
0139 JNC 013E
013B JMP 500
013E CALL 0600
0141 MOV AH,4F
0143 INT 21
0145 JNC 014A
0147 JMP 500
014A CALL 0600
014D JMP 0141
```

First, the program looks to see if there is any command tail, and if there is not, it obligingly puts in *.* to ask for a complete directory listing. If you specify a directory other than the default, you will have to supply the *.* characters at the time of call. Catering for that omission would turn this into an even longer spaghetti program, but you are welcome to try.

The wild cards are loaded into the command tail area at 114 and 11B. Address 1030 contains the heading for the directory listing preceded by the escape sequence that clears the screen:

```
E 1030 1B,"[2JFile name Size Date Time Attributes",0D,0A,0A,24
```

You should type in 11 spaces after File name and Size, and 9 after the other two headings.

At 126 we call a new function of INT 21, 1A, which sets a new DTA, or disk transfer area, away from 80 where we have the file name or wild card set up for matching purposes, and we have located it at 1000. The size of the buffer required is 20 hex characters.

The important business starts at 130, with another new function, this time 4E, which is called "Find first file". What this does is to look at the ASCIIZ string starting at 82 (the 0D terminating the command tail has already been made zero at 108) and find the first file that matches it.

If no file is found, carry is set and AX returns the error code. For normal searches CX is zeroised. If a matching file is discovered, then we are swamped with information which is deposited in the DTA which we have just specified at 1000.

The following is all in hex. The first 15 bytes – 00-14, that is – are reserved by MS-DOS and need not concern us. Byte 15 contains the attribute of the file, whether it is read only, hidden, system, or whatever. 16-17 contain the file time and 18-19 the date, both encoded in a way which will require some nifty decoding.

The file size is in 1A-1D, and the file name itself is stored as an ASCIIZ string starting at 1E. If a first match is found, the program trots off to 600 and following to sort things out, otherwise we jump to 500, where you will need to insert INT 20 to stop the program. I have left the option open here for you, if you wish, to add up the file sizes at the end of the subroutine starting at 600 and to output the total at this point before closing the program down.

Then the related function 4F looks for the next matching file and so we continue until the list is exhausted.

Now for the tricky bit, which will require some patient typing, I'm afraid, so let's take it a bit at a time so that you can see what is happening and check out the program piece by piece. After each chunk I give you, just add a temporary RET instruction so that you can check through what you have done.

First, a piece of housekeeping in which the area of memory starting at 1090, which is to hold our extended directory listing, is cleared to spaces:

```
0600 MOV CX,0060
0603 MOV AH,20
0605 MOV SI,1090
0608 MOV [SI],AH
060A MOV DI,1091
060D REPZ
060E MOVSB
```

You can type REPZ MOVSB on a single line, but DEBUG splits them up into two separate instructions. This clears 60 hex addresses by using a variation on LOOP, REPZ, repeat until zero – which needs to be told what it is to repeat until zero, and in this case it has to MOVSB, move a single byte from the address specified in the source index (SI) to the destination index (DI), then add one to each and decrement CX, and so on until CX is wound down to zero.

If you find it a bit puzzling, change the 20 temporarily to another character, and watch it happen a step at a time.

Now we take the gloves off and get down to the real business. First, the date, which starts with a really fancy piece of programming which I think is neat. See what your view is when you have typed it in and I have had a chance to explain just what is going on:

```
060F MOV AX, [1018]
0612 SAR AH,1
0614 PUSHF
0615 XOR BX,BX
0617 MOV BL,AH
0619 ADD BX,07BC
061D PUSH AX
061E MOV AX,BX
0620 MOV DI,10B8
0623 MOV CX,0004
0626 CALL 800
0629 MOV BX,0020
062C XOR DX,DX
062E POP AX
062F XOR AH,AH
0631 DIV BX
0633 POPF
0634 JNC 0638
0636 OR AL,08
0638 MOV DI,10B3
063B MOV CX 0002
063E CALL 0800
0641 MOV AX, [1018]
0644 AND AX,001F
0647 MOV CX,0002
064A MOV DI,10B0
064D CALL 0800
```

The date of a file is stored as a word. Unfortunately, it is not saved in such a way that a child of five could read it straight off the screen. No, it is packed ingeniously into the word in a way that takes some unscrambling, because one of the values crosses the boundary between the first and second words. I think it will become a little less murky if I give you an example. Here is the two-byte value for the date 6 June 1990:

C214

First, we must remember that it is stored the wrong way round, so if we set it out right way up plus the binary values that go with it, the date becomes:

```
   1    4    C    2
 0001 0100 1100 0010
```

Now comes the complicated bit. Counting from the least significant bit on the right and numbering from zero, the situation goes like this:

```
0-4 = day
5-8 = month
9-0F = year
```

So, we get these values from the binary split up as indicated:

```
00010 = 2
0110 = 6
0001010 = A
```

Day and month make sense, but we are not out of the woods yet. The year is down as A, ten in decimal, which means that the year is given as a value starting at 1980 as zero.

How is all this coped with in the program? First I do something apparently odd – I load the contents of 1018 into AX and shift AH arithmetically one to the right. Next I push the flags on to the stack (PUSHF).

The crafty and somewhat labyrinthine method behind this apparent madness goes like this: AH contains the value 14, the leftmost 7 bits of which contain the year as an offset from 1980, and the least significant bit contains the most significant bit of the month value.

What shifting AH one bit to the right does is to make the AH register contain the seven bits which represent the year, and the state of the carry flag will in a moment tell the program whether the month is a value greater than seven or not. To continue with the year: The value in AH is added to the zeroised BX register at 617. The jiggling around is because you can't mix half a register with a whole one. That is added to 7BC, not a particularly meaningful number until you convert it to decimal: 1980.

That's the year sorted out. Now we deal with the month, which is held in the topmost three bytes of AL plus a one or a zero, depending on the state of carry. So, after converting the year to decimal and storing it at the right point in the buffer beginning at 1090, AX is popped, AH is cleared since we have finished with the year, then AX is moved to the right by a division process and, if the carry flag is set, the topmost bit is added back in.

Finally, with a great sigh of relief, it is converted into decimal and we home in on the easy part, the bottom five bits which are isolated out by the mask 11111 at 644. At each conversion call to 800, the address into which the converted value is to be placed is loaded into DI.

Now we move from the date to the hardly less arduous task of coping with the time. Here is the code:

```
0650 MOV AX,[1016]
0653 XOR DX,DX
0655 MOV BX,0020
0658 DIV BX
065A ROL DX,1
065C PUSH AX
065D MOV AX,DX
065F MOV DI,10C8
0662 MOV CX,0002
0665 CALL 0800
0668 POP AX
0669 PUSH AX
066A AND AX,003F
066D MOV CX,0002
```

*– Program continued on next page –*
```
0670 MOV DI,10C5
0673 CALL 0800
0676 POP AX
0677 XOR DX,DX
0679 MOV BX,0040
067C DIV BX
067E MOV DI,10C2
0681 MOV CX,0002
0684 CALL 0800
```

Again, this is tough going, but really rewarding once you have cracked the problem and you have understood what is going on. First, we load the time from addresses 1016-7. I am taking as an example the time 16:04.48, and you will immediately notice an enhancement on what DIR gives you in that the time is detailed down to seconds, which can be of great value when you are developing short programs and turning data around quickly.

This is the raw material as it is loaded into AX with the binary equivalent underneath:

```
   8    0    9    8
1000 0000 1001 1000
```

The first five bits are the seconds, but if you do a swift calculation, you will find that the largest number you can fit into five bits – 1F – is just 31 in decimal, just over half the number of seconds in a minute, so the information is stored in increments of two seconds.

This means that we not only have to unscramble the seconds, we have to multiply them by two to get the correct answer.

At 655 we start the process. AX is divided by 20 (in BX), which isolates the first five bits of the packed value and deposits them as a remainder from the division into DX. Answer in AX = 0404, and remainder in DX = 0018. Then at 65A we rotate DX left by one bit which, if you think about it for a moment, is the simplest way there is of multiplying by two, just as shifting right does the same for dividing by two.

The answer in AX is sent to the subroutine at 800, and up comes the answer converted to two ASCII characters: 48. Now we turn to the minutes.

You will see that at 668 I first pop AX and then push it back. The reason is to get back the value 0404 and also to save it again for the hours part of the operation. Now we AND AX with the value 1F, which is 11111 in binary, since the next five bytes hold the time in minutes.

After that relatively painless operation, back we come with AX = 0404 again, and this time we want to divide AX by a value which effectively gets rid of the minutes five bits and leaves us with the hours value. Dividing by 40 at 67C does the trick, and one more conversion later we have cracked the hardest part of the exercise.

Now it is all downhill – relatively speaking, that is. The next piece of information I am after is in the byte at 115, and that is the file attribute, of which we shall be seeing more in detail in the chapters on files. Briefly, the attribute byte tells you, according to which bits are set or clear, whether the archive bit is set, whether the file is read only, and so forth.

In this case, I have allowed for all the possible attributes to be expressed by single letters – ADVSHR (where the D stands in for subdirectory). For full details see Appendix C.

At 687-698 the appropriate part of the buffer is loaded with those six letters. Then the attribute byte is moved into AL at 69E, and a loop of six set up. Each time round the loop, AL is ANDed with AH, and if the bit is set, nothing happens, otherwise the letter at the given address is set to a space. To follow it through, take a file – assume it is called FRED – and make it read only like this:

```
ATTRIB +R FRED
```

ATTRIB is an external command and needs to be accessible before you can use it.

Then run the program through, single-stepping the loop to watch the letters A and R being left untouched. The instruction at 6B0 rotates the contents of AH one to the right; in other words, the single bit mask is moved one down the list and with A and R set, the byte value is 20 and the bit pattern is as follows:

```
ADVSHR
100001
```

Here is the part of the subroutine which deals with the attribute byte:

```
0687 MOV DI,10D0
068A MOV AX,4441
068D MOV [DI],AX
068F MOV AX,5356
0692 MOV [DI+02],AX
0695 MOV AX,5248
0698 MOV [DI+04],AX
069B MOV CX,0006
069E MOV AH,20
06A0 DEC DI
06A1 MOV AL,[1015]
06A4 INC DI
06A5 AND AL,AH
06A7 JZ 06AB
06A9 JMP 6B0
06AB MOV BX,0020
06AE MOV [DI],BL
06B0 SAR AH,1
06B2 LOOP 06A1
```

Now an almost trivial task. The file size is held in two words at 101A-101D, and is converted in the next few lines:

```
06B4 MOV AX,[101C]
06B7 MOV CX,0004
06BA MOV DI 10A6
06BD CALL 0800
06C0 MOV DI,10AA
06C3 MOV AX,[101A]
06C6 MOV CX,0005
06C9 CALL 0800
```

Finally, and almost hardly worth mentioning, the name of the file is at 101E onwards as an ASCIIZ string. The last part of the subroutine looks for the zero string terminator, and replaces it with carriage return, line feed, and dollar sign. And the whole lot, from 1090 onwards, is put on screen by function 9.

```
06CC MOV SI,101E
06CF MOV DI,1090
06D2 MOV AL,[SI]
06D4 CMP AL,00
06D6 JZ 06DE
06D8 MOV [DI],AL
06DA INC SI
06DB INC DI
06DC JMP 06D2
06DE MOV AX,0A0D
06E1 MOV [10D9]AX
06E4 MOV AL,24
06E6 MOV [10DB],AL
06E9 MOV DX,1090
06EC MOV AH,09
06EE INT 21
06F0 RET
```

I leave you to add any refinements, like a colon and full stop in the hours, minutes and seconds, and suppressing leading zeroes if that takes your fancy.

That concludes our long and – I hope – informative look at DEBUG, but in the remaining chapters we shall be cranking it up now and again in order to explore more of the hidden depths of MS-DOS.

# Summary

Here are the descriptions of the find file functions, with a reminder about setting up your DTA.

## Find first file

This function is called with AH set to 4E, with CX normally zero, and DX pointing to an ASCIIZ name which will, of course, almost inevitably include wildcards. Alternatively, this routine can be used as another way of checking that a single file exists. If it does not, carry is set and AX contains the error code. The most likely code is 02, which means "file not found".

The disk transfer area contains information about the file. To set up your own DTA, use function 1A with DX pointing to the beginning of an area of memory set aside for the purpose.

The contents of the DTA are as follows:

```
0-14 reserved
15 attribute byte
16-17 time
date
1A-1D size
ASCII name and extension.
```

# Find next file

Of course, this call only makes sense if there has been a previous call of 4E which has successfully matched a first file. The function call is 4F, and the DTA should also have been first sorted out, if necessary, by the program. Do not mess around with the DTA address after calling 4E, because 4F assumes it will find the appropriate information in the DTA on which it can work to get the next matching file.

If a match is found, carry is clear and you are ready to proceed to the next match. If there isn't one, carry is set and AX contains the error code, usually stating that the list of matches is exhausted (02).

# 20

# Caring for the Environment

You might think from the chapter heading that we are going all trendy and are about to take the plunge into Green Computing. You will be relieved to know that the "environment" has nothing to do with computers polluting rivers or creating carbon dioxide emissions on Mother Earth, let alone zapping you with radiation; it is quite simply a special part of the RAM of your PC which can be inspected and altered with care. If you type:

```
SET
```

- from your keyboard if you have Version 3.1 or above, MS-DOS will report what the current contents of the environment are. On the machine I am typing this chapter on, the current settings are:

```
COMSPEC=C:\COMMAND.COM
PATH=C:;\DOS
PROMPT=$p$g
```

Your own listing will at least have the first two lines. The very first line tells MS-DOS where to look for the COMMAND.COM program, in this case the root directory of the hard disk. If you have Version 3.2 of MS-DOS or lower and no hard disk, and you wish to nest batch files without having to load COMMAND.COM each time from the A: drive, you can change things round, provided that you have set up a RAM drive as I have explained at the beginning of the book.

Just add two lines to your AUTOEXEC.BAT file:

```
COPY COMMAND.COM D:
SET COMSPEC=D:\COMMAND.COM
```

That will copy COMMAND.COM to the RAM drive - which, remember, may well be drive C rather than D - and tell the operating system to look for it there rather than expecting it to be sitting in the A: floppy disk drive.

The SET command, then, can be used to change as well as inspect the environment variables. One very important point to note is that, while the variable on the lefthand side of the equals sign is not case sensitive - it is always converted by MS-DOS to upper case - it is "space sensitive"; in other words, you must not, repeat not, leave a space before or after the equals sign. The following are identical:

```
SET fred=hi there
SET FRED=hi there
```

- but these are not identical:

```
SET FRED=hi there
SET FRED =hi there
SET FRED = hi there
```

FRED and FRED plus space are two different variables and are treated as such by MS-DOS in its perverse wisdom. I'm open to the power of rational argument, but it does seem to me strange to be able to include in a variable name the main character - space - which the operating system uses as a separator between commands and the like.

Still, ours is not to reason why. The best explanation one of my erstwhile teachers ever gave me of something I didn't understand was: "It is so because I say so, boy." Things haven't changed a great deal over the years, it seems.

# A bigger and better environment

One of the problems you face with the environment space is that it is miserably small; a mere 160 bytes, and for any serious use of the environment, if you do not wish to be on the receiving end of a message which tells you you are "Out of environment space", you will need to do something about it. If you do get that message, you will find that MS-DOS has inserted as much as it can in the space, and then simply truncated it.

The result could be interesting, especially if you set a prompt, started it by saving the cursor, and the bit restoring the cursor has been cut off in its prime. This is why I issued a couple of warnings earlier in this book when we were designing the mega-prompt which put the date, time and so forth in the top righthand corner of the screen.

As you can see from the list generated when I typed:

```
SET
```

- a record of the current prompt is kept in the environment space, except when you have left it to MS-DOS to display its default prompt. In other words, if your prompt is plain A> or C>, there is no entry in the variable list for PROMPT, unless, that is, you actually type:

```
SET PROMPT $N$G
```

- in which case the default prompt does appear in the list. Again, don't blame me. I just write about them, I don't invent them.

The monster prompt we designed earlier was well on the way to swallowing up all the remaining environment space, and more, and it would almost certainly have done so when it comes to storing the old prompt there too. More of that in a moment. First we must do something about the space problem.

That something is, obviously, to expand the environment, but this is one area where MS-DOS is not very compatible between versions. If you have Version 2, there is nothing official that can be done about the size of the space.

Under Version 3, the story is less painful, thank goodness. You can use the SHELL command to set up a value like this:

```
SHELL COMMAND.COM /E:x /P
```

The ''x'' stands for the number of 16-byte chunks you require, or -for 3.2 and above - the actual number of bytes. Versions 3.2 and upwards allow you a pretty generous 32K - ironically the full RAM size of the BBC B micro of late lamented memory - but 3.1 allows less than one megabyte in all.

In effect, the SHELL command sets up a customised version of COM-MAND.COM at boot-up time and the parameters specified tell the system that it is to be a permanent copy and to have the environment space expanded by the given amount.

## Adding new variables

One of the advantages of the environment variables is that you can add your own, although it seems that they can be unreliable in practice, particularly in Version 3.0, so do try before you buy, so to speak. If they do function properly, you have an extremely potent programming tool available to you, as you will now see.

If you think back to the chapters on batch files, you will remember my attempts at offering advice on how to debug your batch files without having to add and remove ECHO OFF lines and the like as you did so. I suggested adding an asterisk as the first parameter during test mode, and shifting it to take over %0, where its existence could be tested during the running of the file, for example:

```
IF %0 == * ECHO Got to this label all right
```

The problem with that technique, crafty though it is, is twofold. First, you lose the name of the batch file from %0, which in most cases is no great hardship, but more importantly, you can't use this approach when you are developing a batch file in which you use SHIFT, for reasons which hardly need spelling out.

However, this is no problem if you make use of the environment parameters. Create a little batch file like this:

```
SET ASTERISK=NO
IF NOT "%1" == "*" GOTO NOTEST
SHIFT
SET ASTERISK=*
:NOTEST
REM Rest of file...
IF "%ASTERISK%" == "*" ECHO Testing....
```

This sets ASTERISK to the asterisk sign if you are developing a batch file and tests the contents of ASTERISK. Or, you could simply type from the MS-DOS prompt:

```
SET ASTERISK=*
```

And when you no longer require test mode:

```
SET ASTERISK=
```

This version of SET removes the variable ASTERISK from the list altogether, which explains my fussy-looking line which puts double quotes round the odd-looking %ASTERISK%. If it does not exist, it returns the null string and without double quotes or similar you would be on the receiving end of a syntax error. Let's see what the per cent signs mean.

## A PROMPT rearrangement

The best part of the environment variables is that you can not only alter them, but inspect their contents by using yet another variation on the per cent sign theme. As you will remember, %0 - %9 refer to the ten parameters which can be part of the command tail of the batch file name when it is called. In addition, a double per cent plus a single character can be used in the FOR command.

But now, the ultimate use of per cent, as the alternative to quotes bracketing a variable.

To observe what is going on, create a little batch file like this, noting the per cent signs carefully:

```
SET EXPROMPT=%PROMPT%
SET PROMPT=$G$G$G
SET
```

Call it SWAP1.BAT. Then create another batch file called SWAP2.BAT:

```
SET PROMPT=%EXPROMPT%
SET
```

Now run them one after another, and see what happens. Your prompt first changes to a triple chevron, and then back again to its previous state. That means you can switch between the mega-prompt we designed in an earlier chapter and a more modest standard prompt. Both can be set up in the AUTOEXEC.BAT file. This should work even if you don't specify a prompt at start-up time, as the command:

```
SET EXPROMPT=%PROMPT%
```

- and its matching partner will simply return an empty string.

The call of SET without parameters, remember, just lists the variables and their associated phrases, as they are called, and I have included it so that you can inspect the state of the list.

This is quite a powerful technique which unfortunately can, as I have found, be a little quirky, so test it out thoroughly to ensure that it can be run on your system and that it does what it is supposed to do.

One instant application of this technique is to establish a password or passwords for using parts of the system. If you put into your AUTOEXEC.BAT file the lines:

```
SET PW1=GOD
SET PW2=30.6.40
```

- that will enable PW1 and PW2 to be matched against user keying in of passwords to check that usage is authorised. Incidentally, don't use GOD or a birthday like that - they are two of the most frequently-used passwords in the universe.

The password can be tested when a user invokes a batch file, for example:

```
ACCOUNTS 30.6.40
```

The batch file will contain near the beginning a couple of lines like this:

```
IF "%1" == "%PW2%" GOTO OK
ECHO Call the police!
GOTO FAIL
:OK
```

- or possibly something slightly less dramatic, such as "Access denied".
In addition, you can change the PATH if the fancy takes you by storing the current path as something like OLDPATH:

```
SET OLDPATH=%PATH%
SET PATH=D:\
```

## Other techniques

You can use the per cent brackets with batch file commands in the normal way, and this brings us to some intriguing possibilities. First, you can ECHO the current contents of one of the system environment variables, or one of your own invention:

```
ECHO The current path is %PATH%
```

Or - a more intriguing possibility this - you can set up a variable such as the following:

```
SET LIST=*.BAK *.WP
```

- and call it using FOR:

```
FOR %%A IN (%LIST%) DO COPY %%A B:
```

Even more useful is the possibility of holding on to the value of parameters when a batch file is called, even if you SHIFT them out of existence. If you put these lines in a batch file, you will save them for use either later in the same batch file or even in another batch file later on. This listing assumes that you want to save up to five parameters:

```
SET P0=%0
SET P1=%1
SET P2=%2
```

```
SET P3=%3
SET P4=%4
```

Remember to put quotes round the %P1% variables when testing for their contents in case there was no parameter, so that you get the null string instead of a syntax error.

You can be even more devious with the SET command by incorporating part or all of the PROMPT commands themselves in the variable list. If you do this:

```
SET A=$E[1;34;43m
SET B=$E[33;34m
```

- and call them in a batch file:

```
PROMPT %A%
PROMPT
PAUSE
PROMPT %B%
PROMPT
```

- you can change the on-screen colours, or indeed perform any of the tricks that PROMPT itself gets up to. Even more cunning, I discovered, is that you can set a variable to contain a complete command:

```
SET X=ECHO This is a demo of set echoing...
```

Call it like this:

```
%X%
```

The possibilities are quite extensive. Which leads me to a final, useless but entertaining, piece of information. If someone tells you you may not use a single per cent sign in a batch file to generate a sign on screen, because you have to double up to get a result, don't believe them. This combination will work like a charm. Call SET from the MS-DOS prompt:

```
SET Z=ECHO I prefer 10% discount
```

Then call it from within a batch file, and you will see what I mean!

You may have noticed that I tend to use short variable names. That's just to save space. There appears to be no upper limit, apart from the total environment space, to the length of a variable. I tried one 26 letters long and it seemed to work, but who needs that kind of length?

## Nesting problems

One problem to watch out for with SET is that if you have a version of MS-DOS below 3.3, you have to load a new version of the operating system to run a nested batch file which then returns control back to the calling file. This means, in effect, two different environment copies, neither of which can talk to the other.

However, CALL, which was introduced with Version 3.3, does not use this technique at all, so that the same environment is used for the calling batch file and the inner one.

# *21*

# *Key Solutions*

---

A great deal of attention in books on the PC is devoted to the MS-DOS operating system, the memory of the PC, the BIOS, the disk interface and a number of other unquestionably fascinating aspects of the machine, but the poor old keyboard tends to be sadly overlooked. After all, it is just there for you to two-finger type commands on to the screen and into memory, and it's not particularly interesting in its own right.

The time has come to set the record straight and give the keyboard its due. There's a great deal of profit to be gained by getting on familiar terms with the intricacies of the keyboard, and we have already established this to some extent when we looked at the Caps, Num and Scroll Locks in an earlier chapter.

Now we are going to explore the keyboard a little further, starting with the 40 function keys. No, that isn't a misprint: There really are 40 function keys on your keyboard, even if it seems that you have only 10, or – on AT and other machines – 12.

Each of the function keys F1-F10 generates an ASCII value of a rather special kind, and so do Shift+F1 to Shift+F10 and Ctrl+F1 to Ctrl+F10 and Alt+F1 to Alt+F10. That makes 40 keys available in all for particular purposes, and we start by showing you how to customise the Shift+function keys for use with a simple text processor like Rped, supplied with Amstrad computers, which doesn't grab all the possible function keys for its own ends.

Let us assume that you want to incorporate German characters in your text: They are Ä, ä, Ö, ö, Ü, ü and ß. To enter them from the keyboard normally requires you to hold down the Alt key, and then – for Ä, for example – to press the 1, 4 and 2 keys on the numeric keypad and then release the Alt key. That is a pretty tiresome business, and not conducive to the ready flow of ideas or smooth copy typing.

So, it would be nice if we could program the appropriate function keys with the right values, but there is a snag to overcome first, and one which can best be demonstrated by loading up DEBUG once again. Assemble the following instructions, which ask for two successive characters to be typed in at the keyboard:

```
MOV AH,01
INT 21
```

```
MOV AH,01
INT 21
INT 20
```

Then type G to go, and when the program is sitting waiting for you, press the F1 key, you will find that the program terminates normally, but that out of the blue a semicolon appears. If you now save that program and reload DEBUG, this time single step through using P, and you will find after the first call to INT 21 that the debugger gets a mite confused when you press F1. A semicolon appears against the minus prompt, but if you examine the AL register, which records the input character, you will find that it is zero.

What is going on? The function keys, along with some other keys, cannot be accommodated among the normal ASCII character set plus the accents and graphics characters, because a glance at the table in your manual will show that it's fully taken up and there is no room for further expansion. For this reason, the concept of "extended ASCII codes" was devised. These consist of a leading zero followed by a number. The full list of these extended codes goes like this. Under the column marked "value" is the decimal number which follows the zero:

| Value | Meaning |
| --- | --- |
| 3 | NUL (the ASCII null character) |
| 15 | Shift Tab |
| 16-25 | Alt+Q W E R T Y U I O P |
| 30-38 | Alt+Z X C V B N M |
| 59-68 | F1 – F10 |
| 71 | Home |
| 72 | Cursor up |
| 73 | PgUp |
| 75 | Cursor left |
| 77 | Cursor right |
| 79 | End |
| 80 | Cursor down |
| 81 | PgDn |
| 82 | Insert |
| 83 | Delete |
| 84-93 | Shift+F1 – F10 |
| 94-103 | Ctrl+F1 – F10 |
| 104-110 | Alt+F1 – F10 |

So, in order to use PROMPT to reprogram the function keys, it is necessary to add in this leading zero to the redefinition escape sequence. Write a short batch file like this:

```
PROMPT $E[0;84;143p
PROMPT $E[0;85;132p
PROMPT
```

Note that the "p" at the end of the escape sequence must be in lower case, and that you must have ECHO switched ON, otherwise the change to the function keys won't "take". Again the last PROMPT should be different if you want to customise it.

So it's a simple matter to alter the Shift+F1 and so forth keys to suit your requirements. All you need is a list of the character set, which we earlier wrote a program to do, and a little table on the top of the keyboard to remind you which is which.

This is a good illustration of how the SET command can help you. The mechanics of changing the key values are quite straightforward. First set a value to save the current prompt to, then reset the value at the end of the sequence of commands:

```
SET TEMP=%PROMPT%
PROMPT $E[0;84;143p
PROMPT $E[0;85;132p
PROMPT
SET PROMPT=%TEMP%
```

I find this particular variation on the escape sequence useful when typing in a foreign language, as you will find from the above example if you try it out. Instead of having to remember and key in Alt+1+3+0 for e acute, you can simply change the value of a function key, and so on across the keyboard using a combination like Alt+F1 and so forth.

The trouble is that most modern wordprocessors grab these keys for their own use, and on top of that there is only a very limited space allocated by MS-DOS for these keyboard redefinitions, around 200 bytes. So their use is limited, although if you want to do something like convert the keyboard to an AZERTY a few redefinitions can do the trick.

Still, there is nothing to stop you changing the values of the keys from the MS-DOS prompt or when running a batch file, so you could have a menu system which asked you to press F1, F2, and so on, and their values could have been reset to something like:

```
PROMPT $E[0;84;"CHESS";13p
PROMPT $E[0;85;"INVADERS";13p
```

Note that in this case the key redefinition ends with a carriage return code, which means that it presses the Enter key for you, so to speak, as well as generating the program name. Do be careful if you reset the values of the normal keys, as you can end up rather confused unless you set them back to their original values when you have finished with them in their altered form.

## Boxing clever

Only the "normal" ASCII character set can be keyed in directly from an unmodified keyboard. For the rest, you need to hold down the Alt key and type in a three-digit number on the numeric keypad, then release the Alt key before the character pops up on the screen.

If you examine the ASCII values in the range 176 decimal and upwards, you will find a fairly complex set of strange-looking lines which can be put together to draw either plain boxes with a single or double rule, or more complex boxes with different compartments, all neatly joined up together.

It would add greatly to the attractiveness of your programming and, in particular, your batch files if you could harness these design features to make your presentation more attractive, but it is a slow, error-prone business trying to get the boxes just right and set out properly on screen. So here is a natty little program in assembler which does a lot of the dirty work for you. All you have to do, once the program is written, is to incorporate in your batch files or elsewhere this command:

```
BOX 9 12 15 66
```

– where the first two numbers are the row and column where the top lefthand corner of the box is to be located, and the second two are the row and column at the bottom righthand corner of the box.

Here is the listing for you to type into DEBUG, with the address numbers for reference purposes on the lefthand side. Call the program BOX.COM:

```
0100 MOV SI, 0081
0103 MOV AL, [SI]
0104 CMP AL, 0D
0107 JNZ 010C
0109 JMP 0500
010C CALL 0400
010F MOV DI, 1002
0112 MOV [DI], BX
0114 MOV DI, 1012
0117 MOV [DI], BX
0119 CALL 0400
011C MOV DI, 1005
011F MOV [DI], BX
0121 MOV DI, 1025
0124 MOV [DI], BX
0126 CALL 0400
0129 MOV DI, 1022
012C MOV [DI], BX
012E MOV DI, 1032
0131 MOV [DI], BX
0133 CALL 0400
0136 MOV DI, 1015
0139 MOV [DI], BX
013B MOV DI, 1035
013E MOV [DI], BX
0140 MOV CX, 0002
0143 MOV DX, 1010
0146 MOV AH, 09
0148 INT 21
014A ADD DX, 20
014D LOOP 0146
014F MOV AL, BB
0151 MOV [1050], AL
0154 MOV CX, 0002
0157 MOV DX, 1000
015A MOV AH, 09
015C INT 21
015E MOV BH, 00
0160 MOV AH, 08
```
*– Program continued on next page –*

```
0162 INT 10
0164 CMP AL, [1050]
0168 JZ 0172
016A MOV AH, 02
016C MOV DL, CD
016E INT 21
0170 JMP 015E
0172 MOV AL, BC
0174 MOV [1050], AL
0177 MOV AH, 09
0179 MOV DX, 1020
017C INT 21
017E LOOP 015A
0180 MOV AL, C8
0182 MOV [1050], AL
0185 MOV CX, 0002
0188 MOV DX, 1000
018B MOV AH, 09
018D INT 21
018F MOV AH, 09
0191 MOV DX, 1041
0194 INT 21
0196 MOV BH, 00
0198 MOV AH, 08
019A INT 10
019C CMP AL, [1050]
01A0 JZ 01AB
01A2 MOV AH, 09
01A4 MOV DX, 1040
01A7 INT 21
01A9 JMP 019C
01AB MOV AL, BC
01AD MOV [1050], AL
01B0 MOV DX, 1010
01B3 LOOP 018B
01B5 INT 20
```

Now for the subroutine call to 400, which loads the appropriate row and column numbers into the data areas which hold the four corners of the box:

```
0400 MOV BX, 3030
0403 MOV AL, [SI]
0405 CMP AL, OD
0407 JNZ 040C
0409 JMP 0500
040C CMP AL, 20
040E JNZ 0413
0410 INC SI
0411 JMP 0400
0413 MOV BH, AL
0415 INC SI
0416 MOV AL, [SI]
0418 CMP AL, 20
```

*–Program continued on next page–*

```
041A JNZ 041D
041C RET
041D CMP AL,0D
041F JZ 041C
0421 MOV BL,BH
0423 MOV BH,AL
0425 INC SI
0426 RET
```

Then the familiar bell-ringing party at line 500:

```
0500 MOV AH,02
0502 MOV DL,07
0504 INT 21
0506 INT 20
```

And finally, with a sigh of relief, the slots for the four corners of the box and, at 1040, the rather complicated-looking downward and backspace movements to put in the vertical lines:

```
E 1000 1B,"[00;00f",C9,"$"
E 1010 1B,"[00;00f",BB,"$"
E 1020 1B,"[00;00f",C8,"$"
E 1030 1B,"[00;00f",BC,"$"
E 1040 BA,1B,"[B",1B,"D$"
```

Now for an explanation of what the program does. We are already familiar with the technique of reading the command tail from location 81 and following in the PSP, and the first couple of instructions check for the absence of a tail and then calls the subroutine at location 400 four times, once to pick up each of the parameters. If any or all of the parameters are missing, we jump to location 500, where the bell is rung and the program terminated.

If you feel like adding an error message at this point, it's up to you to do so. This is strictly a programmer's tool, so I haven't made it too watertight. The object of the exercise is to take the values keyed in and transfer them to the four escape codes starting at address 1000. One particular snag in doing so is that we have to cope with single digits. The valid values for the box outer limits range from 1-25 and from 1-79.

Fortunately, the escape code for locating the cursor doesn't mind a leading zero, so we initialise the BX register at 4000 with two zeroes. Then the first digit is read in and placed in the BH register. Remember that when the contents of the BX register are stored, they are stored "back to front", so a single "9" placed in BH will look like 3900 in the register, but will be placed in the escape code the "right" way round, as the equivalent of 09.

If the number is more than one digit long, the first digit encountered is shunted from BH to BL and the second digit placed in BH. You can watch this at work by single-stepping through the program. After each call of the subroutine, the contents of BX are stored in the appropriate locations in the area starting at 1000. If you call the program like this:

```
DEBUG BOX.COM 9 12 15 45
D 1000 103F
G 140
D 1000 103F
```

– you will be able to see the escape codes in their "empty" state and then with the numbers each in the right location for printing the four corners of the box. This particular program produces a double ruled box, and the four codes for the corners can be found at 1008, 1018, 1028 and 1038, and two of them perform an interesting role.

Now comes the crafty bit. The instructions from 140 to 146 print the top and bottom righthand corners of the box, for reasons which will now be revealed. The tricky bit of drawing a box when using "normal" decimal parameters typed in from the keyboard is working out the length of the sides of the box without having to indulge in some fairly fancy conversions and calculations. Fortunately, function 8 of INT 10 comes to the rescue.

It reads the character and attribute at the cursor: in other words, it picks off the screen – or rather, the video buffer in RAM – the character at the location where the cursor is sitting, together with its attribute, which gives the foreground and background colour, whether it's intense or blinking and so on. We are not interested in the attribute, just the character, and that is to be found in AL. BH is set to zero to denote the currently active screen.

So what we now do first at 14F is to save the first character we shall be looking for, in other words BB in hex, the top righthand corner of the screen, then we print the top lefthand corner on the screen and then simply keep printing the horizontal double rule character out, checking each time until we reach the top righthand corner of the box, and then we stop. The process is repeated for the bottom line of the box, and as you can see, I've saved a lot of extra typing out by turning it into a simple loop to the CX register value.

Typing across the screen is no problem – that's what computers are rather good at, but typing down the screen, putting in the vertical rules, is quite a different kettle of fish. First, at 180 we load the target bottom lefthand corner value into location 1050, then we print again the top lefthand corner. Keeping the vertical rule in the right place is a bit of a problem. First we have to move the cursor down one and one to the left to line it up for the first character – that's achieved in 18F-194, and if you examine the string beginning at 1040, you will see that starting first time round at 1041 does just that.

I skip past the actual character – BA – the first time round. Now the program is set to print the vertical rules in a neat line, testing in the right place, that is, immediately below the character last printed, for the presence of the bottom lefthand corner. When that task has been completed, I've saved lines of code again by looping back to draw the righthand vertical side of the box. And that's all there is to it.

One word of warning when running the program: I have not built in a check for silly numbers, again because this is a programmer's tool rather than something for general user application, so if you try to draw a box with the righthand side to the left of the lefthand side, or with values greater than the screen size, the program will have one of its nasty turns. Try Ctrl+C to escape back to the prompt, and if that fails, Ctrl+Break.

Now we are in business, but not just for drawing a single box. Not only can we now draw a number of boxes in different parts of the screen, we can also liven up our batch files with a display of animation, a dramatic effect of boxes growing out into the screen.

First we need to make the necessary alterations to BOX.COM and call it BTHIN.COM – this creates a single line box. Now to create the illusion of the box moving out across the screen, and this involves an extremely cunning use of SET. If SET doesn't work properly on your system, do not despair. There is a way round the problem, and I'll tell you that at the end of this listing:

```
ECHO OFF
CLS
CUROFF
SET B1=BOX
SET B2=BTHIN
COUNT 0
:LOOP
%B1% 12 30 14 32
WAIT
%B2% 11 29 15 33
WAIT
%B1% 10 28 16 34
WAIT
%B2% 9 27 17 35
WAIT
%B1% 8 26 18 36
WAIT
%B2% 7 25 19 37
WAIT
%B1% 6 24 20 38
SET B3=%B1%
SET B4=%B2%
SET B1=%B4%
SET B2=%B3%
COUNT +
IF ERRORLEVEL 59 GOTO NEXTBIT
GOTO LOOP
:NEXTBIT
```

WAIT is a simple assembler program which goes like this:

```
0100 MOV CX,FFFF
0103 LOOP 103
0107 INT 20
```

If that's too fast, add another loop if it is too slow, reduce the figure in CX. Alternatively, get clever and work out a program which you can call with a command tail which specifies the length of the wait. That should hold no terrors for you now. COUNT is the looping program we wrote a couple of chapters back.

BOX.COM is copied to BTHIN.COM and patched to change double lines to single. I leave you to do that, but here are the appropriate numbers and characters in hex:

| description | double | single |
|---|---|---|
| top left corner | C9 | DA |
| horizontal line | CD | C4 |
| top right corner | BB | BF |
| vertical line | BA | B3 |
| bottom left | C8 | CA |
| bottom right | BC | D9 |

You will need to make changes both inside the program, and to the data area. Be careful if you use the search facility to find the code for double horizontal line, as it's CD – which is also the machine code instruction INT. So, watch that you don't change the wrong values.

What does the batch file do? This is the really cunning part, probably the programming which has given me most of a kick in writing this book for you. First, we use SET to create environment variables called B1 and B2 which first time round contain BOX and BTHIN respectively.

Then a series of boxes is drawn which start in the middle of the screen – more or less, I leave you to tart it up to suit yourself – and move out towards the edges. Note that the boxes are defined via the environment variables: Double, single, double, single, and so on. When the boxes have reached their outer limits (and I have not gone to the edges of the screen in the above listing; I'm just demonstrating the general principle), what happens next is that I use B3 and B4 to swap the variables round, so next time it is single, double, single, double, and so on, giving the illusion of a constant sequence of boxes moving out from the centre.

I must confess that, even after all these years at the keyboard, I am still amazed at what you can do with humble old MS-DOS and a touch of low cunning. I am sure you can devise other similar patternings with equally eye-catching effects, blending in colour variations, for example.

I assume that you are running this from the RAM drive, otherwise it will be painfully slow, and for those of you for whom SET doesn't work, try calling the programs B1 and B2 and then use COPY to swap them round each time you come to the end of the sequence:

```
COPY B1 B3
COPY B2 B4
COPY B3 B2
COPY B4 B1
```

It will also be necessary to save and restore the cursor before and after each call or set of calls of the BOX program. I have not incorporated this into the program, as you may well be using it in an animation sequence or in conjunction with other programs, so you need to have up your sleeve little programs SAVEC and RESTC, which will contain the necessary escape sequences, and can be written in no time at all.

Here's the program to save the cursor:

```
MOV AH,09
MOV DX,1000
INT 21
INT 20
```

Then:

```
E 1000 1B,"[s$"
```

There is one snag with the box program, and this relates to the fact that the line-drawing process stops when it encounters the next corner – and that could in some rare cases be the corner of a previously drawn square on the screen. So beware.

# 22

# A Moving Display

Now that we have drawn some boxes, it would add considerably to the attractiveness of the text inside them if it could be persuaded to move like those displays in shop windows or news and advertising hoardings.

In case you were wondering: Yes, it can be done and with a fairly straightforward program. If you consider the design parameters of such a program, we need to know on which row and column the display is to start, how many characters can be displayed at any one time, so that they fit neatly into our previously drawn box, the speed we want them to move at, and – last but not least – what the text is that you want to incorporate into the scrolling display.

It occurs to me that we must also take account of a situation in which the text to scroll is actually shorter than the size of the window, so that consideration must be built into the program. Once again, we shall make use of the command tail starting at location 81. When we have ensured that all the parameters and the text are in order and are loaded into memory, the most challenging part of the exercise is the fact that this is to be a rolling buffer; in other words, a point will come when the window will have to wrap round from the latter part of the text to the beginning of the text, if you see what I mean.

In addition, it would be useful to write a version of this program which makes use of function 0B of INT 21; in other words, the check keyboard input status interrupt. Text could be scrolling, say, in one of our boxes at the top of a menu, and continue to scroll until the user hits a key, at which point the program asked for could be loaded once IF ERRORLEVEL has determined which key has been depressed.

The program calls for our old friend DEBUG once more, but before we key it in let us consider the parameters we require. Here is a typical call of the program, which I have named as STRIP.COM:

```
STRIP 12 22 3 29 *** This is a demo ***
```

It looks a bit fiddly to set up, but I found that the best way to get the program functioning correctly was to set the box up from the MS-DOS prompt, and then try running STRIP until it was in the right place, right speed, and right length of string.

Then I made a note of the parameters and incorporated the lot in a batch file.

The first two parameters are the row and column on the screen, the third parameter is the speed in the range 1 (fast) to 9 (painfully slow). The fourth parameter is the length of the string to be displayed scrolling from right to left, and the rest is the string itself, which can be longer or shorter than the window in which it is scrolled.

From a programming point of view, the trickiest part is to persuade the text to scroll properly. First, though, we pick up the parameters from the command tail at 80 and following in the PSP, just as we have done with quite a few previous programs. Here is the main module of the program:

```
0100 MOV SI,0081
0103 MOV AL, [SI]
0105 CMP AL,0D
0107 JNZ 010C
0109 JMP 0500
010C MOV CX,0004
010F MOV DI,1002
0112 MOV BX,3030
0115 MOV AL, [SI]
0117 CMP AL,20
0119 JNZ 011E
011B INC SI
011C JMP 0115
011E CMP AL,0D
0120 JNZ 0125
0122 JMP 0500
0125 MOV BH,AL
0127 INC SI
0128 MOV AL, [SI]
012A CMP AL,20
012C JZ 0133
012E INC SI
012F MOV BL,BH
0131 MOV BH,AL
0133 MOV [DI],BX
0135 ADD DI,+10
0138 LOOP 0112
013A INC SI
013B MOV AL, [SI]
013D CMP AL,0D
013F JNZ 0144
0141 JMP 0500
0144 CMP AL,20
0146 JZ 013A
0148 MOV [1040],SI
014C MOV [1050],SI
0150 MOV SI, [1012]
0154 MOV [1005],SI
0158 MOV AH,0B
015A INT 21
015C CMP AL,00
```

*– Program continued on next page –*

```
015E JZ 0168
0160 MOV AH,08
0162 INT 21
0164 AND AL,DF
0166 MOV AH,4C
0168 INT 21
016A MOV AH,09
016C MOV DX,1000
016F INT 21
0171 MOV CX,[1032]
0175 CALL 0700
0178 MOV SI,[1050]
017C MOV DL,[SI]
017E CMP DL,0D
0181 JNZ 0189
0183 MOV SI,[1040]
0187 MOV DL,[SI]
0189 MOV AH,02
018B INT 21
018D INC SI
018E LOOP 017C
0190 CALL 0600
0193 MOV SI,[1050]
0197 INC SI
0198 MOV AL,[SI]
019A CMP AL,0D
019C JNZ 01A2
019E MOV S1,[1040]
01A2 MOV [1050],S1
01A6 JMP 0158
```

That's the main part of the program dealt with, and although a lot of this covers familiar programming territory, I know how off-putting a pageful of raw assembler can be, so let me go through the listing and explain what is happening.

First, as you can see, we check to see if 81 contains 0D, in other words if the user has failed to put any parameters at all. In this case, we go to 500 where, guess what, this is what you find:

```
0500 MOV DL,07
0502 MOV AH,02
0504 INT 21
0506 INT 20
```

Now a loop is set up at 10C to pick up the four items of numeric data and process them. If any one of them is missing, off we go again to 500 and noisy disgrace. As you see from 117, I make allowance for multiple spaces between parameters, as this utility is likely to be used also by non-expert programmers.

As the first two numbers are going to be used for locating on screen, the BX register, which is set up to receive them, is set to ASCII zeroes at 112, so that when they are deposited at locations 1002 onwards they fit in with the pattern which you should now key in:

```
E 1000 1B,"[00;00f$"
```

Thank goodness, the escape sequence doesn't mind if there is a leading zero. Purely for the sake of easy management of the numbers, what happens is that the first one or two-digit parameter is deposited into 1002-3, and then DI is incremented by 10 hex, and the rest end up rather arbitrarily at 1012, 1022, and 1032.

The down side of that piece of sleight of hand is that it is necessary at 150 to move the second parameter to where it belongs in the escape sequence. Immediately before that, two copies of the start of the text string are set up at 1040 and 1050. Why two? More of that in a moment or so.

Next we set up the loop. At 158 function 0B is set up. This, you may remember, listens in to the keyboard to see if a key has been pressed. If AL is zero, it hasn't, and the program carries on. If a keypress has occurred, then we invoke function 8 to read the character in, AND it with DF to convert it to upper case, and halt the program, leaving that character as the exit code, which means that you can use this display in conjunction with a menu in a batch file and pick up the exit code with IF ERRORLEVEL without further ado.

There is one slight snag with this command, which you will now be in a position to recognise. If some joker presses a function key or any other extended ASCII key, only the leading zero will be picked up, so to give your program a complete set of belt and braces, you could test for an initial zero and then invoke function 8 again if it is detected.

You could even ask for function keys to be pressed, although it would be advisable to adjust the second value so that it is out of the normal ASCII range when you test it with IF ERRORLEVEL, otherwise a semicolon pressed might be mistaken for a function key!

Now at 16A, function 9 outputs the cursor location escape sequence, and we are nearly ready to try outputting the string itself. First, though, the value of the string length needs to be converted from a two-byte ASCII value to a binary digit which can then be counted down via register CX and a LOOP instruction. So, off we go to CALL 700, where the conversion takes place.

Incidentally, in the old programming days I would have been lynched for putting the instructions at 171 and 175 where they are. They really belong outside the loop, since it means recalculating the value each time round, but computers are so fast nowadays that it doesn't really matter. It keeps them busy and out of mischief, that's my excuse. Now for the subroutine at 700:

```
0700 AND CX,0F0F
0704 PUSH AX
0705 PUSH BX
0706 PUSH DX
0707 XOR AX,AX
0709 MOV AL,CL
070B MOV BX,000A
070E MUL BX
0710 MOV CL,CH
0712 AND CX,00FF
0716 ADD CX,AX
0718 POP DX
```
*–Program continued on next page–*

```
0719 POP BX
071A POP AX
071B RET
```

The characters are stripped at 700 to two binary values, the first is multiplied by 10 decimal at 70B and the second one added in. It may look daunting, but it is ground we have covered before. Single step through the routine with a few trial values and you will soon see what is going on.

## Looping the string

Now comes the bit which caused me the most headaches, but which looks ridiculously simple when it is explained. As I said earlier, two copies of the address in the PSP of the first letter of the string are held in memory, one at 1040, the second at 1050. They were put there by the instructions at 148 and 14C.

We are back in the main module after calling 700, the length of the string in binary is safely located in CX, and we now loop from the address pointed to by 1050 for the length of the string. The first problem to solve is what happens at the end of the string in the command tail. It is terminated by the 0D character, remember, and this is what I keep a weather eye open for at 17E.

Each time we go round the loop, SI is incremented by one in order to output the next character in the string, but if we come up against 0D we simply reset SI to the value of the first character in the string (saved in 1040) and keep going.

When the loop count has been exhausted you will see why there were two copies of the start address saved. Let's explain with an example. Say you were scrolling from right to left the text:

**A program by J. Bloggs**

First time round, you would start at "A". Next time, you begin at the space, then at the "p" of program and so on. You could either make the window width smaller than the string, or longer, but in either case we would have to cope with the 0D character.

So, each time round the string, the value in 1050 is incremented, until – and this is where the real catch is – it points to the 0D, and because we don't want to start the next listing from after the end of the string, in that special case it is set to the value of the beginning of the string.

All of which sounds hopelessly confusing, but does make sense when you run the program through and see what's happening. There is just one administrative detail to sort out, and that is the time delay which is in the subroutine at 600:

```
0600 PUSH CX
0601 PUSH BX
0602 MOV CX, [1022]
0606 CALL 0700
0609 AND CX, 000F
060D MOV BX, FFFF
0610 DEC BX
0611 CMP BX, +00
0614 JNZ 0610
0616 LOOP 060D
```

```
0618 POP BX
0619 POP CX
061A RET
```

The number is converted to binary and the loop whizzes round the appropriate number of times. If you find the fastest speed – 1 – too slow, change the value in 60D down from FFFF.

There is one design aspect of the program to watch out for, and that is that the front and end of the strings butt-end on to each other, so to speak. I have deliberately not added a space, so that if you want the string to look right, you can either start it halfway through, so to speak:

STRIP 12 12 3 19 ease press Enter P1

– or use a set of asterisks, which appear in the program as a continuous trio:

STRIP 12 12 2 20 ** Round and round *

This is an extremely eye-catching, attractive and useful little program, especially when done in conjunction with the box-drawing command, and adds visual impact to your batch file commands. You will see it being used to good effect on the disk which can be purchased in conjunction with this book.

And one final thought: To make your text even more eye-catching, why not use one of the techniques described earlier to switch screen modes? That will really give this program a strong impact.

# 23

# Working with EDLIN

---

This chapter offers a general introduction to EDLIN, together with a few tricks you can play with it to help to make it more user-friendly. For those of you completely unfamiliar with EDLIN who wish to use it to type in the programs in this book, Appendix C offers a straightforward guide.

When the microcomputer first came on the market, people's ideas were still very much mainframe oriented, and notions like full screen editing and automatic wrap-round, let alone colour and windows, weren't even a twinkle in the software developer's eye. So, the nearest you could get to a wordprocessor, unless you were very lucky, was a line editor – and one such comes ready-made for your PC.

Called EDLIN, it bears a strong family resemblance to the ED program which was designed for the CP/M environment, and which is about as unfriendly as a piece of software could get without actually biting you. Still, you have to remember that in the early days there was no such notion as user-friendliness, the human computer programmer had to adapt him or herself (almost exclusively himself in those days) to the rigours and constraints of the machine.

There are other family connections with CP/M, the Control Program for Microprocessors, which is/was the operating system for 8080 and Z80 processors, and which is now sliding gracefully into late middle age on the PCW range of computers. IBM was not over-confident that MS-DOS would rule the roost, so there are many compatible features between the two, one of which – the Program Segment Prefix – we examined in our explorations of assembler. And when the Amstrad PC1512 came on the scene, both MS-DOS and DOS Plus, a grown-up version of CP/M, were on offer, though I suspect hardly anyone uses DOS Plus, except occasionally for one feature, the powerful copying routine, PIP, which stands for Peripheral Interchange Program.

Now, though, MS-DOS has become top dog on the Intel range of processors, and seems likely to remain so for the foreseeable future, despite the chippings away at the top end of the market by OS/2. So, here we are in the 1990s about to look at a superannuated piece of software. Is it going to be worth the effort?

The answer, in my view, is a resounding yes – EDLIN is temperamental and does need handling with care, but if you want certain features like control codes, or want to incorporate editing within batch files, EDLIN is for you. And, as we shall see, there is an added bonus or two.

You will find EDLIN.COM on your MS-DOS disk, or on the root directory of your hard disk. To give you an idea of the vagaries of line editors, the one I use on a Prime mainframe, which was devised in the University of Sheffield, and hence rejoices in the name of SHED, will fail if you try to open a new file at the time you summon it up:

`SHED FRED`

This will generate an error message. You have to type plain SHED, and then when you want to save your new file, you use the FILE command to do so. But does EDLIN follow this well-trodden path? Not a bit of it. If you type plain EDLIN, you are on the receiving end of an error message and you are dumped unceremoniously back into MS-DOS:

`File name must be specified`

So we get going with:

`EDLIN FRED`

The second thing you learn about line editors is that they antedate the present soft generation who are coddled with luxuries like context-sensitive help. EDLIN simply responds with a message telling you that this is a new file (an interesting fact which you knew already), then on the next line an asterisk which EDLIN more or less defies you to do something with.

If you get something wrong, you will tend to receive a message as unhelpful as:

`Data entry error`

What we are going to do with it is to issue one of the fourteen one-letter commands which EDLIN allows – in this case I for Insert (followed by Enter, as with all EDLIN commands), and this is what happens:

```
EDLIN FRED
New file
*I
        1:*
```

EDLIN is clearly as fond of asterisks as batch files are of per cent signs. The cursor winks invitingly, and at this point you can type in these four lines of deathless verse, penned in all seriousness by that well-known writer, Anon.:

```
1:*O Moon, when I gaze on thy beautiful face,
2:*Careering along through the boundaries of space,
3:*The thought has often come into my mind
4:*If I ever shall see thy glorious behind.
5:*^C
*
```

After the fourth line, press Enter, then Ctrl+C to exit from Insert mode. The IBM manual tells you that you must press Ctrl+Break, but Ctrl+C works on every machine I have used EDLIN with. In the process, we seem to have gathered a rich crop of asterisks, more of which in a moment.

The first point to note is that, like all editors and wordprocessors, EDLIN has two basic modes – command mode and edit mode. In other words, with any word-processor you are either tinkering with the text (edit mode) or issuing instructions relating to the text (command mode): Saving files, searching for strings, moving paragraphs about, and all the other housekeeping tasks required.

Every wordprocessor or text editor has its own way of distinguishing between the two modes – with windows or control codes in command mode – and EDLIN is no exception. When the asterisk is sitting on the lefthand side of the screen it is in command mode, and when there is a number and a colon plus a cursor – and maybe an asterisk – sitting a tab space into the screen, you are in edit mode.

So far, so good. The not so good news is that, whilst most wordprocessors switch effortlessly and recognisably from one mode to another at the press of a control code or a function key, EDLIN's attitude approaches the burlesque. But before I demonstrate that particular quirk of the system, let us explore some of the features of this line editor.

If you are new to the concept of line editors, you will be surprised that you can't just move the cursor up the screen to edit a previous line – that, after all, is why they are called line editors, and in addition, trying to split a line is quite a challenge, although it can be done – just.

Note that if you type Ctrl+C at any point on a line in text mode you will lose the entire contents of that line, a popular pitfall to trap the unwary. Now let us try manipulating this mini-file. The first task is to show you how to extricate yourself from EDLIN.

That's easy. Type E and you are out of EDLIN with your file safely saved. You can inspect its contents by using TYPE in the normal way. If you want to abandon EDLIN without saving the file or the latest version of the file, type Q – and in a rush of user-friendliness to the head, you are asked if you are sure you want to quit.

To get back with our newly-created file, type:

```
EDLIN FRED
```

– and back comes our asterisk prompt, which it is time to look at in more detail. At this point you are going to have to tread with caution. Type 2 – plus Enter, of course, and this is what happens:

```
2:*Careering along through the boundaries of space,
2:*
```

What EDLIN is trying to tell you at this point is that line 2, marked with an asterisk, is for text editing purposes the current line, and you are now invited either to alter the line or to press plain Enter and leave it as it is. That's the main function of the asterisk when it appears after the colon, to tell you which it thinks the current line is.

You may find in your explorations of EDLIN that serious differences of opinion can arise as to which is the current line, but one thing is for sure, and that is, that EDLIN always wins the argument, so do be particularly careful when, for example, it comes to deleting what, in your estimation, is the current line.

If you want to alter the line, you have all the hard-to-remember features of the MS-DOS command line editor at your disposal. They do take a bit of getting used to and are vastly inferior to what CP/M offers, but here is a reminder of what will happen if you press particular keys at this point:

F1 – Pressing this key puts up one letter at a time from the line being edited on to the screen, so pressing F1 three times results in:

```
2:*Car
```

At any point in the line, you can type in your own replacement text from the keyboard, but – and this is the trickiest point to note – the command line editor is by default in overtype mode, so if you typed in the sequence F1 three times plus "xx" from the keyboard, plus F1 another couple of times, the result would be:

```
2:*Carxxring
```

To insert text, you need to press the INS key, but note that the switch to insert mode lasts only until you press F1 again. It swaps immediately and infuriatingly back into overtype mode. The best advice I can offer with this and the other line editing function keys, is to practise on a piece of text which you don't mind mangling beyond recognition until you get the hang of it.

F2 – I can best explain the workings of this key with an example. Given our line 2 again, press F2 followed by g – and this is what you will see on screen:

```
2:*Careerin
```

In other words, F2 copies up to but not including the next occurrence of the letter you press after it. Perversely, if you press F2 plus a letter not on the line, the pointer remains at the beginning of the line. This process can be continued from the current point on the line.

F3 – Prints out the rest of the line or, if you are at the beginning of the line, it prints out the whole line. This is a particularly useful feature if you are working from the MS-DOS prompt and are, for example, copying selectively from a hard disk subdirectory. If you had typed:

```
COPY C:\WP\LETTERS\PERSONAL\MAR*.WP A:
```

If you also want to copy those files to B:, just press F3, the back delete key twice, and B:. This saves time, especially if your typing is of the hunt and peck variety.

F4 – This does the opposite of F2; in other words, it wipes out the text up to but not including the letter you press after it. So, by way of example, given our line 2 again, pressing F4 plus space will result in nothing apparently happening, but if you then press F1 a few times, you will see that the line up to but not including the first space has been deleted:

```
2:* along through the boundaries of space,
```

Note that both F2 and F4 are case sensitive.

In tinkering with line 2, you can revert to the former state of the line by pressing

Ctrl+C. That will return you to command mode, abandoning any edits made to the line, and pressing 2 plus Enter will put the unaltered line up on the screen again.

F5 – again this is best demonstrated by an illustration, and this time I'll give an example from the MS-DOS prompt. Say you had typed in some whopping great COPY command, but had got the first letter wrong:

`TOPY C:\SUB1\SUB2\SUB3\*.BAK  A:\SUB1\SUB2`

At the end of the line, press F5 and you will have inserted into the buffer that whole line as it stands. Then just press C and F3 and the line will now read:

`COPY C:\SUB1\SUB2\SUB3\*.BAK  A:\SUB1\SUB2`

F6 – creates the end-of-file marker ^Z. More of that later.
F7 – creates an ASCII null, echoed as ^@.
ESC – has exactly the opposite effect to F5. The edited line you are typing in is abandoned in favour of the previous version of that line. So, if you had typed in that huge COPY line, thought you had got it wrong and changed it to TOPY in a fit of madness, you could press ESC and return to the first state of the line.
DEL – In line editing, this steps over the line in the buffer and deletes it. Try this. If you had typed:

`COPYYYYY C:\SUB1\SUB2\SUB3\*.BAK  A:\SUB1\SUB2`

– and realised the error of your ways, you would press F5, F1 four times to get this far:

`COPY`

Then you would press DEL four times, F3 to get to the end of the line, and all would be well. (To let you into a secret, I personally would probably have found it easier to retype the line than leap through all those hoops, but that's just me.)
The next little problem is that when you press Enter in EDLIN, either after having tinkered around with the line or having left it alone, you are back at the command mode asterisk prompt. At this point, some sadist must have resolved to make life as unpleasant as possible for the poor user, since if you press Enter again, you are back in text mode at line number 3.
Try this a couple of times and you will see what I mean. The opportunities for pressing Enter twice by mistake, then a command like I for Insert in text mode, thereby wiping out the contents of the entire line and replacing them with the letter I, are legion, and this is a trap I regularly fall into with EDLIN.
To list the file, you have two options. L displays a specified range of lines, and it also makes assumptions for you if you don't tell it which lines to list. If you just type:

`L`

– it assumes you want to start 11 lines before the current line, and display up to and including what EDLIN thinks the current line is.
Alternatively, you can specify the start and end line, or either:

```
4,22L
12L
,15L
```

The first case is self-explanatory. In the second case EDLIN displays 23 lines for you, starting at line 12. In the third case, you get 11 lines, ending at line 15.

The alternative is P, which stands for page. Hitting P repeatedly gets you through the file a page (23 lines) at a time, starting at the line after the current line and ploughing on until the end of the file or you get bored with the whole idea. You can specify line numbers in a similar kind of way to L.

The really important point to note is that the current line remains the same when you use L, whichever part of the file you are listing, but with P the current line is changed as you move through the file. Watch for the asterisk after the colon to see what I mean.

At this point, it is useful to know how to get to the current line. Just type a full stop, plus Enter, of course, and you will be deposited in edit mode on the current line.

The next commands need careful handling and practising before you use them in anger. Copy and Move are similar one-letter commands which tell EDLIN either to copy or move lines from one part of the file to another. To copy lines 22-40 to line 3:

```
22,40,3C
```

Line 3 becomes the current line. You can add a fourth parameter which tells EDLIN to repeat the count a specified number of times. You can use + or – with the numbers in the first three parameters (if you really want to confuse yourself, that is). M for move behaves in a similar way.

Note two consequences of using these instructions. The first of the lines copied or moved becomes the current line in the file for editing purposes. On top of that, all the lines in the file are dynamically renumbered, so if you have carefully made a hard copy listing of the file with numbers on it, throw it away and start again.

Not too dissimilar is D, which in its simplest form without parameters tells EDLIN to delete the current line, and the line after the one you have just deleted becomes the current line. If you specify a range of lines, like:

```
12,99D
```

– the line after the last one deleted becomes the current line, with the additional point to note that, of course, dear old EDLIN has renumbered the line for you.

I allows you to insert lines from the keyboard immediately before the current line, or if you must, before a specified line:

```
99I
```

After each line inserted, press Enter, and on you go to the next line, all of them obligingly numbered as you type them in. To stop inserting, press Ctrl+C or Ctrl+Break. When you have finished inserting, the line before the one you originally started inserting in the first place – if you follow me – becomes the current line.

There is a search and a replace facility, both of them case sensitive. Either of them can be used as a blunt instrument, like this:

```
1,99Rthis^Zthat
1,99Sfred
```

In the first line, Ctrl+Z is generated by pressing F6. All occurrences of "this" are replaced by "that". In the second line, the editor lands you on the first occurrence between lines 1 and 99 of "fred".

More helpfully, you can insert a question mark before the R or S, to allow you to decide if you want to replace, or if this occurrence is the one you really are searching for:

```
1,99?Rthis^Zthat
1,99?Sfred
```

Omitting either line number assumes the current line. Note two very important traps for the unwary, especially if you are overhasty and hit a key without thinking. Point one is that if you leave out the second string in a replace command, EDLIN will assume you want to delete the search string altogether.

Point two – and even more arcane – is that in both R and S, if you omit the strings after the command, EDLIN reuses the last strings you typed in, which can be very helpful if that is what you intended, and disastrous otherwise.

One more general command: T is used to allow you to read in – or Transfer – another file:

```
Tfilename
```

– and again you can specify a line number before the T.

In the unlikely event that you have a file too big to read into the buffer, you are stuck with editing only what is in the buffer, and you will need to use W to write the existing buffer load to disk, or a specified number of lines immediately preceding the W, and A to append the next chunk of text into the buffer.

If it all gets too much for you, you can always exit using Q for quit. You are first politely asked if you really mean that. After all, EDLIN assumes it has been quite nice to you and you shouldn't want to abandon such a nice friendly editor.

# *24*

# *Practical EDLIN*

---

You may be wondering if I have a good word at all to say about EDLIN, and the surprising answer is yes, I do. One reason is that you can enter control codes directly into EDLIN files, which isn't always either possible or easy with a wordprocessor, and this feature can be pretty useful.

Here's an unexpected application which goes back to the days when files had end-of-file markers to tell the operating system when they had finished. Now it is done in a more sophisticated manner, but the standard end-of-file marker is ^Z and EDLIN still makes use of it. How can that be of value to you?

Well, one of the most hyped areas of computing nowadays is that of security – the world appears, according to the advertising boys and girls, at least, to be full of ill-intentioned villains anxious to hack, bug, or virus their way into our precious software and steal our state secrets.

The best remedy for those nervous of most such invasions is: Time. If you can make it that little bit more difficult and time-consuming for the thief to get at your data, he or she is more than likely to leave you alone and go on to attack someone else. As far as file security is concerned, short of chaining a Rottweiler to your keyboard, one of the neatest tricks for preventing prying eyes from exploring your customer list, secret development projects, or latest literary masterpiece is to put an end-of-file marker at or near the beginning of your file.

You will notice that I wrote "or near" the beginning of the file. If we can doubly confuse the potential data burglar that there is something genuinely wrong with the computer, we may gain even more time. One of the error messages which almost inevitably requires a reset or, if you don't have a reset button, a switch off and reboot, is:

`Divide overflow.`

Now, if we could devise some means of causing our precious data files to issue such a message which should put the fear of God into any potential purloiner of computer data, we could hold off or deter the villain for long enough to preserve the integrity of our material.

At this point, EDLIN comes to the rescue. Let us assume you have a longish data file containing material which you do not want prying eyes to explore, and it is called JOE. At least this makes a change from FRED.

Type:

```
EDLIN JOE
```

– and at the asterisk prompt, type I for Insert and add the following two lines to the front of the file:

```
1:*Divide overflow
2:*^Z
*
```

On line 2, type a carat followed by Z, not Ctrl+Z!

Now E to end the edit, and when you type:

```
TYPE JOE
```

– you will simply get the error message and nothing more. But has the file lost all its data apart from that one line? In order to answer that question, type:

```
DEBUG JOE/B
```

You'll remember that I stated at the beginning of this book that I put MS-DOS commands in upper case for clarity, but that you can use upper or lower case as you please. This is one instance where I advise you to use upper case "/B". There is a bug in some versions of MS-DOS which causes it not to recognise "/b", so use upper case to be on the safe side.

The "/B" parameter tells EDLIN to load the whole file regardless of end-of-file markers, and if you type L you will see our spurious error message and the ^Z character at the beginning of the file which, as always with EDLIN, will be dynamically renumbered:

```
1:*Divide overflow
2: ^Z
3: ... rest of file starts here ...
```

There are two snags to this particular technique. The first is that any astute user calling up DIR will see immediately that the file is far longer than the supposed error message would allow you to believe. Secondly, it is a bit of a bore having all your files beginning with an error message plus end-of-file marker, so the easiest way round both problems, if you have created your own version of DIR.BAT as I described earlier, is to create a batch file which puts the spurious error message into the beginning of files you wish to hide and which also renames DIR.BAT to contain a message stating something to the effect that "This utility is not available on this terminal".

Then you can use a second batch file to switch things back to normal when you come back from your coffee break, visit to the powder room or the off-licence, or whatever.

So, despite its crudities, EDLIN has its uses, and particulary when it comes to typing in assembler listings and the like, since full-powered wordprocessors enter all kinds of fancy codes which you have to strip off, then export the document and re-import it, and with some wordprocessors if you don't watch what they are up to, you may well get ASCII garbage, as they tend to strip off what they regard as non-essential carriage returns and line feeds. Still, EDLIN, could have been a touch friendlier – which brings me to a couple of improvements which can make life a lot pleasanter for the EDLIN consumer.

# Bending EDLIN

If you want to search through the file for a given string of characters, use this technique which finds up to 20 occurrences of a specified string, which ought to be enough for most circumstances:

```
ECHO OFF
FOR %%A IN ("%1" "%2") DO IF %%A == "" GOTO FAIL
IF NOT EXIST %1 GOTO NOTFOUND
ECHO 1,#?S%2> EDBITS
ECHO NNNNNNNNNNNNNNNNNNNNNNY>> EDBITS
ECHO E>> EDBITS
EDLIN %1 < EDBITS > TOTAL | FIND ":"
FIND /C ":" TOTAL
TYPE TOTAL
DEL TOTAL
DEL EDBITS
GOTO END
:FAIL
ECHO You haven't specified a file or search string – or either!
GOTO END
:NOTFOUND
ECHO I can't find the file %1
:END
```

This is pretty crafty way of finding out all the occurrences of a given string in a file using EDLIN and coming up with the line number and the number of occurrences. Agreed, it would be possible to do something similar just with FIND, but this method sets out the line numbers precisely in EDLIN format, and on top of that it involves low cunning and demonstrates techniques you might wish to adapt yourself if you are designing batch files built around EDLIN.

The second line checks for the absence of parameters necessary to make the batch file – let's call it SEEK.BAT – function properly. Parameter one is the name of the file and parameter two is the string you are after. Then we check to see if the file exists, and if all is well on both counts, we move to this odd-looking command:

```
ECHO 1,#?S%2> EDBITS
```

What is happening here is that we are creating the first line of a temporary file, which I've called EDBITS and which you can call what you like, so long as you make consequential changes later in the batch file, the purpose of which is to tell EDLIN to search from the beginning to the end of the file, looking for occurrences of whatever is in %2 and to stop and ask each time if this is the occurrence you are looking for.

Note that there is no space between the %2 and the redirection operator. If you leave a space, EDLIN thinks it is looking for whatever is in %2 plus a space. The next command, the one with a great long string of n's in it which you can extend if you wish, took me quite a long time to get right. First, I tried this:

```
ECHO N> EDBITS
```

– but ended up with either only half of the items I wanted or an error message, or both. Let me explain. The S command has two formats. In the straighforward version it looks like this:

```
Sfred
```

– a search occurs (case sensitive) from the current line for the next occurrence of "fred". Then EDLIN stops, and awaits its master's bidding. Alternatively:

```
?Sfred
```

– carries out a similarly case sensitive search for "fred", but when it reaches the first occurrence, it pauses and asks if that's the one you want. If you type anything other than Y, the search continues, on and on until you say Y or the end of the file is reached.

This is one case where EDLIN doesn't expect you to press Enter after an instruction, so a series of lines in the file EDBITS looking like this:

```
N
N
N
```

– were interpreted wrongly, with EDLIN getting confused at the carriage returns in the midst of the N's. Hence the string of N's one after the other, which took me ages to work out and get correct, followed by a Y, just in case you were looking for a string which occurs more times than there are N's.

The E for end edit command is then added on to the file EDBITS and the search takes place. The result is put into a file called TOTAL, which you can call what you want, but there is rather a nice reason for calling it that:

```
EDLIN %1 < EDBITS > TOTAL | FIND ":"
```

The result is piped into the external FIND command which is told to filter out only lines containing a colon, in other words, occurrences of the string you are looking for. Error messages and sundry other garbage are removed.

The file is passed through the FIND filter with the /C for count instruction. Here is a sample piece of output based on the first few lines of this chapter in draft form looking for the string "file":

```
---------- total: 3
6: assuming your file is called FNAME:
10: - then, after you have been told this is a new file,
28: That sends you to the end of the file, where you can
```

The word "total" appears, apparently by magic, but FIND always puts up the file name when it produces a listing, so we have neatly exploited this feature and made it look meaningful for once.

There is, of course, nothing to stop you from improving this batch file to look for multiple occurrences, like The, the and THE, by putting a SHIFT command after the FIND /C command and checking to see if %2 is empty. If not, cycle round again to a label in preceding the first ECHO command.

It may well also be worth replacing the TYPE command with:

```
MORE | TOTAL
```

– which will give you a paged listing on screen, pausing at the end of every screenful. Additionally, you could remove the line which deletes TOTAL – that will enable you to inspect it subsequently.

## Making amends

Here is a little program and batch file to help you make alterations to files using EDLIN "hands off":

```
0100 MOV AX,3D00
0103 MOV DX,1000
0106 INT 21
0108 MOV BX,AX
010A MOV CX,00FF
010D MOV AH,3F
010F MOV DX,1200
0112 INT 21
0114 MOV SI,1200
0117 INC SI
0118 MOV AL,[SI]
011A CMP AL,2A
011C JNZ 0117
011E MOV AL,1A
0120 MOV [SI],AL
0122 MOV AH,3E
0124 INT 21
0126 MOV AH,3C
0128 PUSH CX
0129 MOV CX,0000
012C MOV DX,1000
012F INT 21
0131 MOV BX,AX
0133 MOV AH,40
0135 POP CX
0136 MOV DX,1200
0139 INT 21
013B INT 20
```

Then enter a filename ASCIIZ string at 1000 like this:

```
E 1000 "CHANGE",0
```

Again, if you insist on having a file yourself called CHANGE, I leave you to make the necessary alterations to this program and the batch file that's coming up in a moment or two.

Set the CX register to 1200 and write the program to disk as CPROG.COM. Then knock together a batch file called REP.BAT:

```
ECHO OFF
CLS
FOR %%A IN ("%1" "%2" "%3" "%4") DO IF %%A == "" GOTO FAIL
ECHO %2,%2R%3*%4 > CHANGE
ECHO E>>CHANGE
CPROG
EDLIN %1 <CHANGE /B
GOTO END
:FAIL
ECHO You have missed out a parameter...
:END
DEL CHANGE
```

What this batch file does is to take four parameters, the first being the name of the file to edit, the second the line number for the replacement, the third the string to replace, and the final one the new string. Note the ingenious use of FOR to check for missing parameters. The next commands must be typed in with great care and need some explaining:

```
ECHO %2,%2R%3*%4 > CHANGE
ECHO E >>CHANGE
```

The repeated second parameter ensures that the replacement only takes place on the specified line. If you leave out the second %2, EDLIN assumes you want to replace to the end of the file. The file CHANGE is created to contain this line, and the next line appends the E, to end edit, to the file.

Now comes the slight problem. I've used an asterisk to act as a delimiter between the search and replacement strings, since we cannot use ^Z as that is the end of file marker. That's why we need the little program called CPROG to look for 2A and replace it with 1A. Once more, if you want to change asterisks, I leave you to tinker with the program and the batch file accordingly.

So what the CPROG program does is to put a ^Z character in the middle of the file, which creates the next problem for us. If we simply typed next in the batch file:

```
EDLIN < CHANGE
```

– our friendly line editor would read in up to and including the ^Z, think it got to the end of the file, and then the whole computer would freeze, since we have redirected input to the file, and the file has, so EDLIN thinks, ended without telling it what to do. So it would all end in tears, unless we can think of a way round it, and that way does exist:

```
EDLIN < CHANGE /B
```

This tells EDLIN to treat CHANGE as a binary file, and include any 1A end of file markers, so we have overcome a double problem and created for ourselves a very user-friendly face of EDLIN.

I have just given the bones of the batch file, and I leave you to pretty it up with a display indicating that this is file X and you are replacing on line such-and-such, and is it all right to go ahead.

At the label FAIL, you could indicate which parameters are missing, and also remove the fourth parameter in line three from the list to allow replacement by nothing, in other words, erasure of the string altogether.

So, those are a couple of ways in which EDLIN can be made more user-friendly for you. I leave it up to your deviousness and ingenuity to devise any further methods of making a computing dinosaur into something bearng a passing resemblance to an electronic thoroughbred.

# 25

# *Conclusion*

---

And that is just about that. We have covered a great deal of ground and put together a number of utilities and programs which I hope will be of considerable value to you.

We have bent the batch file system in ways that it was certainly not designed to bend, and have come up with a number of programs, like the notepad file, which extend its potential in a whole range of different directions.

Most importantly, you will have come a considerable way down the road towards becoming an expert in assembly language programming, and if you want to extend your knowledge even further, look at the recommendations in the appendix on assembler code and the relevant books in the bibliography.

MS-DOS itself is one of those subject areas in computing which never seems to become exhausted. I must confess at times that I am surprised at the richness and variety of interest and information that lies buried beneath the surface of this operating system, and it is one of the reasons why I feel that it will still be around in a modified and upgraded form years from now.

It contains within it enough power and potential for development on a solid base that it is hard to see any real competitor coming to overtake it altogether, unless, that is, someone somewhere has a secret mega-power parallel processing neural network computer which will be chatting merrily away to us in plain English. That's a prophecy which has raised its head many a time since computing began, but I doubt whether the all-talking, all-dancing computer will arrive for a very long time.

And when it does, it may not only sweep MS-DOS and its brethren away, but also cast a cynical eye over us puny humans and throw us aside altogether as being of a far too meagre intellect to be able to cope with the real problems of life, the universe, and everything. In the meantime, continue to enjoy your explorations of MS-DOS.

# Appendix A

# Hex and Binary

---

The object of the exercise in this appendix is to explain the significance of decimal, hexadecimal and binary on your PC, and to demonstrate why this range of number systems is not only necessary, but very desirable in aiding the advanced user to get the best out of his or her machine.

Let's begin by getting one myth out of the way, and that is, that decimal is the "normal" system since, after all, we have five fingers (thumb included) on each hand, and ten toes on each foot. That, however, could equally be an argument for working from the base 20, or even 40. There's nothing sacred about decimal, nor is it necessarily the most straightforward system to function in.

Take oldfashioned pounds and ounces, for example. There are 16 ounces in a pound, as every schoolboy used to know before the world went mad for grammes and kilogrammes. Take the decimal 10 and divide it by 2. Answer = 5. Divide that by 2, and you are already into decimal points with 2.5. By contrast, you can divide good old 16 right down to 1 and not have a single fraction in sight, since it is a power of two.

So there is no truth in the rumour that there is some preordained reason why we should either think in decimal or, indeed, work to a regular number base at all. Going back to ounces: 16 in a pound, 4 in a quarter, and on to stones, hundredweights, and the rest. If you are still not convinced, ask yourself how many seconds there are in a minute, minutes in an hour, hours in a day, and so on. And then go on to inches, feet, yards, chains, furlongs, and the rest.

But, if we are to stray from familiar systems to oddities like binary and hex, then we at least deserve to know what the reasoning is behind them. Why are they so necessary and why is the decimal system so inappropriate?

Let's start with binary. Computer systems work with electronic states which are either "on" or "off". That's a choice between two, so it makes sense to describe them in terms of a number system which functions in two's. It requires just two digits, a "0" and a "1", to describe the numbers in the system. That makes it very simple, but there's a huge drawback to it, as we'll see in a moment, which positively invites the introduction of hex.

Let us try a bit of binary first. Here are the numbers 1 to 7 in binary:

| binary | decimal |
|--------|---------|
| 0 | 0 |
| 1 | 1 |
| 10 | 2 |
| 11 | 3 |
| 100 | 4 |
| 101 | 5 |
| 110 | 6 |
| 111 | 7 |

I hope you can see the pattern emerging in binary. If you work onwards, 8 will be 1000, 9 1001, 10 1010, and so on. The main pattern to spot, though, is obviously that at every power of two, we have the equivalent of 10 in decimal, in other words, a number followed by a string of zeroes:

$$10 = 2$$
$$100 = 4$$
$$1000 = 8$$
$$10000 = 16$$

– and so on and so forth. On the other side of the coin, though, there is no really convenient, easy-to-remember pattern at all between the decimal numbers and their binary equivalents, and it is important that there should be some human-friendly correspondence when it gets to reasonably large numbers, since I would be totally lost trying to work out a way of pinpointing or remembering a number like:

11010011

– or of converting a decimal value like:

3256

– into binary.

To the rescue comes hex, or hexadecimal, to give it its full name. Instead of working to the base ten, hex works – like oldfashioned ounces – to the base 16. First, here are the hex values between 0-15 with their binary and decimal counterparts:

| hex | decimal | binary |
|-----|---------|--------|
| 0 | 0 | 0000 |
| 1 | 1 | 0001 |
| 2 | 2 | 0010 |
| 3 | 3 | 0011 |
| 4 | 4 | 0100 |
| 5 | 5 | 0101 |
| 6 | 6 | 0110 |

*–continued on next page-*

| | | |
|---|---|---|
| 7 | 7 | 0111 |
| 8 | 8 | 1000 |
| 9 | 9 | 1001 |
| A | 10 | 1010 |
| B | 11 | 1011 |
| C | 12 | 1100 |
| D | 13 | 1101 |
| E | 14 | 1110 |
| F | 15 | 1111 |

Now you can see that there is a correspondence between hex and binary, and that is that all the different possibilities in four bits (binary digits) can be represented by a unique hex value. C is 1100, 2 is 0010, and so on. The letters A-F have been imported into the number system simply because we have run out of digits.

The PC works in units of storage called bytes, each of which hold 16 bits, which means very conveniently that they can be described in terms of two hex digits. Here is an example:

11011111 = DF
01000001 = 41

And this means that it is pretty straightforward to convert back and forth, a task that would be almost impossible in decimal.

Let's take the idea a stage further. If you have a byte containing this information:

4142

– which happens to be the values corresponding to the characters A and B, and you wanted to pick out just the second character and find out what it was, you could use a technique called masking, which you will find explained in detail in the chapters on DEBUG, and you will also see that the character sets are created in such a way that it is simple, using a bit mask, to convert from upper to lower case and back again.

Hex, then, is an ideal means of taking all those strings of ones and zeroes which look so confusing and converting them into a form which we poor humans can just about understand. So, hex looks difficult and obscure, but once mastered, it will enable you to work more closely and effectively with your computer, especially when you are dealing with DEBUG and assembler.

# *Appendix B*

# *DEBUG*

---

This is an account of the features of the MS-DOS DEBUG program for reference purposes. In general terms, each DEBUG command consists of a single letter which may have one or more numbers associated with it, or the letter L. In each case, you should type Enter after each command. As elsewhere in this book, I have put all commands in upper case for purposes of legibility – you can use either upper or lower in your own work with the computer, DEBUG doesn't mind.

The commands are given in alphabetical order with notes as appropriate and indications of problems that may arise. Note that the segment number preceding the colon will almost inevitably be different on your machine – I'm just using the value which my AT coughs up at me.

## A – Assemble
Type A followed by a number to assemble instructions into DEBUG. If you type:

*A100*

– you will be greeted with this message and invited to type.

*33C0:0100*

If you make a mistake, DEBUG will pinpoint it and invite you to retype the line. If you press Enter twice, you will be returned to the DEBUG minus prompt.

If you type:

*REPZ MOVSB*

– or a similar command on a single line, DEBUG will place them on succeeding lines, and the instructions:

*JC*
*JNC*

– will be listed as JB and JNB, to which they are functionally identical.

Do be careful to ensure, when changing an instruction, both that you are starting at the correct address, since inserting in the middle of an instruction will have totally unpredictable and probably disastrous results, and also ensure that you are replacing like with like, byte-wise.

In other words, if you want to replace an instruction which occupies three bytes, like:

```
MOV BX,1234
```

– with one occupying one byte, like:

```
POP AX
```

– you should fill the unused bytes with the NOP instruction, otherwise the whole of the rest of the program may be gibberish.

Working the other way round is more difficult. If you wanted to replace this instruction:

```
MOV BX,1234
```

– with this one:

```
MOV BX, [1234]
```

– you would be in trouble since the second takes four bytes, one more than the first. There are two ways round this problem, short of retyping everything that follows. The first is to use M for move, which is described later, but which has its pitfalls. The second is always to include plenty of NOP instructions when you are typing in a program using DEBUG, so that it is less tricky adding instructions at a later stage. I have avoided this practice in the programs listed in the book, simply to prevent you from typing in reams of NOPs, but it is by far the safest approach in designing your own material.

Although I have used a different approach in the body of the book, you can also use A to assemble DB and DW pseudo-instructions into memory.

# C – Compare

Not used in this book, this command allows you to compare two chunks of memory, and reports where differences occur. The command is typed in like this:

```
C 250 L 30 550
```

That compares the 30 hex bytes starting at 250 with those starting at 550.

# D – Dump

This dumps information from memory on to the screen. Examples are given in Chapter 11 of the form of the layout of the dump. The command can be invoked in one of three ways:

```
D
D 100 11F
D 150 L 20
```

The first default call takes the first 80 bytes, starting either from address 100 or from the last address specified. This can easily cause material you require to scroll off the top of the screen, so the next two variations are extremely useful. Number two tells DEBUG to list from address 100 to 11F inclusive, and the third variation tells DEBUG to start at 150 and list the next 20 bytes.

# E – Enter

This allows you to inspect and/or alter information in memory, and works in one of two ways. The simpler method is the one I use in the body of the book for data byte (DB) areas of memory, such as:

```
E 1000 "This is a message",0D,0A,"$"
```

That inserts bytes starting at address 1000. Do watch that you are not overwriting information you require further up the memory. It is easily done, especially when you are altering messages.

Approach number two is more complicated. Type:

```
E 100
```

– and the contents of 100 will be displayed. You can either press Enter to return to the prompt, minus to go back one memory location (to FF), space bar to go forwards one location, (in both cases with the contents of the new location being displayed), or you can type in a two byte value to replace the current value.

# F – Fill

Fills an area of memory with a given value. If, for example, you are unhappy with the spurious code that an area of memory filled with spaces generates, you can change it to NOPs:

```
F 100 500 90
```

Fill from 100 to 500 with the value 90, which is the machine code for NOP. You can mix hex values and ASCII typed in double quotes, that is, if you can think of a reason for wanting to do such a thing.

# G – Go

Tells DEBUG to execute the program which you have either loaded into memory or typed in. The first important point to note is that when a program has run through DEBUG with a message like "Program terminated successfully", or you have run part way through a program, never try and run it again without exiting from DEBUG, otherwise the machine will almost certainly hang.

The most frequent use of G is in conjunction with an address you want to stop at, like:

G 504

– but ensure that the address marks the beginning of an instruction, not the middle of one, otherwise it will never stop. It is possible to put more than one breakpoint, as it is called, after G.

If, as often happens, you want to inspect the changing contents of registers and addresses in a loop, use G to go to the instruction you want to halt at, then T (unless the next instruction is an INT, in which case use P) to single step past that instruction, then issue G with the same address as before. You can't type:

G 546

– and then, when you are at 546, type the same again. DEBUG will just sit there muttering to itself something about silly programmers not realising that I am at address 546 already.

## H – Hexarithmetic
Follow H by two values:

H 120 445

– and DEBUG will tell you their sum and their difference, but will get confused if you put, as here, a smaller value before a larger one, and also if you exceed the maximum permitted value of FFFF.

## I – Input
This is unlikely to be used by you as it refers to inputting a byte from a numbered port. The number input is displayed.

## L – Load
This enables you to load a file or program into DEBUG:

L

It requires that the file has already been made known to DEBUG by the N = name command. Alternatively, L can be used to load sectors direct from disk:

L 1000 0 12 02

This will load into addresses 1000 and following the contents of sector 12 and 13 from the A drive (drives are numbered from zero).

## M – Move
Moves bytes around the memory. Say you are trying to add an instruction to a program at location 145. You might take the rest of the program typed so far and move it well out of the way to, say, location 800:

M 145 1B0 800

Then at 145 you add in your new instructions, which, say, finish at 14A. So:

```
M 800 850 14A
```

– to allow for plenty of characters left over. And all is fine. Only it isn't. What no one tells you is that DEBUG, bless it, tries to be helpful by renumbering jumps to specific addresses. That is usually well and good, since it renumbers them again when you return the rest of the program to its new starting address, but unfortunately it insists on renumbering CALL instructions, sometimes with catastrophic results.

The moral of the tale is, first, practise with M until you understand what it does, and second, always check on JMP, JNC, CALL and similar instructions to check that the addresses are still valid.

# N – Name
An alternative to typing:

```
DEBUG MYFILE.COM
```

– is to type DEBUG without parameters and then:

```
N MYFILE.COM
L
```

Note that naming the file does not, repeat not, load it. You have to do that as well, since you might be naming a file to write to.

# O – Output
The opposite of I for Input.

# P – Proceed
Similar to T for Trace, used in single-stepping, but it carries out an interrupt, or a subroutine, or a repeat string, then halts at the next instruction. So, in this sequence:

```
MOV AH,09
MOV DX,1000
INT 21
XOR CX,CX
```

– if you are single-stepping, use T for the first two instructions and P for the interrupt. Similarly, if you want to hop over the CALL:

```
MOV DX,[1234]
CALL 600
CMP AL,FF
```

– use P to move directly from the second instruction to the CMP.

# Q – Quit

Immediately abandons DEBUG and causes the memory contents to be lost. It is essential to save your program first using W, and possibly also the R for Register command, which comes next in the list.

# R – Register

This command is executed automatically with P and T. If you type it without parameters, the result is a full list of registers, as illustrated in Chapter 12. Alternatively, you can inspect and alter, if you wish, the contents of an individual register.

When determining the size of the file you wish to save, first ensure that the BX register is zero and then set CX to the value you require. Only then should you Write the file and Quit to MS-DOS.

If you wish to display the flags, type:

```
R F
```

You can change the flags at this point by typing the appropriate two-character code, DN instead of UP, for example, to change the direction flag.

# S – Search

To search an area of memory, type:

```
S 1000 2000 "DIR"
```

– or:

```
S 2000 4000 0B
```

– or a mixture of hex and values in strings. Note that the values in strings are case sensitive. The result will either be nothing, if no match has been found, or a list of addresses which indicate where the match begins. This is a powerful tool, useful in patching programs, as demonstrated in the body of the book with COMMAND.COM.

# T – Trace

Single-steps through a program. If you put a number after the trace, it will execute that number of instructions, putting up the register contents and flag states after each instruction.

Do remember that any number you put after T is in hex, so 20 means 32 decimal instructions, quite a few screenfuls of information.

# U – Unassemble

Tries to convert the contents of memory locations into valid assembler code. Again, it can be followed by values exactly like D. Note that if you try and unassemble in the middle of an instruction, you will either get garbage, or an implausible but wrong instruction, or a subtle blend of the two.

If you want to see instructions around address 14B but you aren't sure whether

14B is the beginning of an instruction, try:

```
U14B
U14C
```

– and so on, until the instructions make sense to you.

## W – Write
Takes the contents of memory as specified in the BX and CX registers and saves them to a file named either as a parameter to DEBUG when you called it, or with the N command.

## A note on segments
If you change the segment, or if you inadvertently stroll into the middle of an interrupt, you can issue an R command to inspect the segment values, so that you can find out where you are. To override the current segment to find out where an INT finishes, type:

```
U DS:100
```

– to unassemble instructions starting at 100 in the segment specified in DS.

# Appendix C

## 8086 Instruction Set

This is a list of the most common 8086 instructions, together with comments, most of which have been used in the course of this book. For a complete list, see the book by Wyatt recommended in the bibliography. His book also includes the enhanced instruction sets for the 80286 and 80386, together with those of the numeric coprocessors.

If you're not sure how these instructions operate, experiment using DEBUG, watching particularly for any change in the state of the registers and flags. Here is a list of the flags:

```
OV   DN   EI   NG   ZR   AC   PE   CY
NV   UP   DI   PL   NZ   NA   PO   NC
```

In the first line they are set, in the second clear. They mean, in order:

```
Overflow
Direction
Interrupt
Sign
Zero
Auxiliary carry
Parity
Carry
```

In what follows, there are many references to bytes and words. As a reminder, a byte is an 8-bit value and a word is two bytes. So the AH register is an example of an address which can hold a byte, and the AX register of a word. Another reminder:

```
MOV AX,1234
```

refers to an actual value, whereas:

```
MOV AX,[1234]
```

refers to the contents of address number 1234.

References to the source and destination operands have the following meaning:

```
MOV AL, 99
```

– means move from the source operand 99 to the destination operand AL.

Please note again that my aim has been to introduce you to a subset of 8086 assembler to enable you to write programs using DEBUG and to get a general feel for assembler. If you decide to go further and use a full-blooded symbolic assembler, which enables you to give names to labels and addresses, I recommend the shareware product called A86 assembler which, with its parallel debugger D86, is the product I use to develop commercial software. It is widely advertised and readily available via shareware marketing companies.

The MASM assembler which forms the basis of the books by Norton and Miller is less user-friendly and far more bureaucratic. Norton's book is, none the less, recommended for its description of 8086 programming instructions and techniques. Here now is a description of the main assembler instructions in alphabetical order.

## ADD

Can be used with either an 8-bit or a 16-bit register. Here are a couple of examples:

```
ADD AX, DX
ADD AL, [1080]
```

To take the first example: it means add the contents of AX and DX and put the result in AX.

## AND

Compares bit by bit, and sets bits in the destination operand only when both are set. Example:

```
MOV AX, 4C56
MOV BX, 00FF
AND AX, BX
```

The result in AX is 0056, since the lower four bits of BX are set and the rest is zero.

## CALL

Loads the IP register with the address after CALL, saves the return address on the stack. The subroutine is executed until a RET instruction is encountered, then we return to the calling code.

## CLD

Clears the direction flag so that instructions like REPZ MOVSB will work in increasing memory addresses. This is the default state of the flag, and appears on the register list as UP. (The opposite is DN – see STD).

## CMP

Compares bytes or words, and sets the flags accordingly. Example:

```
CMP BX,DX
JE 500
```

If the two are equal, jump to the instruction starting at address 500.

## DEC
Decrement a byte or a word by one.

## DIV
Divide. If you are dividing a byte, the assumption is that the contents of the AX register are divided by whatever you specify as an operand:

```
MOV AX,1234
MOV BL,2
DIV BL
```

The result is stored in AL, the remainder in AH.

If you are dividing by a word, on the other hand, it is assumed that DX:AX is being divided. The result is held in AX, the remainder in DX.

## INC
Increments the value of a byte or word by one. It can also be applied to an address:

```
INC BX
INC [1234]
```

## JC and JNC
Jump if carry, or if not carry. The first instruction is functionally identical to JB or JNAE, and you will find that DEBUG alters any JC you type to JB.

JNC is functionally identical to JAE and JNB, and DEBUG puts up JNB if you type JNC.

## JE, JG, JGE, JL, JLE, JNG, JNGE, JNZ
That's a selection from the "jump if" set of instructions, some of which duplicate each other. JNZ, for example, is the same as JNE in function.

They should cover just about every contingency. Reading from left to right they are: Jump if equal; jump if greater; jump if greater or equal; jump if less; jump if less or equal; jump if not greater; jump if not greater or equal and jump if not zero.

All the jumps should, of course, be followed by an address which points to the beginning of an instruction.

## JMP
Jump unconditionally, again to a specified address.

## LOOP
LOOP to the given address, decrementing CX each time until CX is zero. It is up to you to ensure that CX has a sensible starting value and that you do not interfere with the value during the loop, otherwise it could go on for some time. One way of

protecting yourself is to PUSH and POP CX if you are designing a long loop, and certainly if you want to create an inner loop.

## MOV

Move from source operand to destination operand. Note that it doesn't make sense to try and move a byte to a word, and vice versa. DEBUG will not approve if you try. If you want, say, to put a value in AL into the CX register to set up a count, use this technique:

```
XOR CX,CX
MOV CL,AL
```

That first zeroises the whole of the CX register for you.

## MOVSB and MOVSW

Powerful commands which need to be set up carefully. The first moves a single byte, the second a word. You first put into SI the source address for the move, and into DI the destination address. Then you put the number of bytes into CX. Take a deep breath and type:

```
REPZ MOVSB
```

– to move the number of bytes specified in CX. A technique to clear an area of memory to, say, spaces, is to put the value 20 into the first address (let's say it is 1050), and move it like this:

```
MOV SI,1050
MOV AL,20
MOV [SI],AL
MOV DI,1051
MOV CX,100
REPZ MOVSB
```

Whether you are working up through the memory or down depends on the state of the destination flag. See CLD and STD.

## MUL

Like DIV, it depends on whether you are dealing with bytes or words. In the case of bytes, AL is multiplied by the operand and the result goes into AX. If it is a word, the contents of the whole of AX are multiplied by the operand and the result goes into DX:AX.

Note that this implies you should not have a value lurking in DX that you may want later, and this kind of consideration is important in arithmetical operations.

## NOP

Does nothing. Use it as a filler when writing code, and for leaving spaces to enable you to add in instructions.

# OR

A logical bitwise or. If bits in both operands are set to one, the destination operand has the corresponding bit set to one.

## PUSH and POP, PUSHF and POPF

Put a register or the flags on to the stack, and remove them. Remember, it is last in, first out. The stack is located by default at the top of the code segment.

## RET

Return from a subroutine.

## ROL and SAL

Two of the rotate instructions, moving bits left and right. The difference is that the rotate instructions move bits round in a circle, so to speak, whereas the arithmetic ones lose bits off whichever end you are moving to.

Note that DEBUG is not happy with all these instructions, and will only let you rotate one bit at a time. Multiplying and dividing by powers of two are another way of arithmetic shifting.

## STD

Makes the direction flag point downwards.

## SUB

Subtracts source from destination and stores result in destination operand.

# *Appendix D*

# *MS-DOS Versions - A Brief Overview*

In general, all the programs in this book work with Version 3.1 and above of MS-DOS. Verson 3.0 may cause problems with environment variables, but that is a relatively small area.

The biggest drawback of Version 2 is that it doesn't come with VDISK.SYS or equivalent for installing a RAM drive.

On the subject of internal commands, you should note the following:

*IF EXIST*

Under Version 2, this command can only search in the current directory, which seems a pretty horrendous shortcoming until you recall that all you have to do to check for the existence of a file is to alter the directory first using the CD for change directory command.

*ECHO*

The rules for using ECHO to create a blank line are pretty complex. If you want to write something generally valid, it is best to create a file with a blank line in it, or a short assembler program which can specify the number of blank lines.

As far as external commands are concerned, Version 3 offers a variety of new facilities, including these to which reference is made in this book:

Under Version 3.0, ATTRIB is introduced, to enable you to alter some of the file attributes, notably archive and read-only.

VDISK.SYS enables you to create a RAM drive.

And under Version 3.2, XCOPY allows bulk copying of files; much quicker than plain COPY.

Various modifications of existing commands have been made as MS-DOS has developed over the years.

For a general introduction to the history of MS-DOS, see Duncan's *Advanced MS-DOS Programming*, and for a detailed account of the different internal and external commands, see Somerson's *DOS Power Tools*, both listed in the bibliography.

# *Appendix E*

## *EDLIN Without Tears*

Here's a basic guide to how to use EDLIN in order to input, review and modify the programs in this book with the minimum amount of pain and anguish.

The general procedure goes like this: type the program into a file using EDLIN, then top it and tail it with A, R CX, N, W and Q commands to DEBUG. Then run DEBUG using redirection. Sounds difficult? Here is a simple example of the bell-ringing program (again). Type it in, using EDLIN as described below, together with the DEBUG commands which cause it to be assembled, and then the CX register is set to the right value for saving the program, and it is written to file. Finally, DEBUG is exited from and then you can reload it:

```
A 100
MOV AH,02
MOV DL,07
INT 21
INT 20
R CX
20
N BELL.COM
W
Q
```

Then run DEBUG, using redirection. Assume this file is called BELL:

```
DEBUG < BELL
```

In fact, this looks a suitable case for a batch file. So, to make things really easy, type just the assembler code into a file called BELL, and then create this batch file - let's call it ASSEM.BAT:

```
IF "%2"=="" GOTO FAIL
ECHO OFF
ECHO A>TEMP
TYPE %1>> TEMP
ECHO R CX>> TEMP
ECHO %2>> TEMP
ECHO N %1.COM>> TEMP
ECHO W>> TEMP
DEBUG %1.COM < TEMP
GOTO END
:FAIL
ECHO You've missed a parameter - or possibly both!
:END
```

What this little life-saver does is to assume that you have written the assembler into a file and that you know how many bytes you want to save. The first parameter should be the file name, the second the number of bytes to save.

The output will be a .COM file created from your input file. So, if we have a file called BELL:

```
ASSEM BELL 20
```

– will create a file BELL.COM 20 bytes long. Keep an eye open for error messages during the running of DEBUG. That will tell you where your typing has gone wrong. Then simply work on the file using:

```
DEBUG BELL.COM
```

## Using EDLIN

Inputting is pretty unstressful. Simply type something like this, assuming your file is called FNAME:

```
EDLIN FNAME
```

– then, after you have been told that this is a new file, type:

```
I
```

– and then insert away a line at a time until you have either finished inputting or want to pause for breath, then press Enter followed by Ctrl+C. EDLIN will put up line numbers for you as you go along. To exit, type:

```
E
```

If you want to return later and add lines, type:

```
EDLIN FNAME
```

– and then type:

```
A
```

That sends you to the end of the file, where you can start appending away line by line. When you want to stop, proceed as at the end of an inserting session as just described.

To review the contents of a file, load EDLIN in the usual way and type:

*P*

This will give you the contents of the first page of the file. Keep on pressing P until you get to the end of the file or you have had enough, then again press:

*E*

– to exit. While paging through the file, keep a note of the lines which contain errors.

The chapter on EDLIN gives you more advanced techniques for altering the text. Here are the simple EDLIN commands for this purpose:

If you have missed out a line, use I for input, preceded by the number of the line you want to insert in front of. Type in the line or lines, each followed by Enter, and then press Ctrl+C.

If you want to delete a line, use D preceded by the line number. If you want to delete more than one - say lines 12-15, this is the form:

*12,15D*

To alter a line, the simplest way of all is to press the line number plus Enter, at which point you will see, assuming the line number is 24:

        *24:*MVO AL,99*
        *24:**

Just retype the line and press Enter.

Those are the basic minimum instructions for you to get EDLIN working.

# *Appendix F*

# *Bibliography*

---

This is a list of the books which I have found most useful in delving into MS-DOS during the time I've been writing about it. It's not intended to be an exhaustive account of every last title on the subject - far from it, since there are far too many works around which duplicate material found in others or where there is a great deal of overlapping.

Alongside the details of each book, I offer a brief account of what you might expect to find inside. In some cases, I would advise you to take a wealthy friend or a rich aunt to the bookshop with you. The going rate for a computing paperback, even though it is large format and runs to several hundred pages, is over twenty pounds, and one book on the list that follows - *DOS Power Tools* - weighs in at just under forty pounds, and that's money, not pounds and ounces. One word of advice before you purchase: ensure that the book you are after covers your version of the operating system, if that's the kind of information you are after. I've tried to indicate where appropriate which versions are considered.

You may notice that I recommend more than one book for many of the aspects of MS-DOS, like batch files or DEBUG, for example. This is simply because each book approaches the subject in a different way, and that there is no "last word" on any aspect of the system. Even this book doesn't aspire to offer the "Last word" on MS-DOS!

Angemeyer, J., Fahringer, R., Jaeger, K. and Shafer, D. *Tricks of the MS-DOS Masters,* The Waite Group, 1987. (Ver.1-3.1)

Silly title for a super book for anyone keen to get the best out of MS-DOS. Particularly good on batch files and redirection, pipes and files. Large sections of the book are given over to add-on software and add-on boards, so check that the contents are really what you are after. I found it worth buying for the chapter on batch files alone.

Angermeyer, J., Fahringer, R. (and others too numerous to mention). The Wait Group's *MS-DOS Developer's Guide*, Second Edition, The Waite Group, 1989.

This is a book for the advanced user, including topics such as TSR programs, real-time programming, devices, recovering lost data, and a technical description of the differences between the various versions of MS-DOS.

DeVoney, C. *MS-DOS User's Guide,* Second Edition, Que Corporation, 1987. (Ver. 1-3.1)

A clear and detailed introduction to the MS-DOS commands and to the system generally. Recommended if you can't make sense of your manual, or if you would like a readable account of what MS-DOS has to offer.

Duncan, Ray. *Advanced MSDOS Programming.* Second Edition, Microsoft Press, 1988. (Ver. 1-4)

Here you will find a detailed account of all aspects of the operating system, from the video display to file management, and from interrupt handlers to installable device drivers. I find it most useful of all, though, for its clear account of all the INT 20, INT 10 and other interrupts which make MS-DOS the powerful and portable operating system it is.

Hogan, T. *The Programmer's PC Source Book*, Microsoft Press, 1988.

Hardly a compulsive read, this is a compilation of tables about every last aspect of the PC, from CPU chip pinouts, the video adapters, the complete DEBUG and EDLIN command sets, to hex tables and Microsoft Windows.

Lai, R. *Writing MS-DOS Device Drivers*, Waite Group, 1987.

This is a one-topic very advanced account of device drivers which covers every last gory detail of the subject. Well written and lucid, but you really have to be a committed and knowledgeable user to get the best out of it.

Miller, A. R. *Assembly Language Techniques for the IBM PC*, Sybex Corporation, 1986.

Written for MASM assembler, this book offers a good introduction to the registers, interrupts and other aspects of the PC which you need to master before you can write your own code. The main programming part of the book shows how to write macros in MASM.

Norton, P., and Socha, J. *Peter Norton's Assembly Language Book for the IBM PC*, Brady Books, 1986.

Describes the MASM assembler. A readable introduction, but obviously biased towards the proprietary assembler.

Norton, P., and Wilton, R. *The New Peter Norton Programmer's Guide to the IBM PC and PS/2*, Microsoft Press, 1988.

Peter Norton is one of the gurus of the PC, and his Utilities for examining, modifying and rescuing disks are known throughout the PC world. This is a comprehensive introduction to all aspects of the operating system. More than most of the books on this list, it can be read from beginning to end out of interest, but I have found it also contains a great deal of detailed information not printed in other supposedly exhaustive guides.

Somerson, P. *DOS Power Tools. Techniques, Tricks and Utilities*, Bantam Books, 1988. (Comes complete with a 5.25 inch disk of utilities.) (Ver. 1-3)

Put together by the editor of PC Magazine, it runs to a massive 1275 pages and covers every aspect of MS-DOS from the user's point of view. Especially recommended are the chapters on the keyboard; EDLIN; DEBUG; batch file techniques; and different screen video modes. Sometimes repetitive and wordy, not always exhaustive, but certainly the best encyclopedia-type book on MS-DOS around, even if it doesn't cover MS-DOS 4.

Uffenbeck, J. *The 8086/8088 Family. Design, Programming and Interfacing*, Prentice Hall, 1987.

An advanced technical reference manual to all aspects of using the 8086. Advised only for the experienced user, particularly if you are interested in interfacing the 8086 with external devices.

Wilton, R. *Programmer's Guide to PC and PS/2 Video Systems*, Microsoft Press, 1987.

Just about every last detail on the video systems of the PC. Assumes a knowledge of assembly language programming.

Wolverton, V. *Supercharging MS-DOS*, Microsoft Press, 1986. (Comes with a 5.25 inch disk) (Ver. 1-3.2)

This is a well-written "post beginner's" manual which you might find useful to reinforce some of the material in this book. Don't expect any advanced stuff on assembler or video systems, though.

Wyatt, A. L. *Assembly Language Quick Reference*, Que Corporation, 1989.

This is an almost indispensable work of reference for the assembly language programmer. It lists and briefly explains all the instruction sets for the 8086 family of processors, including the 80386. In addition, there are sections on the mathematical coprocessors.

Young, M. J. *MS-DOS Advanced Programming*, Sybex Corporation, 1988. (Ver. 1-4)

For this book, a knowledge of the programming language C or of assembler is assumed. It's an in-depth analysis of topics like the BIOS, interrupts, device drivers, and memory management. More of a reference work than a gripping read.

# INDEX

# An Invitation

Sigma Press is the largest independent publisher of computer books in the United Kingdom, and also has a very active leisure publishing division. Marketing and distribution of our computer books has been handled for 10 years by John Wiley & Sons Ltd, the UK subsidiary of a major US publisher.

We always welcome proposals for new books, and can ensure a rapid and informed response. In addition to mainstream computer topics, we particularly welcome book proposals in specialist areas, sometimes too difficult for larger publishers to grapple with.

Books on software or hardware developed mainly in the UK and Europe are also a speciality, as we are closer to these markets than our US competitors.

To assess your proposal, we need:

❑ a contents list

❑ a sample chapter (if available)

❑ an estimate of the final length of the book

❑ an estimated completion date

❑ a list of competing books – with an indication of why yours is necessary

❑ where relevant – names of two experts in your area from whom we can ask an opinion about your book

If you have any questions, or would like to discuss your proposal informally, contact:

Graham Beech
Commissioning Editor
Sigma Press
1 South Oak Lane
Wilmslow
Cheshire SK9 6AR

Phone:  0625 – 531035     Fax: 0625 – 536800